Irvin S. Cobb

IRVIN S.
COBB

THE RISE AND FALL OF
AN AMERICAN HUMORIST

William E. Ellis

UNIVERSITY PRESS OF KENTUCKY

Scholarly publisher for the Commonwealth,
serving Bellarmine University, Berea College, Centre College of Kentucky, Eastern
Kentucky University, The Filson Historical Society, Georgetown College,
Kentucky Historical Society, Kentucky State University, Morehead State
University, Murray State University, Northern Kentucky University, Transylvania
University, University of Kentucky, University of Louisville, and Western
Kentucky University.
All rights reserved.

Editorial and Sales Offices: The University Press of Kentucky
663 South Limestone Street, Lexington, Kentucky 40508-4008
www.kentuckypress.com

Library of Congress Cataloging-in-Publication Data

Names: Ellis, William E. (William Elliott), 1940- author.
Title: Irvin S. Cobb : the rise and fall of an American humorist / William E.
   Ellis.
Description: Lexington : University Press of Kentucky, 2017. | Includes
   bibliographical references and index.
Identifiers: LCCN 2017019630| ISBN 9780813173986 (hardcover : alk. paper) |
   ISBN 9780813173993 (pdf) | ISBN 9780813174006 (epub)
Subjects: LCSH: Cobb, Irvin S. (Irvin Shrewsbury), 1876-1944. | Authors,
   American—20th century—Biography. | Humorists, American—20th
   century—Biography. | Journalists—United States—Biography.
Classification: LCC PS3505.O14 Z65 2017 | DDC 818/.5209 [B] — dc23
LC record available at https://lccn.loc.gov/2017019630

Member of the Association of
American University Presses

To all those who love American humor,
but especially for my grandchildren,
Andrew, Elise, Jordan, Caitlin, and Meredith,
and my great-grandsons, Liam (deceased) and Cooper.

Contents

Photographs follow page 118

Introduction

Immortality is fleeting. Life moves on. The style of a writer, the words of a politician, the deeds of a businessperson can soon become nullities as the world's tastes modernize. To be relevant in the future, an author's words must be apropos beyond the bounds of time.

In *The National Parks: America's Best Idea,* a television program produced by PBS documentarian Ken Burns and a companion book of the same title written by Dayton Duncan, humorist Irvin S. Cobb (1876–1944) is quoted extensively in a segment about the grandeur of the Grand Canyon. "I think my preconceived conception of the Canyon was the same conception most have before they come to see it for themselves—a straight up-and-down slit in the earth, fabulously steep and fabulously deep; nevertheless a slit. It is no such thing!" Cobb declared. "Imagine . . . the very heart of the world . . . laid bare before your eyes! . . . There is nothing between you and the undertaker except six thousand feet, more or less, of dazzling Arizona climate." Commenting on casual tourists who take a hurried look over the rim and then quickly depart, Cobb was particularly dumbfounded by "one bored young man" who asked, "in the patronizing voice of an experienced traveler, 'is there anything interesting to see around here?'"[1]

Cobb excelled at observing the comical in almost any situation. The mule ride into the Grand Canyon offered him an opportunity to make a droll comment on the innocent travails of life—something that became his trademark. Descending Bright Angel Trail, he noted that he and his companions were "as nervous as cats and some holding to their saddle-pommels with death grips." Then:

All at once you notice that the person immediately ahead of you has apparently ridden right over the wall of the canyon. A moment ago his arched back loomed before you; now he is utterly gone. It is at this point that some tourists tender their resignations—to take effect immediately. . . . Nearly always there is some man who remembers where he left his umbrella or something, and he goes back after it and forgets to return. . . . The natives will tell you the tale of a man who made the trip by crawling round the more sensational corners upon his hands and knees.

The true beauty came at the bottom. "You realize that this canyon is even more beautiful when viewed from within than it is when viewed from without," Cobb marveled. In another section of the documentary and book dealing with graffiti in the canyon, Cobb is quoted again: "Also, you begin to notice that it is most extensively autographed. Apparently about every other person who came this way remarked to himself that this canyon was practically completed and only needed his signature as collaborator to round it out—so then he signed it and it was a finished job."[2]

To be quoted this way in 2009, sixty-five years after one's death, is an honor not to be dismissed. Who was Cobb, and why is his story worth telling now? Foremost, Cobb was a consummate wordsmith who knew how to engage a reader with just the right amount of tongue-in-cheek self-deprecation. He could frame a scene, create characters with personalities, insert a twist, and use human interest to tell a story. He could paint a humorous scene just as easily as a horrific one. Cobb himself was never dull. A bit pompous at times and long-winded as a writer, Cobb may seem too sure of himself, too southern, and too benevolently racist for the modern reader, but he was a well-known newspaperman, essayist, short story writer, humorist, and movie personality in the early twentieth century. Cobb is largely unfamiliar to today's readers, and through this biography, I hope to establish his place as an important writer of a century ago, and perhaps at least some of his original works will be read again.

1

The Making of
an American Humorist

American humor comes in many forms and has multiple influences. The southwestern frontier, the antebellum South, and the post–Civil War era are important factors in interpreting the life of Kentuckian Irvin S. Cobb. In the latter third of the nineteenth century, life and humor in the small-town South would have evoked the ethos of a post–Civil War world beset by recent memories of a "Lost Cause," economic struggles in a burgeoning industrial age, and a world racially divided into black and white.[1]

This environment produced one of the best known and most important humorists of the early twentieth century, a man who rose from a humble background to achieve fame and fortune as a newspaperman; as a writer of short stories, novels, and movie scripts; and eventually as an entertainer on radio and in motion pictures. The story of how he gained such heights and then fell into disrepute if not near ignominy illustrates the history of humor in Kentucky, the Upper South, and the nation. However, Cobb's story is important in its own right, and it is one worth telling, as it exemplifies the pace of change in his lifetime.

Irvin Shrewsbury Cobb was born in Paducah, Kentucky, on June 23, 1876, the oldest son of Joshua and Manie Saunders Cobb. His siblings included sisters Manie and Reubie and brother John. Paducah, an important port on the Ohio River at the mouths of the Tennessee and Cumberland Rivers, had more in common with west Tennessee and the Deep

South than with other parts of Kentucky or the midwestern states. Moreover, according to Berry Craig in *Kentucky Confederates,* "while slavery
was waning statewide, it was waxing in the [Jackson] Purchase," which
was like "the South Carolina of Kentucky" because so many of its leading citizens wanted to abandon the Union. Central Kentucky and the
Appalachian region had more Union than Confederate representatives in
the Civil War armies, but rebels predominated in the Jackson Purchase.
Irvin's uncle Major Robert Cobb led "Cobb's Battery" throughout the
war. Irvin's father was a student at Georgetown College when the war
broke out, and he joined the Confederacy at age twenty-one. Although
there were no major battles in the Purchase, the presidents and generals
of both the Confederacy and the Union knew that control of this area
was crucial to winning the war. In the immediate post–Civil War era,
repression of freedmen was common in the Purchase, and the Ku Klux
Klan operated without reservation. Violence was rife: the Jackson Purchase, comprising only seven counties, accounted for a higher percentage
of lynchings than any other region of Kentucky from the end of the Civil
War to 1940. Irvin Cobb came of age in this milieu of rigid segregation
and sometimes violent racial strife.[2]

Cobb described his lineage as "mostly Celt myself—North of Scot-
land and South of Ireland, with some Welsh and a little English mixed
up in my strain" (his geographically challenged notions were humorously
intended). The name Irvin, Cobb claimed, came from "an aunt of mine,
of romantic tendencies," and Shrewsbury came from "my father's dearest
friend," a Confederate compatriot. Owing to his father's loss of sight in
one eye and ill health due to his Civil War service, the Cobbs lived with
his mother's family during most of Irvin's formative years. Manie and her
parents were among the elite in the busy river port of Paducah. Her father,
Dr. Reuben Sanders, was a stalwart citizen, a man of means and substance
in the community, and somewhat famous for his use of atropine to quell
an outbreak of cholera. Her husband Joshua, who had difficulty making
a living and often depended on his father-in-law for income, became an
alcoholic. Manie, however, was a strong-willed and nurturing wife and
mother. From his father, whom he described as a "perky little red bantam"
because of his red hair, Irvin inherited wide-set eyes and bushy eyebrows.
From the maternal side he got his grandfather's height—about six feet
when he was full-grown—and black hair. The young Kentuckian's early

life became more difficult as his father's will to live lessened. In his last memoir, Cobb lamented that Joshua "set about drinking himself to death so that we might have something to live on until my Grandfather Saunders' estate was distributed and my mother got her share. He had health though and was strong, and to accomplish this took four hard years. They were four hard years on my mother, too. The memory of them still is like a scar burnt in my brain."[3]

Cobb attended the public schools of Paducah until age fifteen, when he was "chucked out of them for general cussedness." His school record must have been spotty. He was not very good at mathematics, especially the multiplication tables. "At grammar school," he admitted, "I got through Ray's Higher Arithmetic by the simple expedient of doing their Latin for certain of my classmates while they did my problems for me." One year at a nearby private school under the tutelage of Professor W. A. Cade, whom Cobb recalled as "one of the most lovable most impractical men I ever knew," had a great influence on his life. What Cobb lacked in formal schooling he obtained by listening, observing, and traveling around his own small part of the world, consisting of Paducah and its environs along the Ohio River.[4]

Cobb interacted with the river men whose steamboats plied the Ohio and crowded the town's wharf. The Cumberland and Tennessee Rivers flowed into the Ohio just above Paducah, adding commerce and occasional floodwaters to Cobb's hometown. Paducah was also a railroad hub, and the Illinois Central connected it to major cities. The young Cobb drifted in and out of businesses and through the busy streets, where he absorbed the speech, local color, humor, and life of a small town. Paducah had a decidedly southern flavor and was located in a part of Kentucky that had avidly supported the Confederate cause. The war remained a vivid memory for many. Cobb knew many Confederate veterans as well as a few Union men, and he absorbed their tales of the war. Moreover, African Americans made up a large minority of the population there, including some in Cobb's own household, and they added another dimension to the life of a young white boy struggling to find his way. With typical embellishment, Cobb told his old friend Fred Neuman, "I *was* Tom Sawyer." (Neuman would later write a flattering biography of the man who became Paducah's favorite son.) Wayne Chatterton, in an excellent literary critique of Cobb, maintained: "What Hannibal had been to Samuel

Langhorne Clemens, Paducah was to Irvin Cobb." The young Kentuckian always seemed to be searching for ways to stretch his talents. From an
early age, Cobb liked to sketch, and when he was in his teens, four of his
drawings were published by *Texas Siftings* magazine—but they "forgot to
send me a check," Cobb chortled later in life. He also collected Native
American relics and continued to do so until he died. About his surroundings he had unbounded inquisitiveness.[5]

The young Cobb also read extensively. His grandfather Reuben and
uncle Jo (Joel Shrewsbury, who instructed Cobb in Latin) encouraged his
reading by opening their libraries to the precocious boy. He delved into
"stock literary classics" of the day, including Defoe, Scott, Cooper, Dick-
ens, and Maupassant, as well as "dime novels" and the even more juvenile
literature known in the argot of the day as the "nickel library." Cobb would
later write about the importance of the latter in his development, given
its straightforward moral lessons. In addition, Cobb absorbed the plays of
Shakespeare. He was as familiar with James Fenimore Cooper as he was
with Ned Buntline. Southern humor of the Sut Lovingood variety penned
by George Washington Harris permeated Cobb's thinking and writing
throughout his career. He carried a great store of knowledge about history
and literature, which held him in good stead. He apparently remembered in
great detail everything he read and observed. If Cobb had a fault, it was that
he was a compulsive talker, which often got him into trouble as a student.
Later, some friends and particularly foes complained of an intrusiveness
that tended to dampen conversation. Robert H. Davis, who became one of
Cobb's best friends as well as a "crony and hunting companion," once commented bluntly: "Damn it, he knows everything"—or least he appeared to.[6]

In the South, storytelling was pervasive and was considered an art
form. Verbal and written storytelling was an important cultural value and
was a common part of everyday life. Cobb learned this art by listening
to and observing his parents and grandparents, Uncle Jo, and Judge William Sutton Bishop (the model for "Judge Priest" in some of Cobb's best
fiction), as well as the African Americans he interacted with every day. It
cannot be overemphasized that his upbringing occurred in a prototypical
New South–Lost Cause milieu. His relationship with blacks was paternalistic, and he told "darky stories" all his life, according to his daughter.
He no doubt heard and used the "N-word" early and often, and his thinking continued to be influenced by the racial atmosphere of his youth until

his death in 1944. Cobb was exposed to the cultural climate of the late nineteenth century, which included minstrel shows, fairs and carnivals, and the showboats that plied the lower Ohio River.[7]

Two African Americans had a profound influence on Cobb's early upbringing, and he acknowledged their importance in his life in his last memoir. The family cook, "Mandy," served "uninterrupted" for forty-two years and "was the fractious but affectionate despot of the kitchen department." Cobb recalled with fondness the day she drove him out of her domain armed with a skillet for "filching" a delicious "fried pie." His mother gave him "one of the worst whippings I ever got"—not for stealing the pie but for "the infinitely worst crime of calling Mandy 'an ole black nigger' as I fled with my spoils." In contrast, "Uncle Rufus," the family's handyman, "was tolerant of small transgressions and ready to shield the transgressors" from the consequences of their childlike pranks. Cobb enjoyed joining the former slave in his cabin for a hearth-baked sweet potato and listening to the old man's "buggerman tales." According to Cobb, these stories were not in the Uncle Remus mold but the "pure essences of Ethiopian nightmare and making dreadful the wild things and the harmless tame things, as well." Sooner or later, Cobb would be called to bed, which was "a grief and a shock to my enthralled soul." Though the tales were frightening, at "the very next chance I got I'd go back, like a drug addict, for a fresh spasm. I wonder how many years' growth I lost under Uncle Rufus' fascinating treatments." Like many white southerners of his age and time, Cobb developed a paternalistic, even loving view of African Americans, but he never harbored any thoughts of full equality for them. Like most Kentuckians of this era, he believed in the Lost Cause of the Confederacy. Later in life, Cobb would struggle with his southern heritage as the world inexorably changed.[8]

Another influence on Cobb was religion—or the lack thereof. On more than one occasion he described rebelling against his Calvinist Presbyterian upbringing. As he explained in *Exit Laughing*, "I don't believe I could have been more than eight years old, or maybe ten, when some vague adolescent sense of the plain fitness and fairness of things bade me secretly to revolt against a plan of unutterable, unendable punishment for poor faulty fallible mortals, let alone for innocent babes whose baptisms had been overlooked." Having to dress up for Sunday services, and then being unable to play for the rest of the day, was only slightly offset by sumptuous southern-style dinners. Even reading was confined to something biblical and uplifting on Sunday afternoons. For his entire adult life, Cobb shunned formal religion. However, the moral lessons of the Bible appeared to have great meaning for him. Despite his seemingly wide knowledge of the Bible, Cobb never had an evangelical view of Jesus, whom he described as "the first great gentleman of recorded history and greatest gentleman that ever, in any age, walked upon this earth. And if that be blasphemy, I'm proud of it." He claimed in his last memoir that "long before I grew out of short pants," Uncle Jo had converted him "to tolerance of all creeds whatsoever, counseling that I must never set myself against the practice of any faith but only against its narrow-minded practitioners, if any." Or, as he described himself in a *New York Evening World* column: "In religion he is an innocent bystander." Although he was associated with many organizations, Cobb never became a member of the Masonic order, which many men joined if for no other reason than to enhance their careers. No doubt he eschewed its religious base. He reserved the highest praise of a religious group for the Salvation Army because of its efforts in World War I: "I stand ready to salute these people as what surely they are—the Shock Troops of the Lord."[9]

At age sixteen Cobb's formal education ended, primarily because of his grandfather's death and his father's dissipation. He was forced to go to work, driving an ice wagon. In mid-January 1893 Cobb's father persuaded the proprietor of the *Paducah Evening News* to hire the teenager as a "cub reporter." Unpaid at first, in keeping with newspaper custom, Cobb was told to go out in the community and look for stories. He soon found his niche and began to write about anything and everything he observed— wharf news, personals, court proceedings, accidents, and anything else that piqued his interest. At the end of three weeks, he received his first paycheck; in two years, he was making $10 a week. The challenges came early. In 1896, at the tender age of nineteen, Cobb took over the newspaper when the managing editor left abruptly. This probably made him the youngest editor of any daily paper in the nation. Cobb later wrote: "I'm sure I was the worst managing editor of any age in the United States. I was reckless, smart-alecky, careless, gaudy in my enthusiasms, a dynamic builder of lurid headlines. I rarely let a dull fact hamper my style." Joshua Cobb had died a year earlier, and Irvin was now the sole breadwinner for himself, his mother, and his two sisters.[10]

Cobb gained a world of knowledge and experience as an editor. He became adept at rewriting, finding advertisers, handling a small staff, and negotiating the intricacies of local and state politics. The editorship did not last long, and Cobb relished the chance to go back to developing his own stories and covering the offbeat sides of events. His ambition to leave Paducah soured after "four fevered nightmarish weeks" at the *Cincinnati Post*. Cobb moved back home and got a job with the *Paducah Daily Democrat*. Almost marking time, he covered many interesting stories and developed a distinctive style, never short of words or description. Cobb had already learned the art of writing long articles for "space rates"— that is, the longer the article, the bigger his paycheck. This also avoided the need to pad columns with uninteresting "fillers." One such story was about the hanging of a black man that Cobb knew well. Cobb's article was what he called a "commonplace" or straight news rendering of the story, but he did not reveal until years later that he and another young man played a part in the event. When the condemned man's feet touched the ground, they immediately grabbed his legs and dug out the ground with their feet so that he could be fully suspended and strangle to death without any more suffering.[11]

At age twenty-one, Cobb received the opportunity of a lifetime for a small-town newspaperman when he got wind of a breaking story with national notoriety. As reported by the *Chicago Tribune* on December 1, 1897, Christopher Merry and his accomplice James Smith killed Merry's wife for the paltry sum of $7.78 and then escaped a police cordon in Chicago. They worked their way south, riding the rails and walking a good bit of the time as winter deepened. Thrown off a freight train en route from Louisville to Memphis, Merry and Smith found themselves in Fredonia in western Kentucky in mid-December. From there, they walked to Kuttawa. Merry's feet finally gave out, and the two men were identified and thrown in jail in Princeton, Kentucky. At first, Chicago officials could not believe the culprits had ended up in distant Kentucky. But when news of their capture reached the city's newspapers, the *Chicago Tribune* contacted several local reporters and advised them to cover the story. "I was the only country correspondent of the whole lot who obeyed," Cobb recalled. "I went."[12]

"Swollen with a sense of my importance," the young Kentuckian caught the first train from Paducah to Princeton, a distance of about fifty miles. He joined a throng of locals and other reporters outside the jail looking for information. Remembering that his father had been a friend of the town's mayor, he used that connection to meet the sheriff and gain entry to the jail. Merry and Smith found the young reporter's appearance rather comical, with his "broad-brimmed hat and . . . budding mustache," but "they talked," Cobb recalled. He listened, fascinated by their narrative, and scooped the other reporters by dominating the local telegraph to relay his story to Chicago. In the opening sentence, he referred to himself as an "industrious Kentucky newspaper correspondent," but no byline accompanied the single-column article that appeared on December 16, 1897. The next day Smith confessed. In his second report to the *Tribune*, Cobb got two full columns for the kind of reporting he relished—a firsthand account with copious details. Merry "is the brains of the pair," Cobb reported. "The bottoms of Merry's feet are absolutely raw. He cannot wear shoes and can hardly hobble," but "he said if his feet healed, he would jump from a car window on the homeward trip."[13]

No doubt Cobb embellished the story when he retold it in *Exit Laughing*, but the truth was a worthy enough tale. He received $100 and expenses for his two days of work. Merry and Smith were returned to Chicago under heavy guard. A University of Chicago professor pronounced Merry a "typical degenerate" prone to alcohol abuse who smoked five to ten packs of cigarettes a day. The *Tribune* relished this type of sensationalism, as did most of the press of the day. Merry was executed in late April 1898. Cobb had gotten a taste of big-time newspaper work by covering this great drama, but for the time being, he did nothing more than serve as a stringer for big-city dailies while keeping his job in Paducah.[14]

If Cobb appeared destined for bigger and better things, it did not come easily. He took a job with the *Louisville Evening Post* in early November 1898. The competitive Kentucky newspaper market included the much better financed *Louisville Courier-Journal* and the *Louisville Times*, as well as the *Evening Post* and its morning partner the *Louisville Herald*. Edited by Confederate veteran Richard W. Knott, the *Evening Post* boasted on its masthead, "If New and True, Not Otherwise," and it sold for two cents per copy. Cobb quickly settled in as a statewide reporter.[15]

In late January 1900 Cobb traveled to Frankfort to cover the ongoing dispute over the 1899 gubernatorial election involving Republican William S. Taylor, Democrat William Goebel, and John Y. Brown, the candidate of a dissident Democratic Party faction. Taylor appeared to have a slight plurality of votes over Goebel, and the Board of Elections certified his election by a 2–1 vote. The Democratic-controlled General Assembly refused to accept the results and called for an investigation. Lawsuits, legislative shenanigans, and armed bands of men threatened the outbreak of civil war in Kentucky.[16]

Cobb covered all these events for his newspaper and was in the state capitol on January 30, 1900. As Goebel and his two armed bodyguards approached the building, gunfire rang out and Goebel fell, mortally wounded. When Cobb heard the gunfire he rushed outside and was nearly shot by a Frankfort policeman who mistook him for an assassin. Cobb helped carry Goebel to the Capitol Hotel, three blocks away. Governor Taylor called out the State Guard, while Cobb telegraphed his story to Louisville. Meanwhile, Goebel's supporters in the General Assembly had him declared governor and administered the oath of office to the moribund Democratic leader. Goebel died four days later, and Lieutenant Governor John C. W. Beckham was sworn in as governor. For the next several months, Cobb covered the events as investigations were made, Taylor fled to Indiana, and indictments were handed down. In the end, several criminal trials were held, but the mystery of who shot Goebel was never solved.[17]

Cobb, like many writers, continually searched for projects that would allow him to exploit and demonstrate his talent. At least as early as 1900, he began to write short stories—if not on paper, then at least in his fertile mind. His Paducah background conjured up such tales as "Fishhead," a macabre story set on the mysterious Reelfoot Lake; it did not appear in published form until thirteen years later. Cobb probably told this story to friends before committing it to paper.[18]

While at the *Evening Post,* Cobb began to write a semiregular column called "Sourmash" in mid-1901. It had no byline, but it indulged his predilection for humor and provided the first inkling of what would soon become his career. Sometimes he also wrote poems. For example, on May 28, 1901, he published "As Our Eastern Friends See Us," about Kentuckians' violent tendencies as perceived by easterners. The poem—a takeoff on "Ten Little Indians"— begins: "Ten little Kentuckians sitting in a line, One kicked another's leg, then there were nine. Nine little Kentuckians lying hid in wait, One let his hammer slip and then there were eight."

The poem ends: "Ten little Kentuckians sleeping in a row, 'Died from natural causes,' as the verdicts show." Cobb later admitted, "My poetry was so wooden that it fairly creaked at the joints, but I could turn it out by the yard." Quips about current news stories, often based on incongruity or absurdity, included these examples: "A steel bridge fell against the Chicago River the other day, but bounced off without doing any material damage to the surface of that classic stream." Or, "The fellow over in St. Louis who voted eighteen times in the recent municipal election cannot rightfully be called a repeater. He comes nearer being a machine gun." Knott also allowed Cobb to make editorial comments, such as taking on famed South Carolina senator "Pitchfork" Ben Tillman. "How nice it would be if . . . Ben Tillman were hoist with his own pitchfork," or, "If you don't believe Senator Tillman is a great statesman, just ask him." When asked in 1937 why he never compiled the popular "Sourmash" columns in a book, Cobb replied: "It was pretty bad." However, it was a forerunner of the humor that would make him famous and prosperous.[19]

This style of humor was reminiscent of the short squibs and barbs written by many editors and columnists of the day. Two practitioners of that art that Cobb would have come across in Kentucky were George D. Prentice, editor of the *Louisville Journal* until 1868, and Henry Watterson, who edited the *Louisville Courier-Journal* from 1868 to 1918. During Cobb's time in Paducah, the *Courier-Journal* had a wide circulation and influence.[20]

In addition, Cobb came in contact with other newspapermen and personalities. Kentuckian Keats Speed, who also worked for the *Louisville Evening Post*, went on to become managing editor of the *New York Sun*. Cobb and Opie Read, a newspaperman and southern humorist, enjoyed each other's storytelling company. Kent Cooper, longtime leader of the Associated Press, and Ray Long would later play important roles in his life. During the Spanish-American War, reporters, particularly those who traveled to foreign countries, became important figures in the American press as the "yellow journalism" rivalry between the Pulitzer and Hearst newspapers heated up. Reporter Richard Henry Dana's name became known to most Americans because of his daring exploits. Though still a minor figure, Cobb understood the power of the press, calling this turn-of-the-century era the beginning of the "time of the Great Reporter."[21]

While working for the *Louisville Evening Post,* Cobb kept in close contact with his family and others in Paducah. Cobb's life changed dramatically with his marriage in 1900 to Laura Spencer Baker of Savannah, Georgia. They had met when Laura was in Paducah visiting relatives. Cobb was immediately taken with the vivacious girl from a well-to-do old southern family. She was not as readily attracted to the tall, gangly, none-too-handsome newspaperman. As described by their only child, Elisabeth, they were distinctly different in a number of ways. Laura was from a well-established family in an old southern city, while Paducah was basically a raucous, unkempt river town. "Her youth was as happy as his was not," explained Elisabeth. Long after their wedding, Cobb's mother tried to hold on to her son, and there was undying jealousy and possessiveness on her part.[22]

After a wedding trip to Washington, DC, cut short when they ran out of funds, the young couple returned to Kentucky, where Cobb covered the trials of Caleb Powers and then Henry Youtsey for the murder of William Goebel. In one instance, the Cobbs took a brief trip to Cincinnati during a lull in a trial he was covering in Georgetown. In his absence, the trial took a crucial turn, and Cobb had to rush back to meet the deadline for his afternoon paper. He obtained a copy of the day's trial transcript and dashed off 4,000 words by telegraph to Louisville, with embellishments, as if he had actually been at the courthouse. Though some might doubt Cobb's explanation of events, it at least proved his resourcefulness as a storyteller, if not his integrity as a reporter.[23]

Having had experience covering important events outside his home base, Cobb must have thought about his next career step. He was lured back to Paducah in late 1901 by state and national Democratic Party leader Urey Woodson, who had organized a new newspaper, the *Paducah Daily Democrat*. Cobb again became managing editor of a daily for the paltry salary of $22 a week. When the paper later became the *News-Democrat* and was acquired by the Democrat Publishing Company, Cobb's salary increased to $30 a week. Cobb was not obsessed with money, but his livelihood remained a great concern because he had so many others depending on his support. Irvin and his younger brother John, who also worked at the Paducah paper, apparently had a disagreement, perhaps about contributing to the upkeep of their mother and sisters. John moved to Memphis and they never communicated with each other again. Sister Reubie proved to be something of a recluse and never contributed to her own livelihood. Her younger sister Manie also had to be supported until she married. Given his family circumstances, Cobb was always concerned about money.[24]

Cobb suffered from a barely submerged inferiority complex, feeling like he was always looked down on by the "establishment," whether in Kentucky or elsewhere. This was not an unusual reaction for someone who had dropped out of school at an early age to support his family. Images of the South as "other" and the southerner as "stranger" fit Cobb throughout his life. He never lost the sense "that he had been cheated," according to his daughter Elisabeth, "and nothing ever made it up to him." She recalled, "He was the touchiest man alive and I am sure that there are hundreds of people who have felt the rough end of his tongue." Moreover, he never lost his accent and, according to Elisabeth, even cultivated a southern drawl beyond his natural western Kentucky twang, perhaps to rail against a hostile world where his accent might be scorned. Beneath the exterior of a quintessential southern gentleman–raconteur was a curmudgeonly "outsider" who constantly had to prove that he belonged at the top of whatever heap he found himself in.[25]

"I guess no man ever worked harder than I did," Cobb recalled of his nearly three years with the paper in Paducah. As managing editor he handled just about everything, including reading "most of the proof" and contributing his own long stories and columns to the eight issues printed each week. "I ate many of my meals on my desk, a fork in one hand and a pencil in the other, doing snatches of work between bites and taking bites between snatches of work." Though proud of what he produced, Cobb realized he was merely treading water in Paducah, as well as working himself to death.[26]

The *News-Democrat* claimed to have a greater circulation (about 3,000) than any Kentucky paper outside of Louisville, but Cobb found it challenging to fill its pages and make a profit at a price of three cents per copy. When Buffalo Bill's Wild West and Congress of Rough Riders of the World visited Paducah, the paper warned of the usual swarm of pickpockets that would also be in attendance. Before the first Pure Food and Drug Act was passed, it ran advertisements for "Ozmanlis Oriental Sexual Pills," "Dr. Taller's Buckeye Pile Cure," and other patent medicines. The paper left no doubt about its political and sectional sentiments. After John C. W. Beckham won the governorship in his own right in a special election held on November 6, 1900, and the Democratic Party won resounding victories in the general election of 1901, the paper exulted, "Praise God from whom all blessings flow. Kentucky Republicanism has had its day." Moreover, Kentucky remained within the "Democratic arch and the vast breastwork of the solid South." The paper found the lynching of a black male in Hodgenville, who had allegedly forced a fifteen-year-old white male "to commit an unnameable act," an honorable conclusion. In this milieu, Cobb began to write an occasional humorous column, "The Moving Throng." And he continued to write short squibs to strike at political foes. For example, "Fugitive W. S. Taylor says he is going into a manufacturing business in Indiana. He is well-fitted for certain lines of manufacturing. He once ran a murder foundry in Kentucky."[27]

Laura, known as "Lolly" to Irvin and a few others, encouraged her husband's ambition to move away from Paducah, in no small part owing to the rivalry with her mother-in-law. She also believed her husband's abilities were being wasted at the small-town newspaper, where he invested so much time and received so little pay. After living in the more cosmopolitan Savannah, she did not enjoy the small-town atmosphere of the Ohio River port. Laura had also visited New York City once and had immediately fallen in love with the big city. "So I guess she started working on him just about right away," claimed Elisabeth. Both their lives were complicated by the birth of their daughter, who had health problems.[28]

In 1904 the twenty-eight-year-old Cobb decided to make the move to a big city such as New York or Chicago. After all, his two stories for the *Chicago Tribune* had made a big splash, and he had covered the Goebel murder and the subsequent trials better than anyone else in Kentucky. Apparently, Laura persuaded him to set his sights on New York City, and he admitted "the lure of New York, which comes to every newspaper man at least once in his life was stretching out to me and tightening its grip on me every day." He knew others who had made the move to New York newspapers, and he had enough confidence, with a hint of foreboding, to believe that he too could find a career there. Laura arranged for her father to loan Cobb $200 to go and seek his dream job in the big city, while she took their now much healthier daughter to live with her parents in Savannah for a while (it would be nearly a year before they were reunited in New York City). Cobb finally decided that if he wanted to make a move, the time was right.[29]

Cobb undoubtedly embellished the story of finding his first job in Gotham, but given the turbulent nature of the newspaper business in the big city, the tale is still amazing. Cobb took a train to New York City in early August 1904 and moved into a sweltering boardinghouse. He had a letter of recommendation from Urey Woodson to the editor of the *New York Evening World,* giving him a slight advantage, and he knew a friend from Paducah who had gotten a job as a reporter. But Cobb soon discovered there were no jobs available on the *Evening World,* and his friend had just lost his job at another paper. To fill up his time, he explored the big city with all the enthusiasm of the proverbial country bumpkin of the Kentucky variety.[30]

As Cobb told the tale: "I did not know much of anything about New York except that I was going to break in." He empathized with the immigrant standing on the deck of a steamer "because, to all intents and purposes, I was an alien then too, and was coming to a brand-new world myself." For two weeks he made the rounds of the morning and evening papers, with no luck. No editor would even give him an interview. In desperation, Cobb devised a brassy letter—what he called an "inspiration"—in which he proclaimed he was exceedingly well qualified for any position on any paper. "This is positively your last chance," he wrote. "I have grown weary of studying the wall-paper design in your anteroom. . . . Unless you grab me right away I will go elsewhere . . . and your whole life hereafter will be one vast surging regret." Cobb paid a stenographer to make thirteen copies, which he signed and mailed. The next day the *Evening Sun*'s managing editor invited Cobb into his office and hired him. He immediately wired Laura of his good fortune but did not mention the paltry starting salary of $15 a week. When Cobb returned to his boardinghouse he found that other offers had arrived by mail, but he stuck with his first choice. Soon the young Kentuckian was working as a "legman," gathering information for breaking stories that he sent by telephone to a "rewrite man." The first months were grueling. After writing a story about the "Tenderloin" district, he got offers from two other newspapers, but he decided to stay at the *Sun* for the time being. Proud to having gained a foothold as a big-city reporter, Cobb later concluded: "I've only one regret—I waited until I was nearly twenty-eight years old to break into New York [actually, he had already turned that age on June 23]. I only wish I had done it at eighteen."[31]

2

Big-City Newspaperman

Seeking work and success in New York City may have seemed like a daunting task for a small-town newspaperman in 1904, but several Kentucky writers had already gained substantial national status by the turn of the twentieth century. For example, in 1903 *Publisher's Weekly* listed five books written by natives of Kentucky among its "top-ten best-seller list." This was "quite an achievement for one state," according to Kentucky state historian James C. Klotter. In particular, the books of James Lane Allen, John Fox Jr., Annie Fellows Johnston, and Alice Hegan Rice were being read by a national audience at the time Cobb moved to New York City. Moreover, Henry Watterson's editorials made the *Louisville Courier-Journal* a nationally important newspaper.[1]

Cobb's first year in New York proved most difficult because he spent it alone, with his wife and young daughter still living in Savannah. He had no knowledge of how New York City newspapers were run but quickly learned the ropes. By the time Cobb took his job with the *Sun*, that paper had fallen on somewhat hard times. The *New York World, New York Herald,* and *New York Times* were the leading papers in the city, generating more revenue and better coverage than the *Sun.* Cobb, at the bottom of the pack of reporters, could not help recollecting his short, ill-fated trial in Cincinnati. The morale of the *Sun's* staff was low, with lots of turnover, and Cobb became a telegraph watcher again. However, he soon demonstrated that he had the talent to be more than a legman or a rewrite man and developed stories on his own.[2]

Cobb worked long hours and received some small raises, but he was still not earning enough to bring his wife and daughter to New York.

Spending his first Christmas in the city without his family was depressing. Then he got a chance to edit an early, or "lobster," edition of the *Sun,* further demonstrating to his bosses that he had both talent and a sense of responsibility. After personally covering a murder in a district of the city that he knew well, he got another raise. Although his salary of $30 a week still left him a little short, it was enough to reunite the family. Irvin, Laura, and daughter, "Buff" (a nickname given to Elisabeth by a maid in Savannah), became bona fide New Yorkers, taking up residence in a small boardinghouse. However, Cobb continued to put in long, grueling hours working nights at the *Sun.*[3]

The transplanted Kentuckian got a break when the *Sun*'s managing editor sent him to New Hampshire in August 1905 to cover the Portsmouth Peace Conference, a result of the diplomatic efforts of President Theodore Roosevelt. Representatives from Russia and Japan traveled to the port city to negotiate the end of the Russo-Japanese War, a conflict demonstrating Japan's ascendancy in the Pacific. Roosevelt wanted a peaceful settlement to enhance the Open Door policy of the United States and to ensure that Japan did not dominate Russian interests. After private meetings with Roosevelt, the conferees descended on the naval base at Portsmouth for the important work of resolving their rivalry in Asia.[4]

Well-known journalists from the United States, Europe, and Asia reported on the communiqués of the conferees as well as their daily trips back and forth from their hotels in Portsmouth to the naval yard where the meetings took place. Few details of the conference proceedings were made public, which stymied the reporters' quest for substantive stories. Cobb, however, submitted descriptive columns about how the diplomats were dressed and the food prepared for them, as if these were the most important stories of the day. And the public loved reading what we would call "human interest" stories today. Several pieces by the *Sun*'s rising star were reprinted in Europe. Cobb perfected a writing style that, while verbose, was always interesting to readers. For example, commenting on the comings and goings of the Japanese and Russian diplomats, Cobb noted: "The underlings of their two staffs, the secretaries to secretaries, are the lobby favorites. They chat with the debutantes, past, present, and future; pose for photographs and look pleasant generally when they aren't busy upstairs."[5]

"Watching the Peacemakers" became a popular pastime for the

Americans vacationing in the coastal resort town, according to Cobb. He also found the foreign correspondents entertaining, as the "hotel resounds with their babel of languages. Energetic little Frenchmen talk over the tables on the back piazza with grave-eyed calm faced Russians. Italians match their quick gestures with the lordly flourish of the Spaniards." Cobb was amused by the pretentiousness of the foreign correspondents' "decorations," as they all appeared to be beribboned. He (and his readers) also took an interest in the diplomats' churchgoing routines. One Sunday, Cobb reported, the Russians attended the local Episcopal church en masse, but the Japanese could not get there because of a faulty auto. Cobb even found the Japanese love of flowers interesting. The Kentuckian's racist view of the Japanese, who were often referred to as "Japs" in the press, drew no criticism when he declared that the Japanese diplomats "all look like boys, but any Japanese looks like a boy until he is nipped by actual old age." Cobb reported with glee when the size eleven shoes of Russian plenipotentiary Sergei Witte were mixed up one morning (the diplomats placed their shoes outside their rooms each evening to be shined) with those of another Russian who wore size seven. Meanwhile, on the front page of the *Sun*, the news was limited to speculation about what had gone on behind closed doors. On the second page, Cobb's stories imparted a sense of levity to the important treaty negotiations.[6]

The reading public loved Cobb's offbeat style, which included considerable tongue-in-cheek humor. While Roosevelt won the Nobel Peace Prize for his efforts in maintaining the status quo in the Pacific, Cobb's journalistic star rose. "Laura never had to live in a boarding house again," according to biographer Anita Lawson, and the young couple and their daughter moved into a proper New York apartment.[7]

The time appeared right for the transplanted Kentuckian to move up in the world of journalism. After his reporting coup in Portsmouth, Cobb received several offers, but he accepted the one from Joseph Pulitzer's *Evening World*, a rival of Charles A. Dana's *New York Sun*. Pulitzer had bought the *New York World* in 1893, pledging to dedicate it to the "cause of the people." Within a few years, the *World* became the most profitable paper in New York, and in 1897 Pulitzer introduced the *Evening World* at a cost of one cent per copy (most important big-city newspapers had multiple morning and evening editions). With the three leading papers in New York housed side by side in impressive skyscrapers on Park Row, the

World, the *Tribune,* and the *Times* waged an intense and often acrimonious competition for news, advertisements, and notoriety. These were the days of yellow journalism, when sensationalism was rampant and most newspapers, including William Randolph Hearst's *New York Journal,* would do just about anything to sell copies.[8]

Managing editor Frank I. Cobb (no relation to Irvin), hired by an ailing Pulitzer in 1904, "gave the *World* its brilliance and style," according to one newspaper historian, and its progressive editorials commanded much respect. Irvin Cobb's initial salary was $60 a week, and for the next six years he increased his role at the newspaper and honed his skills as a writer. Cobb found himself in a somewhat tense situation at the *Evening World* because the paper expected all its writers to engage in sensationalism. In 1898 Charles E. Chapin, known as "Hard-boiled Charlie," had become city editor of the *Evening World* and intensified the "if it bleeds it leads" style of journalism. In his last memoir, Cobb described Chapin as "a tremendously competent, sometimes an almost inspired tyrant with a kind of occult instinct for detecting an unsuspected or craftily hidden sensation"; he was a man who loved the "news" and only that. Apparently, there was no love lost between the two men. Upon hearing that Chapin was ill, Cobb was quoted as saying, "Let's hope it's nothing trivial." Chapin even reported the statement in his own memoir, claiming that Cobb's words were, "Dear me, let us hope it is nothing trivial." Cobb did, however, make friends with fellow *Evening World* employees Bob Davis and Don Seitz. The Kentuckian also improved office morale by holding a daily "levee" in the city room, where he regaled coworkers with his stories.[9]

Having proved his worth as a reporter, Cobb was assigned to cover the trial of Henry Thaw for the murder of Stanford White. This sensational story was front-page news across the nation in 1906–1908. White, a renowned architect and designer of the original Madison Square Garden, had allegedly violated Evelyn Nesbit, who was now Thaw's wife. Evelyn personified the beautiful, narrow-waisted, luxuriant-haired Gibson girl and had been in show business before her marriage. She told her husband that, when she was a teenager, White had raped her. The distraught Thaw, scion of a wealthy Pittsburgh family, shot White three times in a melodramatic encounter on the rooftop garden of White's masterpiece. "You deserve this," Thaw allegedly said. "You have ruined my wife." The Thaw case had all the sensational elements the public loved: a wealthy man had dallied with a New York beauty and been killed by her furious husband. The ensuing trial became the first in a long line of famous criminal proceedings dubbed the "trial of the century." It attracted large crowds and a lot of newspaper attention. Other papers used numerous reporters to cover the story, but Cobb did it alone, providing as much as 12,000 words of coverage each day in the "space rates" tradition. Famed attorney Alan M. Dershowitz, in an introduction to Gerald Langford's *The Murder of Stanford White*, called the case one that changed American ideas about such crimes forever. The trial's fame and the public's fascination with it lingered well into the twentieth century with the movie *The Girl in the Red Velvet Swing*, released in 1955. Even in the twenty-first century, Paula Uruburu's *American Eve: Evelyn Nesbit, Stanford White, the Birth of the "It" Girl, and the Crime of the Century* found a ready and interested market.[10]

Thaw's first murder trial in early 1907 pitted the wealth of his family against the formidable legal authorities of New York City. The facts of the case seemed simple enough: Thaw had shot an unarmed man. However, the circumstances, the actors both on- and offstage, the daily proceedings, the delays and legal maneuverings, and the testimony and cross-examination became the stuff of legend. Cobb estimated that he wrote "over five hundred thousands of words [in longhand] before it was over," during one of the worst winters in the city's history. Thaw's wife testified that, as a teenager, she had been raped by White. But she also testified that, after her marriage, her husband had stripped her of her robe and lashed her with a "cowhide whip" in a rented Austrian castle. Thaw's periodic irrational outbursts only added to the drama. Yet during the trial, the New York Lunacy Commission studied Thaw's behavior and declared him "rational now" and sane. In mid-April 1907 the jury of twelve men split, with seven voting in favor of the death penalty and five voting for acquittal. Thaw was immediately returned to the city jail known as the Tombs.[11]

All of Cobb's stories illustrated his attention to detail and his ability to write long and rather complicated articles about this ongoing drama. One modern critic, however, scourged Cobb's reporting style. In a critique of trial reporting in the early twentieth century, Robert Mason denounced "Irvin S. Cobb's 600,000 plus words of slobber" about the 1907 Thaw murder trial for the *New York Evening World* as an example of the "Carnival Atmosphere" that prevailed, proving that "law and disorder used to be the press' bread and butter." But at the time, sensationalism was popular, it sold newspapers, and it provided reporters like Cobb a good living.[12]

All the while, Cobb kept up his original humor column, "New York thro' Funny Glasses." These short pieces lampooned and satirized life in the big city. Editor Chapin found Cobb to be "a crack reporter in addition to being an accomplished writer. My only quarrel with Cobb was that he insisted on posing as a humorist. His idea was to turn even the most serious and tragic happening into a laugh." But that was part of Cobb's genius, and it was the way the small-town Kentuckian viewed life in America's largest city.[13]

During the Thaw trial, subjects of the "New York thro' Funny Glasses" columns could be anything that interested Cobb. About the atmosphere on Wall Street just before the crash of 1907, Cobb claimed: "Hence also the current impression that under the climatic influences of the financial district the Milk of Human Kindness turns to brie cheese in twenty minutes." Before the trial, Cobb alluded to Nesbit in one of his humorous columns about athletic women and their attire: "But when the summer's over it won't be the athletic girl who has captured the son of the Pittsburgh millionaire or the heir to the largest distillery in Peoria. No indeedy. The capital prize will have been drawn by a wise virgin with three inch heels and a five-inch waist, whose idea of a violent exertion is to sit in a rocking chair on a hotel veranda in a girly-girly frock and develop dimples." Sometimes his column took the form of a letter to "Dear Green," and he ended it, "Yours, Hi." Commenting on an uprising of an American Indian tribe "in the former wild and woolly West," Cobb maintained that it was doomed from the start because they wore eastern clothing rather than traditional tribal attire. Many of these columns seem racist today, belittling to women, and even prejudiced against the poor. Comparing American comic opera to the English variety, Cobb declared, "Going to an English comic opera is something like eating a mildly indigestible dressing in your salad and then falling to sleep and having slightly incoherent dreams for two hours and a half." Cobb occasionally contributed humor under the name "Grinnan Barrett."[14]

The young transplanted Kentuckian enjoyed the theater, and New York City offered dozens of plays, musical comedies, and dramas, as well as classical music performances, most evenings. Cobb even tried his hand at writing for the stage. *Funabashi* was a musical comedy with shades of *Madame Butterfly*, or, as Cobb described it: with "a wrinkled backdrop showing Mount Fujiyama, the prima donna just naturally had to be a Japanese maiden and the tenor a United States naval ensign—we had to pick a tenor who could wear the ensign's uniform, so his voice didn't much matter." It was panned even by the critic for his own paper, who feared, tongue in cheek, that the play "May Bring on that Japanese Trouble." Cobb joked that in five weeks the play drew poorly, with only 500 paid admissions during the last two weeks, but "attendance did pick up nearly fifty percent . . . on the very last night—the ushers all brought their wives." Adding insult to injury, Cobb claimed that he never received the "agreed advance royalty of five hundred dollars." When a Paducah friend who had attended the musical told him *Funabashi* was "funny," Cobb replied: "It's all funna, no casha." Thus, Cobb's first foray as a librettist turned into a comedy of errors. He also began writing other skits and scenarios, including "Mr. Busybody" for young comedian Ed Wynn. Cobb's other attempts in this field met with mixed results in the years ahead, but he proved to be incredibly productive in other areas.[15]

Meanwhile, Cobb continued to report on the day's sensational stories. The second Thaw trial in early 1908 proved to be just as exciting as the first one. More testimony revealed White's compulsive interest in very young women. Evelyn testified about the "red velvet swing" episode, which titillated readers. At White's famous "House of Mirrors" on West Twenty-Fourth Street, two young girls swung in velvet swings, kicking their "heels through paper parasols" attached to the ceiling, while "Stanford White looked on and applauded." In addition, Thaw's mother declared that her son was insane, much to his annoyance. This time, the unanimous jury found him not guilty by reason of insanity. "Thaw Taken to Madhouse, Vigorously Protests" claimed the headline accompanying Cobb's coverage of Thaw's trip to the "Asylum for the Criminally Insane at Matteawan." The melodrama continued for years. At one point, Thaw escaped from the asylum, only to be recaptured a few days later just over the New Hampshire border in Quebec. Evelyn filed for divorce and resumed her vaudeville career. Cobb wrote years later that Evelyn Nesbit Thaw was "the most exquisitely lovely human being I ever looked at—the slim, quick grace of a fawn, a head that sat on her faultless throat as a lily on its stem, eyes that were the color of blue-brown pansies and the size of half dollars, a mouth made of rumpled rose petals." These were the words not of a hard-bitten reporter but of a man "smitten" by her charm, just as Stanford White and Henry Thaw may have been.[16]

Cobb claimed in his last memoir that he might have played a role in saving Thaw's life during a rehearing of his case. If declared sane and found guilty, he could have been executed. When asked privately by the presiding justice about Thaw's state of mind, Cobb replied: "Judge, he's as crazy as a creek crane." Cobb said the judge thanked him, asked him to keep their conversation secret, and returned Thaw to the asylum. The story did not end there. Thaw was eventually released and was revered by many for protecting his wife, and he maintained a profligate lifestyle until his death. He and Evelyn never reunited, but their romance, White's murder, and its aftermath became the first big crime story of the twentieth century.[17]

Meanwhile, even though Cobb still considered himself an outsider in many ways, he joined the New York City literary cognoscenti, a group of journalists, novelists, dramatists, actors, actresses, and others. "A gregarious man like Cobb soon found himself and his funny stories welcomed into some very glamorous company," according to Lawson. He became one of the earliest members of the Algonquin Round Table, and he and his family occasionally stayed at the hotel for extended periods; he often ate meals at the Algonquin even when he was not living there. Other "stars" of the Algonquin literati included Richard Harding Davis, Booth Tarkington, Gertrude Stein, and H. L. Mencken. One of the legendary stories about Cobb during this time involved one of the other "Algonquin wits," Franklin O. Adams, "whose square-topped head and long-nosed, long-lipped face was much caricatured." When entering the hotel lobby one day, Cobb noticed a newly installed stuffed moose head and with "mock horror" exclaimed, "My God! Somebody has shot Frank Adams." Cobb joined other Manhattan clubs, including the Lambs, the Players, and the Dutch Treat Club. He read drafts of the early plays of Eugene O'Neill at the Lambs and met Theodore Dreiser at the Dutch Treat Club. Although he enjoyed such gatherings, Cobb remained a "family man." He tried to be "in bed by ten-thirty if he could manage it," because of his demanding job and the need to make a living and support his family. But being exposed to popular writers of considerable talent expanded his horizons and encouraged his desire to write fiction.[18]

Cobb's star rose rapidly, and he became one of the most popular writers in New York. By early 1908, he was offered a three-year contract by the Pulitzer papers, with a base salary of $7,500 a year and permission to sell other writings his paper did not use. Still in his early thirties, Cobb hit his stride and began to branch out, displaying more and more of his writing talents, particularly humor. By then, the *Evening World* had become a "modern" newspaper in many ways, with a popular full-time sports columnist, Bozeman Bulger; "Betty Vincent's Advice to Lovers"; reviews of plays and operas; cartoons (often outrageously racist); a profusion of photographs and illustrations; and hard-hitting editorials of a progressive nature, as well as advertisements for such establishments as Macy's and Bloomingdale's.[19]

Cobb never became part of the inner circle of Pulitzer's *New York World* organization, but he deftly served that organization on one major occasion. The *World* led a campaign to investigate the Roosevelt administration's negotiations over acquisition of the Panama Canal. Although the courts found no wrongdoing, Roosevelt felt aggrieved and sued Pulitzer's newspapers for the false accusations. Eventually, the furor struck closer to home when one of Roosevelt's kinsmen urged William Travers Jerome, "the spunky, explosive district attorney" who had prosecuted Thaw, to issue an arrest warrant for Pulitzer for "malicious misstatement." There was no love lost between Jerome and the *World,* but he did nothing. Cobb recalled that "Mr. Pulitzer's higher-ups, the big ones and the medium-sized ones and the little teeny-weeny ones, went straightway into dire panic," fearing that they would all go to jail. After these executives spent large sums on lawyers and detectives to discover the reason behind Jerome's inaction, the *Evening World*'s managing editor called Cobb into his office and then dispatched him upstairs to the inner sanctum of leadership. Believing that Cobb was a "friend" of Jerome, they asked the reporter to quiz the district attorney about his intentions.[20]

The two men met in a bar, and Jerome suspected the reason for Cobb's visit. According to Cobb's 1941 reconstruction of the event, Jerome said: "Well, Kentuck, what's on our mind—if anything? Not that I couldn't make a guess." As it turned out, Jerome had no intention of pursuing the matter, even though he believed the *World* had often attacked him without provocation. In retribution, he said, "I've let King Pulitzer—and his gang of sycophants—stew in their own juice." Cobb returned to the paper's offices on Park Avenue within fifty minutes, and despite being given an unlimited expense account, he claimed only ten cents for round-trip streetcar fare. When he reported his findings, the newspapermen immediately telephoned Pulitzer, and "for the first, last and only time in my life," Cobb said, "I heard the voice of Joseph Pulitzer," who expressed his relief. As a postscript, Cobb noted in 1941: "No official notice was ever taken of this performance. I was pledged not to mention it myself. But at intervals for weeks thereafter and upon the slightest provocation my name would go up on the bulletin board as the recipient of a cash award for merit—usually on the strength of some commonplace story covered according to commonplace rote. The thing got to be an office scandal. Fellows went around calling me 'Teacher's Pet' and wondering how I accomplished such larceny." Cobb had found a secure place at the Pulitzer papers.[21]

3

From Newspaperman
to Short Story Writer

With his humor column in the *Evening World* and other ventures in
that genre, Cobb joined a long tradition of writers whose style of humor
endeared them to Americans in the nineteenth and early twentieth centuries. Samuel Clemens (Mark Twain) was the most famous of the lot; his
extensive writings established him as a "moralist-humanist" whose fiction
took up for the oppressed, opposed corruption, and satisfied American
and even international tastes. Twain was every young reporter's hero. Soon
after Cobb arrived in New York, he interviewed the venerable author, then
in his seventies. According to Cobb's daughter, he "did meet Mark Twain,
being sent to interview him and finding him a cross old man in a room
stained and evil-smelling from tobacco juice, and exceedingly rude to a
boy who worshipped him." Twain, of course, had a persona (or he developed one) to fit his image of the westerner-cum-easterner who spun tales
from his earliest days in California to his last days in Connecticut. He
embraced the role, with his long white hair and mustache, linen suit and
string tie, cigar clenched purposefully in his mouth, and a look of outward disdain for the world.[1]

Cobb's appearance also aided his development as a master humorist.
Whereas Twain became patriarchal, almost biblical, Cobb evolved into a
prototypical southerner. A person's image is often intimately connected
to how his or her writing is projected to the public. In Cobb's case, photographs and illustrations of him in various poses often accompanied his
humor pieces. Beginning just after he joined the *Evening World,* Cobb

"suddenly ballooned into a fat man," according to one biographer, which "he attributed . . . to his newly acquired desk job; probably prosperity and a more settled home life." Cobb's daughter described the transformation as he took up his new assignment: "At the same time he began to plump up. One day he was a long, lean, Gary-Cooper-legged boy, the next a fat man." However, the process did not occur overnight, as pictures from his early years at the *Evening World* do not show an overly chubby face. It took several years for Cobb to develop the large stomach that became part of his persona, along with his bulging eyes, bushy eyebrows, and cigar protruding from his mouth. These characteristics became more pronounced as he aged, and he would often write about his eating habits, his girth, and his health problems in the years ahead. As Cobb recalled in one of his lengthy autobiographical pieces, as a thin, six-foot-tall sixteen-year-old he was known to his friends in Paducah as "Bonesy," but "when I got fat I capitalized my fatness in the printed word. I told how it felt to be fat."[2]

Cobb turned out excellent coverage of straight news stories, as well as commentary on horse shows, baseball, prize fighting, and political rallies and conventions. Most of his front-page reportage for the *Evening World* was not accompanied with a byline, but his style became unmistakable. His offbeat subjects, attention to detail, and humor became staples for *Evening World* readers. The public enjoyed and appreciated his stories of several thousand words. One of his 1909 articles about an important New York City horse show was so memorable that a *New York Tribune* columnist insisted in 1921 that this was the only such piece "we have ever read through." He continued, "That was the story, by the way, when Mr. Cobb achieved the perfect simile by saying that Mrs. W. E. Corey, with a pair of emerald earrings, looked like a Lenox Avenue local [train]." Cobb displayed his natural sense of humor in his *Evening World* column "New York thro' Funny Glasses." He chose an old artifice—the somewhat bewildered rube in the big city—for these columns, and he would use other devices throughout his career. Cobb admitted it was not always easy to be funny and to turn out column after column, but he succeeded better than most writers in the early twentieth century.[3]

To Cobb, "in its essence, humor merely is tragedy standing on its head with its pants torn." He claimed that some writers had a keen sense of satire and could recognize the ridiculousness of life, but they were always looking down on the world "in a rarefied atmosphere of intellectual purity." This type of person laughs *at* the world, not *with* it, and is not part of it. "It is such a one who says, 'What fools *you* mortals be,' never, 'What fools *we* mortals be.'" According to Cobb, the true humorist would always be saying between the lines, yet perfectly recognizably: "'My poor friend, you're an awful ass, addicted to all manner of nonsensical performances. But in your most asinine moment you never came anywhere near to being the ass that I am. So in all humility, as one ass to another let's sit down here together and talk about ourselves and our failings. For the Lord knows we'll have plenty to talk about.'" Cobb asserted, "Mark Twain developed this captivating artifice to a point approximating perfection." In Cobb's estimation, contemporaries such as Bill Nye, Opie Read, and Robert Benchley, as well as Gracie Allen and Dorothy Parker, followed this line. Canadian Stephen Leacock agreed with Cobb's basic estimation of humor when he wrote: "Humor may be defined as the kindly contemplation of the incongruities of life and the artistic expression thereof." A twentieth-century New Zealand humorist espoused the same understanding of humor: "It is healthy to accept the world is full of bumbling fools only if you understand you are a fully qualified bumbling fool yourself."[4]

In Cobb's first long-running humor series for the *Evening World*, "New York thro' Funny Glasses," he used his small-town Kentucky perspective to make observations about the big city. But did the big city change this small-town southerner? In some ways, Cobb began to view the world a bit differently. In one column, he explained how a white southerner might react in Gotham, where the color line was not as rigidly drawn as in his native state. Sitting across from "the crowning product of the Freedman's Bureau—a gentleman of the complexion of a fountain pen"—on a streetcar, Cobb's imaginary southerner is distressed but doesn't confront the African American, as he might have in his hometown. "Five minutes [later] he is passing his colored brother the horse-radish" in a diner. To top it all off, the transplanted southerner has even lost his inherent manners, failing to give up his streetcar seat to a female passenger. "He believes in letting her stand," Cobb wrote, and doesn't even complain when she steps on his toes. Was Cobb learning about the complexities of race as well as adjusting to the exigencies of life in the big city?[5]

In addition to writing his popular column, Cobb continued to cover front-page news stories, including whenever a big circus came to town, having inherited his father's love of the big top. His style of reporting was easily identifiable because of his insertion of droll, understated humor whenever possible. Never a fan of William Jennings Bryan, for example, he parodied a speech by Bryan in 1908 that was unmistakably Cobbesque. He also reported about the ongoing problems of Thaw and other high-profile criminals.[6]

Other experiments in humor for the *Evening World* included "Little Journeys to the Homes of the Big Dubs," which was accompanied by a cartoon of Cobb shopping in a haberdashery. An unsigned column titled "Notes of a Southern Journey" ran for several weeks in 1909, and it could only have been written by Cobb. He enlightened his northern readers with typical deadpan descriptions of a trip to South Carolina. "Rice is served as a vegetable at all meals in Charleston and eaten with salt and butter. The Yankee habit of putting it into pudding dishes is regarded as a mistake." He observed, "Mistletoe abounds everywhere except where the pretty girls are, and the pretty girls abound away from the mistletoe. Such guarantees of both—are both wasted." He quipped, "The Fig trees are full out on the streets of Charleston. They are no longer used for garments." His southernness became obvious in the fourth installment. Discovering "colored" workmen at the Charleston navy yard, he declared them to be slow workers "until the whistle blows to stop work, when they develop the energy of a Brooklyn crowd in a bridge crash in their scramble to get away from toil. It seems funny to have a naval yard full of non-voters." However, in "Notes on a Journey West" Cobb reserved some of his critique for the insularity of New Yorkers when he declared, "Everything becomes 'West' when the train leaves Albany."[7]

The transplanted Kentuckian exemplified the racial attitudes of many white Americans in the early twentieth century. The *Evening World,* for instance, often included cartoons of black boxers that exaggerated racial stereotypes and negated their skills in the ring. So Cobb was apparently following company policy when he heaped his worst racial invective on heavyweight boxing champion Jack Johnson. In a "Funny Side of Sports" segment, he wrote about "Mistah Artha' Johnsing licorice colored gladiator" and his upcoming bout with retired heavyweight champion James J. Jeffries. Johnson defeated Jeffries in a much ballyhooed match in Reno, Nevada, on July 4, 1910. It was a one-sided fight from the first round, as Johnson toyed with the old champion. As one of Jeffries's handlers "threw in the sponge," Johnson landed a vicious right that downed the "white hope." Riots erupted in several American cities—some because of race-baiting, and others the result of African American celebrations. Many white commentators asserted that Jeffries had been drugged. Cobb later attended an interview show where Johnson, anxious to cash in on his celebrity, answered questions from the audience. Cobb wrote about this experience in racially charged words that can only be described as a tirade. In a column titled "One Hour with Mistah Jack Johnson," Cobb declared, "I don't believe he will ever fight another championship battle, but if he does and should meet a real fighter, I believe white supremacy will come back into its own again." Cobb then continued his diatribe: "I am surprised no one has so far likened his physical make-up to a crate garden truck. His skull is the shape of a 40-cent Georgia watermelon. . . . He has a nose that's the very image of a young onion half-buried in a rich loam, and when he opens his mouth and shows his teeth you think of a roasting ear of spring corn." Fixated on his denunciation of Johnson, Cobb described the black prizefighter as having a "body lithe as a black snake . . . a slew-footed coon they'd call him in his native Galveston." Cobb's view of Johnson was shared by most white Americans during one of the worst periods of racial strife in American history known, ironically, as the Progressive Era.[8]

Cobb loved all sports. As a youth, he had once dreamed of baseball stardom. After becoming a reporter for the *Evening World,* and once he was given some leeway to choose his own subjects of interest, he often wrote about the New York City baseball teams. This was the heyday of the New York Giants and manager John McGraw. To a lesser extent he also covered the Brooklyn Dodgers and the New York Hilltoppers (later known as the Yankees). Cobb observed that while the grass "is greener and smoother" at the Giants' Polo Grounds, "the peanuts at the Hilltop are infinitely superior." The *Evening World* sometimes ran front-page stories by Cobb about the crowds and the sports scene, while sportswriter Bozeman Bulger covered the actual inning-by-inning playing of the game. "Quaker (Philadelphia Athletics) Fans Out Do Giant Followers in Outbursts of Joy," read the headline of one of Cobb's pieces in which he described the enormous crowd attending a World Series game. When the Giants returned to New York, Cobb claimed with some hyperbole, "We write our story in a Niagara Sound that deafens us," referring to a crowd estimated at 50,000. Before the days of radio, Cobb found a way to provide vivid details for his readers, writing as if they had joined him in witnessing the event.[9]

One of Cobb's most successful humor columns in the *Evening World*, "The Browe Brothers—Hiram and Loerum," ran for several years. A play on the clash of highbrow and lowbrow culture, "Hiram" and "Loerum" often commented on the news of the day, with the latter usually coming out on top. When discussing the possibility of a second term for President William Howard Taft, Loerum declared, "From where I sit it looks very much to me like one term at the White House, followed by several others raising chickens out in Ohio." When commenting on former president Theodore Roosevelt's reported throat trouble, Loerum asked, "When did Teddy stop talking long enough for a doctor to look down him?" Cobb's dislike of William Jennings Bryan, which coincided with the *World's* editorial policies, also found its way into "The Browe Brothers." Given Bryan's prohibitionist beliefs, Loerum declared the Nebraskan had no chance of winning the 1912 Democratic nomination for president. "And, anyway, how could a Nebraska Democrat go to the next National Convention wearing a white ribbon (a Prohibitionist symbol) in his button hole and nothing on his breath and look the Tammany delegates and the Kentucky warhorses in the face?" Cobb excelled at the one-line zinger that laid an argument to rest, at least for him. "New York thro' Funny Glasses" and "The Browe Brothers" remained staples for about four years, until Cobb left the Pulitzer paper.[10]

Beginning shortly after Cobb joined the *Evening World*, a very brief unsigned column, "Cos Cob Nature Notes," ran periodically on the editorial page. Cos Cob is actually an old settlement and current neighborhood in Greenwich, Connecticut. The wording and understated humor have all the earmarks of Cobb's style. Although other columns have been attributed to him by other biographers and writers, to my knowledge, this one has never been mentioned. These very short pieces included what was purportedly personal information about local residents or events. For example: "A new Billy Goat is the latest excitement in Riverside, a pleasant little suburb of Cos Cob." "Winter is a pleasant season if you look at it right." "Our citizens observed Groundhog Day much as usual. Some went to the Post Office, others took the trolley to Horseneck." "John Bole's donkey sounds reveille at 5:30 A.M. and taps at 9:30 P.M." On one occasion, the author mentioned a friend who had been "brought up" on Kentucky bourbon. The "Cos Cob" pieces would disappear for a while and then appear every few days. One noted, "Gus Scott says the fish are so eager to be ketched that they just jump in the boat." Cobb's other humor columns never appeared in the same issue of the *Evening World* as "Cos Cob." Who else would have written this final line to a column: "Roses and honeysuckle are in bloom, and the night air bears a scent of paradise"? After Cobb left the *Evening World* and moved on to the *Saturday Evening Post,* he apparently made periodic submissions of "Cos Cob" to the former paper. Perhaps to supplement his income, he turned out such observations as "The garter snakes are out with their new spring suits on" and "The pie plant, sometimes called Rhubarb, is now in full refulgence and some has gone to seed." "Pie plant" is a distinctively southern name for rhubarb. Perhaps I am wrong, but these columns bear unmistakable characteristics of Cobb's style.[11]

Cobb's successful humor writing in the *Evening World* led his bosses to find a place for his work in the *Sunday World Magazine,* which included sports, women's news, and other features with voluminous pictures and illustrations. In 1908 Cobb began to experiment with a new series called "Hotel Clerk," which appeared in the *Sunday World Magazine* until February 1910. The fictional setting is the "Hotel St. Reckless," where the clerk and his fellow hotel employees, primarily the house detective, make wry comments about the happenings of the day and the foibles of their fellow human beings. In these columns, the transplanted Kentuckian often took the side of the downtrodden, but he could just as easily make cynical comments about President Theodore Roosevelt and other notables. In one piece, when the house detective asked, "'What's Teddy going to Africa for?' The Hotel Clerk replies, 'For a dollar a word.'"[12]

While Cobb took up for the common people in his writing on racial, social, and economic injustice, he could also take a swipe at his fellow white southerners in a backhanded way. When John D. Rockefeller gave $1 million in 1908 toward the fight against hookworm in the South, Cobb observed, tongue in cheek:

It's a question in my mind whether the people down there want the hookworm dispossessed from their midst by a rank outsider from the north. From what I can learn, intimate association with

Brer Hookworm and his interesting household is productive of a most soothing languor. The owner of one of these pleasant domestic pets doesn't care whether school keeps or not. All he craves is the shady side of the house, a couple of hound pups for company and a little bait of hoe cake a la pellagra three times a day. . . . His greatest physical exertion is voting the Democratic ticket once a year. But just picture what'll happen to his peace of mind when some Yankee comes around and deprives him of his private zoo.

He went on to declare that the cured southerner would "resent being filled with a sudden and uncomfortable restlessness that'll start him out hustling for a job. With him slavery and work are synonymous, and if anything work is the more synonymous of the two."[13]

The "Hotel Clerk" columns were always highlighted by humorous illustrations. Like the columns, the art was stylized and puerile, following a pattern that appealed to Cobb's editors and the reading public. Making fun of politicians such as Taft, Roosevelt, Bryan, and Joe Cannon became a regular feature. Racial issues came up occasionally, and although Cobb condemned lynching, he continued to disparage African Americans in his sardonically humorous way. "We can't isolate him, because if we did we'd have to learn to pick our own cotton and this, when done under the noonday beams of the ardent Southern sun, is represented to be an undertaking bordering on the irksome." Cobb offhandedly criticized the plight of blacks but offered no way to alleviate the problem. "Anyway, he fills a niche here," he continued. "At handling a bay mule he stands without a peer, and his wife can beat anybody in the world frying a chicken." A serious commentary was always followed by comic relief as Cobb, in effect, explained his "southern" view of African Americans to his big-city white northern audience.[14]

By 1911, Cobb was taking home $99 a week from the *Evening World* and another $51 for his contributions to the Sunday paper. Apparently afraid that the other reporters might be envious of his extra pay, the Pulitzer organization paid Cobb at the window reserved for regular staff rather than at the one designated for those making more than $100 a week. Cobb sometimes received as many as four checks, including bonuses, in addition to his work for the McClure syndicate, which reprinted some of his columns. When McClure's did not promptly mail him a check,

Cobb would jokingly plead, "I'm needing the dough." Cobb also ventured into writing advertising copy. Beginning as early as 1909, he wrote pamphlets such as "Talks with the Fat Chauffeur," on the virtues of the new Ford Model-T, for which he chose to take a $500 fee rather than Ford stock. "You Can Afford a Ford," Cobb proclaimed in one of the five self-described "screeds" he wrote in three days. With this extra income, he took a summer vacation.[15]

As Cobb's income increased, he succumbed to the trend of moving to the suburbs, as did many other well-to-do New Yorkers. In 1907 the Cobb family moved into a "plain little box of a house" in the Park Hill suburb of Yonkers, according to daughter Buff (aka Elisabaeth). It was during this period that the "Cos Cob Nature Notes" began to appear anonymously, which I believe were Cobb's comic comments on the suburban lifestyle that he found both enjoyable and ironic. Laura Cobb immediately planted a garden, as she would do every time the family moved. Over the next five years, the Cobbs developed a typical suburban lifestyle. Father went off to work by rail each morning and returned each evening. Buff enjoyed the atmosphere and recalled attending various church services with other families in the community. "From the synagogue to the Catholic chapel," she said, "they made me welcome, odd little visitant that I was." She explored the neighborhood, meeting all the families within walking distance, and introduced her father to a man who would become very influential in his life, George H. Doran. "Our first-and-second mortgage leafy fastnesses faced stern end to across the rocky soil (beautiful garden-spot of the prospectus) of 50' × 100' lots in this mountainous region of Westchester," recalled Doran. "Observant Elisabeth, his precocious daughter of six, after contemplating the rear and kitchen end of our shady nook, hastened to inform her parents that we new-comers (name unknown) must be attractive people, for we had such nice garbage." For five years the Cobb and Doran "bungalows stood back to back." Eventually, the Canadian-born Doran would publish forty-two books written by Cobb.[16]

Relocating to Yonkers whetted Cobb's appetite for other moves. He turned the experience of finding cheap real estate, the mythical "Abandoned Farm," into a humorous piece that appeared on August 15, 1909, in the *Sunday World.* Eventually, this would evolve into longer pieces in the *Saturday Evening Post* and *The Abandoned Farmers,* a book published by Doran in 1920. The next major move for the family came in 1916, and although it was not exactly to an abandoned farm, it was to an old estate Cobb named "Rebel Ridge," a nonproductive sixty-acre farm near the town of Ossining in Westchester County, New York. Wherever he lived or visited, Cobb found material for his writing projects. By means of exaggeration and other stratagems, he could always find humor in the ordinariness of life.[17]

Except on the matter of race, Cobb was surprisingly progressive if not liberal. He showed no opposition to the women's movement, which focused on gaining the right to vote. In one "Hotel Clerk" column, the clerk informed his detective friend that in England, "Bobbies don't use clubs like the American cops. They don't need them. They're a brawny manly lot—Almost any two of them are equal to the task of beating a woman into immortality without the use of any tools whatsoever." Through the hotel clerk, Cobb noted, "If the New York woman wants to smoke, she'll smoke." Throughout the life of these columns, Cobb demonstrated his disdain for spirituality, stuffy religious organizations, political shenanigans, Prohibition, the wealthy, and any type of pretentiousness that he deemed silly.[18]

Beginning with the February 13, 1910, issue of the *Sunday World Magazine,* Cobb developed another motif for his humor: "Live Talks with Dead Ones," in which he carried on imaginary conversations with famous deceased people, the first being St. Valentine. Through Shakespeare, Cobb made fun of the modern theater, having the great playwright lament the dearth of important issues in the plays of David Belasco, a Broadway favorite at the time. "Your musical is especially designed for the tired business man," claimed the Bard. The following week, a conversation between Henry VIII and Brigham Young touched on the suffrage issue: the English monarch admitted his predilection for ending his wives' lives and pointed out that Young would be outvoted by his multiple wives. Other "Live Talks with Dead Ones" included such luminaries as Edgar Allan Poe and Spartacus.[19]

While on the *World* staff, Cobb also developed "The Diary of Noah" and "The Gotham Geography" as platforms for his humor in the *Sunday World Magazine.* All the while, he kept up his midweek column in the *Evening World,* as well as covering news events.[20]

Over the next three decades, Cobb turned out an immense amount of copy for newspapers and then magazines; he wrote short stories, plays, and novels and even tried his hand at movies. He was never short of ideas. As explained by his daughter, "He worked hard, and when I say hard I mean terribly hard." However, the work could be trying. When one of his colleagues had difficulty keeping up his humor columns, Cobb said: "When the best of them doesn't feel funny, which is most of the time, he just doesn't feel funny and that's all there is to it." Cobb "suffered from nightmares," fearing "that someday his head would stop working for him" and he would be unable to turn out material. He made a lot of money and spent it on homes, travel, good food and drink, and his family. He was not always frugal, as his daughter claimed: "It is very hard after years of privation not to spend most, if not all, of that green stuff with the Presidents' pictures on it, once it does start pouring in."[21]

At the time Cobb arrived on the New York City publishing scene, the major forms of entertainment were still limited to print and live performances, including minstrel shows, vaudeville, theater in various forms, circuses, and sports such as professional baseball, college football, and boxing. Popular culture of the late nineteenth and early twentieth centuries evolved as more discretionary income became available to a growing middle class. Burlesque and vaudeville would soon be joined by silent motion pictures as this form of entertainment became available in most urban areas. Chautauqua was also part of the American cultural scene, and well-attended circuits crisscrossed rural and small-town America every summer until the advent of radio and "talkies" in the 1920s. Both the "high" culture of the legitimate theater and classical music and the "low" culture of Tin Pan Alley, the blues, and ragtime became big businesses and competed in the marketplace. Writers such as Cobb reported on many of these cultural events. Cobb knew what interested readers, and his writing style appealed to that audience.[22]

During his time at the Pulitzer papers, Cobb joined the cognoscenti of the New York media. This was the heyday of print journalism, before radio came on the scene in the early 1920s and sound was added to the silver screen. Other writers such as Damon Runyon enjoyed Cobb's companionship; he delighted in meeting new people and introducing them into his circle of friends. Cobb continued his "serious" reporting but was willing to do almost anything that brought in a generous income. When he signed a new contract in 1908, Cobb's salary increased to $7,500 a year. "Whether it was true or not, I was called the highest paid reporter in this country and perhaps in the world," Cobb noted in *Exit Laughing*. Moreover, he was allowed to sell his material to other outlets through the McClure syndicate. "Frequently my income for a single month was upwards of a thousand dollars—and did I count myself a darling of prime luck!"[23]

For all his success, Cobb was not satisfied with newspaper work alone. There never seemed to be enough money to support himself, his wife and daughter, and the three Cobb women back in Paducah. Buff recalled how her father dealt with his dilemma: "So he stewed and he fretted and he worried and longed, and hoped and doubted. And walked, a million miles or so, up and down, twisting and twisting the buttons on his vest. That was the sign of strain. When one had to sew and sew and sew again the buttons back on Irvin's vest, and around them appeared a perfectly slick, shiny circle of cloth worn napless by his unconscious incessant gesture— he was worried." The pressure Cobb put on himself was enormous.[24]

A storyteller from his childhood days, Cobb soon turned to short fiction. He had a wellspring of stories in his mind, based on either characters he had known or composites of individuals. Apparently, a number of people encouraged Cobb to write fiction, and Laura and several of his reporter friends offered their support. Former *World* political writer Samuel G. Blythe, who had taken a job with the *Saturday Evening Post* in 1907, told Cobb that *Post* editor George Horace Lorimer would welcome a story by Cobb. The $500 he had made writing advertising copy for Henry Ford made it possible for Cobb and his family to spend six weeks in the summer of 1909 with the Blythes in the Adirondacks. There, both men worked on their fiction while relaxing with their families.[25]

While Cobb worked on several stories that he termed his "grim tales," the primary outcome that summer was "The Escape of Mr. Trimm." Cobb based much of his fiction on his childhood experiences in Kentucky, as well as the stories he had covered as a reporter from western Kentucky to Louisville to New York City. "Trimm" came to mind after Cobb covered the trial of Charles W. Morse, "former head of the iniquitous Ice Trust and a notorious Wall Street marauder whose manipulations got him snarled up with the law." Though sentenced to prison, Morse "was too smart to stay there." Cobb fictionalized what would happen to such a scoundrel who did not have the luck or the political pull of a Morse in

"The Escape of Mr. Trimm." Among other ideas he worked on that summer were the first "Judge Priest" stories, which became his most popular
and best remembered pieces of fiction.[26]

Published in the *Saturday Evening Post* on November 27, 1909, "The
Escape of Mr. Trimm" is one of Cobb's most anthologized stories. It contains elements that would be repeated in Cobb's later fiction. The story is
about a wealthy man who has risen to great heights, primarily owing to
his nefarious methods, but who eventually receives his comeuppance. In
effect, it is a morality play. Unfortunately, as both Cobb and his readers
knew, in the real world, the guilty often evade punishment, the wealthy
have special privileges, and there is no complete justice.[27]

The story is worth reading today as an example of what the early-
twentieth-century public enjoyed, particularly in a popular, influential,
"middlebrow" magazine like the *Saturday Evening Post*. Somber illustrations by F. R. Gruber added to the gravity of this tale, which war-
rants retelling here. After several trials and appeals, Hobart W. Trimm,
"recently president of the Late Thirteenth National Bank," which he had
driven into bankruptcy, is about to be transferred from the Tombs in
New York City to federal prison. Well treated while in the local jail, with
catered meals and a corner cell, Trimm assumes he will receive more of
the same in prison during his thirteen-year sentence. His lawyer assures
him that he will have a drawing room on the train taking him to prison
and that all the wheels have been greased.[28]

Then things begin to go terribly wrong for the Wall Street manipula-
tor, for whom Cobb and his readers have no sympathy. Deputy Marshal
Meyers, assigned to take Trimm to prison, slips "a new and shiny pair
of Bean's Latest Model Little Giant handcuffs" around the miscreant's
wrists. Hoping to spare Trimm the embarrassment of a gawking crowd,
the warden had planned to sneak him and Meyers out a side door. "But
New York reporters are up to the tricks of people who want to evade
them," and "around the wall of the Tombs came pelting a flying mob
of newspaper photographers and reporters, with a choice rabble behind
them."[29]

To add insult to injury, Trimm discovers that he has no drawing-room
reservation on the train and is forced to sit with Meyers in a smoking car.
Then the first of several twists, similar to those in the stories of O. Henry,
occurs. The train is involved in a collision. Trimm miraculously escapes

injury, but Meyers is killed. Trimm wanders about for the next several days, evading detection, until he reads in a newspaper that his body has been identified as one of those killed. In a pattern that would be evident in all Cobb's stories, he adds detail after detail, perhaps too many for the flow of the plot. But in 1909, most "short" stories were written in the same fashion. Of course, the arrogant Trimm decides to take advantage of the situation, contact his lawyer, obtain most if not all of his secreted $4 million, and strike out for foreign parts.[30]

However, even after extensive machinations, Trimm finds that the accursed handcuffs cannot be removed. His arms and wrists redden and swell, and the handcuffs tighten with every attempt to escape them. A small boy runs away in terror at the sight of the increasingly deteriorating banker. Trimm finds brief succor at the camp of a tramp, but even there he is rebuffed in his attempt to overawe the "knavish-looking vagabond," who threatens to turn him in. "Of a sudden, Mr. Trimm became the primitive man. He was filled with those elemental emotions that make a man see crimson" and shoved the tramp over a cliff. The rain and the cold, the pain of the ever-tightening handcuffs, his hunger and hopelessness finally drive Trimm to surrender himself to the local police chief. When the policeman declares that Trimm is dead, according to the newspapers, there is only one thing to do: "Slowly, with struggling effort, he raised his hands into the chief's sight." Cobb describes them in great detail: "And at the wrists, almost buried in the swollen folds of flesh, blackened, rusted, battered, yet still strong and whole, was a tightly-locked pair of new model handcuffs." But when the chief offers to remove the cuffs, Trimm declares: "'They can wait. . . . I have worn them a long, long while—I am used to them. Wouldn't you please get me some food first?'"[31]

The story was an overwhelming success, and Cobb was paid $500 for it. Lorimer assured Cobb that the *Saturday Evening Post* would publish his work on a regular basis. To Cobb, the thought of cutting himself free from the grinding work at the *Evening World,* covering newsworthy events and writing two humor columns, was attractive, but he was hesitant to make another major change in his life and give up his secure income. However, he was already branching out. For example, a month before his story appeared in the *Post, Popular Magazine,* a literary journal founded in 1903, published Cobb's "Tale of the Hard Luck Guy." In contrast to "The Escape of Mr. Trimm," this piece relied on Cobb's established writing style, which the magazine promoted as "decidedly humorous in a vein that is the author's own." At the end of that story, a suicidal man asks the narrator for some money "because, he said, he still had his family pride left and it would look more respectable if he had money on his person when the body was recovered." In the coming years, Cobb would be confronted with the quandary of writing what sold best—his humor—or branching out into serious fiction.[32]

4

Crossroads Again

Success, Fame, and Fortune

For Irvin Cobb, the period from 1911 through 1914 was one of the most productive in his career. Despite the success of "The Escape of Mr. Trimm" in 1909, he remained on the staff of the *New York World*. Cobb was not ready to forgo a steady paycheck for what seemed to be a risky move to the *Saturday Evening Post*. He was in no hurry to leave his comfort zone.

Cobb suffered from anxiety all his life. Extreme apprehension can lead to illness and despair, but Cobb was driven to overcome his anxiety by both his need to support his family and his ambition to be successful. He had already proved that he could earn a substantial income; however, owing to his lack of formal education, his upbringing in small-town Paducah, and financial pressures, he always felt like something of an underdog. He had an understandable sense of "missing something," as his daughter Buff revealed; he had a chip on his shoulder and could be quite defensive on occasion. Perhaps his talkativeness and his tendency to dominate conversations, which some found charming and others found offensive, came from this feeling. For example, Ring Lardner liked Cobb, but the Kentuckian's telling of one "funny" anecdote after another wore on him. After one such incident when "Cobb did all the talking," Lardner retaliated by writing, "Mr. Cobb is never so happy as when he is amongst his books of which he has a complete set." One of Lardner's biographers reported that "Cobb did not find it amusing."[1]

Several times in his life when Cobb had found himself at a crossroads,

anxiety and doubt had nearly overwhelmed him. Up to this point, however, he had always found the courage to push himself and take a chance.
Now he faced another such crossroads in his writing career.

Cobb, like most writers of proven ability, was always looking for new
outlets for his talents—not only to earn a living but also to establish a
place for himself in American literature. After being in New York City for
less than a decade, Cobb had hit his stride. He could hold his own in the
most competitive newspaper field in America as well as write humorous
columns that engaged a wide reading audience. And now he had broken
into fiction. The question was, how far could he go in this new genre?
Moreover, would Americans' taste in fiction change in the early twentieth century? As Wayne Chatterton explained, Cobb's short stories, which
involved a "long, leisurely development," became dated as more "modern,
highly selective, 'functional' forms of short fiction" evolved after 1920.
In short, Cobb's type of short fiction was becoming dated even as he perfected it. Could he change his style to fit the new trend?[2]

Nonetheless, Robert Davis, editor of *Munsey's Magazine* from 1904
to 1925, declared in 1912 that Cobb was already more productive than
other, more famous writers. "I know of no single instance where one man
has shown such fecundity and quality as Irvin Cobb has so far evinced,
and it is my opinion that his complete works at fifty [Cobb was thirty-six
at the time] will contain more good humor, more good short stories, and
at least one bigger novel than the works of any other single contemporane-
ous figure."[3] Though obviously a "puff" piece to praise his friend, Davis's
opinion would have been shared by Cobb's many friends and admirers.
According to Davis, "There appears to be no phase of human emotion
beyond his pen." After the appearance of Cobb's first short stories, he
effused: "Thus in Irvin Cobb we find Mark Twain, Bret Harte and Edgar
Allan Poe at their best."[4]

Davis related a conversation he had with Cobb after attending the
funeral of Joseph Pulitzer on a "bleak November afternoon in 1911."
Watching a crowd of people as they rode the streetcar, Cobb said, "'It
reminds me of a river, into which all humanity is drawn. Some of these
people think because they are walking up-stream they are getting out of
it. But they never escape. The current is at work on them. Some day they
will get tired and go down again, and finally pass out to sea.'" Somewhat
befuddled by Cobb's remarks, Davis asked: "'What's on your mind?'":

"Nothing particular," Cobb said, scanning the banks of the great municipal stream, "except that I intend to write a novel some day about a boy born at the headwaters. Gradually he floats down through the tributaries, across the valleys, swings into the main stream, and docks finally at one of the cities on its banks. This particular youth was a great success—in the beginning. Every door was open to him. He had position, brains, and popularity to boot. He married brilliantly. And then The Past, a trivial, unimportant Detail, lifted its head and barked at him. He was too sensitive to bark back. Thereupon it bit him and he collapsed."[5]

Davis explained that Cobb then "ceased talking. For some reason—indefinable—I respected his silence. Two blocks further down he took up the thread of his story again": "'One evening, just about sundown, a river hand, sitting on a string-piece of a dock, saw a derby hat bobbing in the muddy Mississippi, floating unsteadily but surely into the Gulf of Mexico.'" After another silence, Davis asked Cobb what he was thinking of calling the novel. When he did not answer, Davis suggested "The River." Cobb replied, "'Very well, I'll call it The River.' He scrambled down from his seat. 'I'm docking at Twenty-seventh Street. Good-by. Keep your hat out of the water.'"[6]

Davis doubted the novel would be called "The River," but he believed it would end unhappily. Was Cobb thinking out loud, describing the "great American novel" he hoped to write someday, or was he just amusing his friend with a few whimsical thoughts? Was he anxious about his own career, indulging in an allegorical musing about his own talents and his dread of unfulfilled dreams? Did Cobb sense that his inventiveness, the creativity evinced in his range of writings, had reached a watershed?[7]

Cobb stayed with the *World* for two more years before joining the staff of the *Saturday Evening Post* full time in January 1912. He continued to write some pieces for the *World* and other publications, always on the lookout for extra income. During this time, he likely wrote the occasional "Cos Cob Nature Notes" that appeared in the *Evening World.*[8]

Cobb's decision to leave the *World* and work full time for the *Saturday Evening Post* caused him almost paralyzing apprehension. "He told me that when the first week rolled by, and payday came, though not for him, he went near crazy," wrote daughter Buff. "He could concentrate on nothing; he just stayed near a telephone, so that if the pressure grew unbearable he might call the *World* at any moment, and ask them to take him back. And he twiddled two sets of buttons off his vest." Cobb's wife apparently handled these challenges with more courage and resilience than he did. "But if he was timid, wife Laura was not," claimed George Doran in his autobiography. Having this support at home must have comforted him.[9]

Cobb worked hard on his short story writing, and "The Exit of Anse Dugmore" appeared in the December 17, 1911, issue of the *Saturday Evening Post.* Another of his "grim" tales, "Anse Dugmore" is based more or less on the history of feuds in eastern Kentucky that Cobb knew so well. The story is simple enough. After spending some years in prison for his murderous activities, Anse is pardoned by the governor owing to his impending death from consumption. Still bent on revenge, Anse heads home, where he learns that his wife and two children are now living with his archenemy Sheriff Wyatt Trantham. With rifle in hand, he heads toward denouement with Trantham. Cobb excelled at making his characters lifelike. Before meeting the governor, Anse is described as "merely a rack of bones enclosed in a shapeless covering of black-and-white stripes. On his close-cropped head and over his cheekbones the skin was stretched so tight it seemed nearly ready to split. His eyes, glassy and bleared with pain, stared ahead of him with a sick man's fixed stare." True to his developing style, Cobb added an O. Henry–like twist to the simple tale. As the nearly dead Anse waits to ambush Trantham, he watches his enemy halt his horse and take objects out of his saddlebags to admire them—toys intended for Anse's own children for Christmas. When Anse's body is discovered with his finger still on the trigger, "his finders were moved to conclude that the freed convict must have bled to death from his lungs before the sheriff ever passed, which they held to be a good thing all around and a lucky thing for the sheriff."[10]

By the time Cobb joined the *Saturday Evening Post,* it had already been radically changed by George Horace Lorimer, who assumed editorship of the Philadelphia-based magazine in 1898. It was part of the Curtis Company, which also published the very lucrative *Ladies' Home Journal* as well as other journals and books. Lorimer soon transformed the *Saturday Evening Post,* the oldest such publication in the United States, into the premier weekly magazine in the nation. It contained editorials, news items, opinion, humor, short stories, and authoritative pieces by the finest writers both nationally and internationally. The *Post, Cosmopolitan,* and *McCall's* competed for a "middlebrow" audience in early-twentieth-century industrial America. Lorimer is credited with not only improving the *Post*'s circulation but also creating a standard for such publications and incorporating his vision of what America and Americans should be and represent. With a weekly circulation of more than 1 million and growing, and full of highly profitable advertisements, the *Saturday Evening Post* was arguably the finest and most successful magazine of its day.[11]

Lorimer wrote unsigned editorials in each issue highlighting his progressivism. A noted artist or illustrator contributed an outstanding piece of art for each cover, with Norman Rockwell being the most famous. "The Boss," as Lorimer was called, collected a stable of writers who covered news that competed with the daily newspapers and authors who wrote nonfiction and fiction that was often better than that offered in literary magazines. David Graham Phillips, Samuel G. Blythe, Isaac F. Marcosson, Will Irwin, Mary Roberts Rinehart, and many others contributed over the years. In Cobb, Lorimer had not only a first-class reporter and essayist but a budding writer of fiction as well.[12]

As Cobb told the story, Lorimer approached him about joining the *Saturday Evening Post* after they had attended a banquet of the American Publishers' Association in New York City. Riding in one of a "squadron of chartered hansom cabs" through Central Park, Lorimer broached the subject. "How about hooking up with the *Post* when your time's up at the treadmill down in Park Row?" "I'd like it," Cobb quickly replied. Lorimer explained that Cobb would be expected to turn out a column at least every two weeks, but more often if assignments came in, and could also do freelance work. Cobb would even receive advances but only under the stipulation that he would promptly produce a column. No contract was signed because Lorimer said he did not believe in them, wanting production without any encumbrance. And, Cobb took that chance.[13]

Once on the "official" staff of the *Saturday Evening Post,* Cobb contributed one piece, either fiction or nonfiction, nearly every other week for more than a decade, as well as publishing occasional stories and other pieces elsewhere. His third story in the *Post,* "An Occurrence up a Side Street," followed the same "grim" pattern as his first two. However, this one was about the seamy side of city life. In one of his shortest stories,

Cobb's protagonists were two urban criminals. In his career as a reporter, he had undoubtedly written about such real-life villains.[14]

The two characters—a man and a woman—are complete scoundrels who are desperate to escape New York City after their murderous activity. To avoid a police cordon, they sneak back into the building where they committed their crime, a bit of irony that Cobb used often in his tales. They cannot leave because a policeman is now guarding the door of the apartment house. Each is looking to get rid of the other, thinking they will be able to evade the authorities more easily if they are alone. Ensconced in the hot, stuffy room, the man peels an overripe peach and cuts open the pits, drawing a plethora of green flies that take on a collective life of their own. The man had planned ahead of time to get rid of his accomplice by spiking a glass of cheap champagne with poison, using the pungent smell of peach pits to mask the odor. Meanwhile, the woman has armed herself with a ten-inch-long hat pin. After offering her the drink, the man settles back. Suddenly, she strikes from the side. "The needle point of the jet-headed hatpin entered exactly at the outer corner of his right eye and passed backward for nearly its full-length into his brain— smoothly, painlessly, swiftly. He gave a little surprise gasp, almost like a sob, and lolled his head back against the chair rest, like a man who has grown suddenly tired." The green flies descend on his face, as the woman unwittingly takes a celebratory drink of the poisoned champagne. "She put the glass down steadily enough on the table; but into her eyes came the same puzzled, baffled look that he wore, and almost gently she slipped down into the chair facing him. Then her jaw lolled a little too, and some of the flies came buzzing toward her." The circle is completed, the guilty die horrible deaths, and with a Poe-esque ending, the green flies thrive as they envelop the murderers. Lorimer and the *Post*'s readers were entranced with Cobb's story, his characterizations, and his sense of drama.[15]

Cobb easily found other outlets for his fertile mind and pen. In April 1911 "The Trail of the Lonesome Laugh" appeared in *Everybody's Magazine*. Here, Cobb explained how difficult it was to be a humor writer. "A comedian can do the same things and say the same things night after night," Cobb exclaimed with frustration. "If a writer uses his own best quip oftener than twice per annum, some unpleasant busybody with a scrapbook or a good memory will draw the deadly parallel on him and shoot him down as he wings." In October of that year, *Munsey's* published "The Perquisites of Public Life," a sarcastic slap at the trappings adopted by a new US congressman. In "Who's Who at the Zoo," which appeared in another New York City monthly, *Hampton-Columbian Magazine,* Cobb wrote about a visit to the Bronx Zoo. "It is the largest Zoo and the completest and the most highly perfumed in the world." Apparently, everything Cobb wrote during this period found a publisher and produced a paycheck.[16]

Some of Cobb's early humor pieces in the *Saturday Evening Post* were only mediocre. For example, his short story "An Open Season for Ancestors" and his article "In the Haunt of the Deadly a La" were not memorable. It seemed as if Cobb were using the old formulaic writing he had done for the *World.* However, Cobb's audience adored these pieces, which poked fun at the search for respectable genealogies and the unnecessary tampering with chicken recipes, respectively.[17]

In his series of "Judge Priest" stories, Cobb found a gold mine. The early twentieth century was "the heyday of popular short fiction," and writers like Cobb developed stock characters they could return to time after time. According to Lorimer biographer Jan Cohn, these characters were "stereotypes deeply embedded in American popular consciousness," and "as such, they reaffirmed popular attitudes and strengthened the values and prejudices of the broad middle-class, middlebrow community that made up the audience of the *Post.*" The first story, "Judge Priest—Murder Witness," published in the *Post* on October 28, 1911, was an instant success. Eventually, there would be forty-two stories and two short novels about the "authentic, bourbon-swilling Kentucky Colonel," as described by *Newsweek* in 1944. But Priest was much more complex than that. Cobb created a character that resonated with the *Post*'s readers, regardless of their region. To Norris Yates, Priest "bears some resemblance to earlier southern crackerbox types." Jeanette Tandy declared that Priest "upholds the tradition of the kindly old Southerner." Cobb actually molded Priest's character out of an amalgam of several real people he had known, including William Sutton Bishop, judge of the First Judicial District of Western Kentucky. Many of Cobb's contemporaries immediately recognized the resemblance.[18]

In a chapter of *Exit Laughing* titled "Stir in Three and Skim off One," Cobb maintained that although Bishop's personality predominated, the character of Priest also included "a trace of my father, but only mental attitudes here, not bodily aspects; and an occasional touch taken from my fellow townsman and crony, Hal Corbett." But for the most part, "he was a reincarnation of the late Judge William S. Bishop and physically almost altogether was Judge Bishop—the high bald forehead, the pudgy shape, the little white paintbrush of a chin whisker, the strident high-pitched voice which, issuing from that globular tenement, made a grotesque contrast, as though a South American tapir had swallowed a tomtit alive and was letting the tomtit do the talking for him." Future vice president of the United States Alben W. Barkley began his career as a lawyer in Paducah in 1901 while Cobb was still editing the newspaper there, and Judge Bishop presided over many of his trials. "All [Cobb] did in writing his stories was to demote the judge from a bishop to a priest," Barkley humorously remarked in his autobiography. Bishop had other qualities that Cobb obviously admired. "The habits and the traits embodied in this triple-sided composite portrait mainly were his too: his exterior dovelike gentleness under which deceiving surface lurked a serpent's shrewdness; his deftly concealed manipulations of local politics; his cultivated affectation of using a country jake vernacular when off the bench and his sudden switch to precise and stately English when on it; his high respect for the profession that he followed and for the office that he held so many years; his divine absent-mindedness, his utterly unreasonable fear of thunderstorms." However, there was also a lot of Joshua Cobb in the judge. For all his father's faults, Cobb dearly loved him, and he idolized Confederate veterans like him as heroes of the Lost Cause. Other biographers of Cobb say much the same thing. Perhaps most succinctly, Yates described Judge Priest as "a paternal fixer-up of other folks' troubles and a pillar of law, justice, and mercy in a town much like Paducah, Kentucky in the eighteen-nineties."[19]

In the first Judge Priest story, the wily jurist is not presiding over a trial in his native Kentucky but serving as a character witness in a Tennessee murder trial. "Words and Music" is a simple story. John Breckinridge "Breck" Tandy, the son of one of the judge's Confederate comrades in arms, has been indicted for murder. Everything seems to be against the young man. He shot and killed his antagonist, who did not fire his weapon, and there were no witnesses. He also has a Yankee lawyer, a congressman from Indiana. As Cobb describes them, the spectators in the audience are totally against Tandy, being led in their animosity by

Aunt Tilly Haslett, who "made public opinion in Hyattsville," the scene of the trial. Even though it appears to be an open-and-shut case, Judge Priest asks to be put on the stand at the close of the trial. He knows that many on the jury and in the audience are former southern soldiers or their kinfolk. In his vernacular southern drawl, he asks his Jewish comrade in arms, Herman Felsburg, if he can borrow some change to purchase a "sweetenin' dram" and then ambles away, telling the defense attorney that during his testimony, "I may ramble." Priest instructs Felsburg to find the "saddle-colored darky" he had seen playing a "juice harp" and instruct him to play a tune on cue during his testimony. The next day, Priest is the last witness and "rambles" on about his life in general and his connection to the defendant. He is humble to a fault. When asked if he was in the "War of the Rebellion," Priest retorts that he was in "the War for the Southern Confederacy" and served as "a private soldier in the Southern army." The audience immediately warms to Priest, including Aunt Tilly, who goes to sit beside Tandy's distraught wife as the judge tells about fighting to save Hyattsville from a Yankee invasion in 1864. While Priest testifies to the good character of the defendant, Felsburg signals the Negro musician to play a Confederate tune. The outcome is never in doubt as the jury, in "only six minutes," finds Tandy not guilty.[20]

In about 8,000 words, Cobb created a simple, secure world that his readers could identify with, even if they lived in New York City or Los Angeles. Longtime *Louisville Courier-Journal* editor and Confederate veteran Henry Watterson called it "one of the finest short stories he had ever read." Though Cobb would refine his Judge Priest stories over the next three decades, the basic elements remained constant. The scene was usually southern and the main characters were southerners, both white and black. Some of the same characters, such as Felsburg and Sergeant Jimmy Bagby, appeared time and again. The black characters were typically depicted as fawning African Americans who were devoted to their white betters. One of these was Jeff Poindexter, Priest's shambling aide, whom Chatterton described as "The Ubiquitous Factotum." Poindexter soon began to appear as a main character, sometimes taking over the story. He often saved the old judge and others from poor judgment and dire circumstances; he was even a central figure in solving a crime while visiting New York. Cobb's type of racism, though benevolent by the standards of the Deep South, was endemic. Chatterton conjectured that Cobb had once envisioned Jeff becoming more of a central character. However, in a 1915 article Cobb is quoted as disingenuously lamenting, "I just couldn't keep that lazy nigger on the job." Cobb wrestled with his racial views even as he developed a reputation as an enlightened southerner living in New York City.[21]

From 1911 until the 1937 publication of *Judge Priest Turns Detective,* the wily Kentucky jurist remained a staple for Cobb fans. The public just couldn't get enough of Judge Priest. Cobb, his contemporaries in Paducah, and later writers and biographers saw aspects of real-life people in the characters in the Judge Priest stories. Undoubtedly, people Cobb knew formed the basis for Priest and his cohorts, but they also represented stereotypical personalities who would have been recognizable to many small-town residents, particularly those in the South. Set roughly a decade on either side of 1900, the stories fit the romanticized sensibilities of all audiences. Why? An "intersectional accord," with some few exceptions, had apparently settled the issues leading to the Civil War. Race relations had not progressed since the time of Cobb's boyhood. Although the 1890s to 1920 would be called the Progressive Era in American history, it was not so for African Americans. Segregation had been achieved by state law (de jure) in the South and by practice (de facto) in the North. The Supreme Court's decision in *Plessy v. Ferguson* (1896) appeared to end any public discourse on the issue when it found that it was constitutional for railroads to offer "separate but equal" accommodations. By implication, restaurants, schools, hotels, and other meeting places could legally separate the races based on the individual rights of the owners of such places. Though more common below the Mason-Dixon Line, lynching of blacks occurred elsewhere as well. It was in this milieu that Judge "Fightin' Billy" Priest became a "star" of magazine stories, books, and eventually motion pictures. William Allen White, an arbiter of American culture in the early to mid-twentieth century, called Cobb's Priest stories "a nice blend of hiccupping nostalgia and conscious, deliberate, downright deception." However, White also admitted that "he enjoyed the Judge Priest tales."[22]

No matter how much the stories changed over the years, the character of Judge Priest stayed largely the same. What Yates described as "the nation-wide cult of the Old South manifested in the movie *The Birth of a Nation* (1915) and a string of prose romances culminating in Margaret

Mitchell's *Gone with the Wind* (1936) also helped to sustain the demand for more tales about Judge Priest." At least into the mid-1930s, a consensus of the American reading public considered Judge Priest not just a lovable southern character but also a national icon. Though conspicuously missing from *Dreaming of Dixie,* a book about the commoditization of the South in literature, radio, and movies in the early twentieth century, Cobb played an important role in making the idealization of the antebellum South and the South of his youth acceptable to the general American public. Cobb's "southern accent," which he could accentuate for effect, and his ability to "imitate a negro to the great degree of perfection" proved acceptable to his northern audience and a source of pride to his southern one. Reunion of North and South was completed at the expense of African Americans. There is no evidence that Cobb questioned the ideals of the antebellum South that had merged into those of the New South. The progressive ideas of Walter Hines Page or the later, more intense criticisms of W. J. Cash would not appear in Cobb's prose.[23]

While he was developing Judge Priest, Cobb also contributed a series of stories, "Judge Hightower of Kentucky," to the *St. Louis Post-Dispatch* in December 1911. These pieces resembled the Judge Priest stories published in the *Saturday Evening Post* and may have been written as a prototype for Judge Priest but sold to a "southern" newspaper. In one of the stories, Hightower explains to a protagonist: "About the time when I might have been adornin' the classic halls of learnin' I was scoutin' around my native land with a carbine rifle tryin' to detain your Gen. Sherman." There is no evidence of other Judge Hightower stories. Of course, the entrepreneurial Cobb was always seeking additional income and readily obtained it by selling stories to newspapers and magazines throughout the country.[24]

As the relationship between publisher George Doran and Cobb progressed from being neighbors in Yonkers to becoming close friends, they had professional dealings as well. Their circle of friends included most of the literary elite of New York City and the Eastern Seaboard. Doran worked with British publisher Hodder and Stoughton to bring its authors to American audiences. *Old Wives' Tale* by Arnold Bennett was Doran's first best seller and helped him attract other authors, both British and American, that his clientele would enjoy. In a splashy publicity campaign, Doran brought Bennett to the United States in mid-October 1911. During a whirlwind tour of the eastern states to showcase Bennett, Cobb sometimes joined the entourage. In Philadelphia, Lorimer hosted a luncheon for the author that included terrapin stew as the first course, a typical regional dish. According to observers, Bennett said, "A sort of turtle, eh?" and pushed back his plate. He left soon thereafter for another engagement. The other attendees were incensed by the Englishman's supercilious attitude, if not outright insolence, but according to Lorimer's biographer, Cobb "restored everyone's spirits by rising to his feet and proposing a toast: 'To Arnold Bennett, our late but not lamented guest, whose presence has made us all the fonder of his absence.'"[25]

Cobb dutifully wrote a piece about the visiting Englishman for *American Magazine* the next year, complimenting his fiction. Though Cobb found Bennett's behavior in Philadelphia reprehensible, he did not comment on it publicly until years later in his autobiography (and ten years after Bennett's death). Cobb observed that Bennett had never overcome his lower-middle-class origins. "He was overly brusque toward those he deemed to be his inferiors, nervous in the presence of persons of large consequence. . . . Because of the inflexible caste system of the English— a plan of selection lacking among the Irish and more or less among the Scotch—it is difficult for one of them to escape from his type grouping. Materially, he may rise up into the sunshine, but spiritually he accepts his predestined place in the cellar" (an eloquent put-down if ever there was one). Critiquing American reporters in his journal entries in 1911, Bennett scolded: "No one knew less of my books than they did. They want you to write their interviews for them." In the next sentence he parenthetically declared: "Women so infernally badly dressed." Bennett's 1912 book about his brief tour of a few eastern cities, *Your United States,* was both critical and complimentary. He commented most favorably on American children, using Buff as an example. Upon meeting her at a dinner at the Cobbs' home, he found her charmingly uninhibited. Though he used Buff's name in his journal, he did not do so in *Your United States:* "when her parents discomforted her just curiosity by the same mean adult dodge of spelling words, [she] walked angrily out of the room with the protest: 'There's too blank much education in this house for me!'" At the age of seven, Buff was what Cobb called "a saucy chit," writing in his autobiography in 1941. In 1911 Cobb was happy to see Bennett return to his native England. For the remainder of his life, Cobb detested English upper-class pretentiousness.[26]

Settling in at the *Saturday Evening Post,* Cobb produced a steady flow
of articles in 1912, writing at least twenty-five, or an average of one every
two weeks. Cobb's work became eagerly anticipated fare in the magazine—his humor columns as well as short stories and comments about
contemporary life. Articles titled "Music," "By-Products of Baseball,"
"Art," "Duds," "Literature," "Law," and "Holidays" testified to Cobb's
versatility. He continued to live in Yonkers and did most of his writing at
home, traveling to Philadelphia when necessary.[27]

Cobb manipulated his audience to accept his views of the contemporary South. "The Mob from Massac," published on February 10, 1912,
presented a side of Priest and the South that Cobb wanted to convey to
his growing audience. In this story, Priest steps in to prevent a possible
breach of justice by challenging a mob determined to lynch a "little" black
man falsely accused of violating the honor of a young white girl. Coinci-
dentally, Priest is in the middle of a tough reelection campaign, and he
is physically exhausted on an oppressively hot summer day. He is awakened by his Negro servant Jeff, who rushes into his office. "'Jedge! Jedge!'
he panted tensely. 'Jedge Priest, please, suh, wake up—the mobbers is
comin'!'" Facing down the mob with an old pistol, the heroic Priest saves
the accused by threatening to kill the first man who steps over a line in
the dirt. Cobb excelled at staging a dramatic scene. "His thumb drew
the hammer back and the double click broke the amazed dumb silence
that had fallen like two clangs upon an anvil. The wrinkles in his face all
set into fixed, hard lines." Like all the Priest stories, this one ends trium-
phantly for the judge. The sheriff apprehends the real guilty party, who
dies in a gunfight, and Priest wins reelection by an overwhelming vote.
When the results of the election are announced, "a yell . . . ripped its way
up and through and above and beyond the mixed and indiscriminate
whoopings of the crowd. This yell, which is shrill and very penetrating,
has been described in print technically as the Rebel yell."[28]

In 1912 Cobb hit his stride as a *Saturday Evening Post* regular. While
he continued to add to his Judge Priest repertoire, he also wrote other articles with a comedic motif. Four articles, "Tummies," "Hair," "Hands and
Feet," and "Teeth," were collected into his first book, published in 1912
as *Cobb's Anatomy.* It was so successful that it went into several editions.
With numerous illustrations by Peter Newell, Cobb accentuated his growing reputation as a fat man with all the problems of the "little" man.[29]

Cobb found the right words to present himself as "the epitome of the funny fat man" belittled by society—in effect, someone with the problems of the little man writ large. "It is all right for a thin man to be grouchy; people will say the poor creature has dyspepsia and should be humored along," Cobb explained. "But a fat man with a grouch is inexcusable in any company—there is so much of him to be grouchy. He constitutes a wave of discontent and a period of general depression. He is not expected to be romantic and sentimental either. It is all right for a giraffe to be sentimental, but not a hippopotamus." Elsewhere in *Cobb's Anatomy,* he accentuated how the little man is mocked or ignored by those who are in control. In the case of a dentist, there is no defense. "You have words with him, or at least you start to have words with him, but he puts his knee in your chest and tells you that it really doesn't hurt at all, but is only your imagination, and utters soothing remarks of that general nature. He then exchanges the crochet needle for a kind of an instrument with a burr on the end of it. This instrument first came into use at the time of the Spanish Inquisition but has been greatly improved on and brought right up to date." Even a modern reader can recognize these same sensations during a visit to the dentist's office.[30]

The *Saturday Evening Post* continued its position as the most widely read "middlebrow" magazine in America, touting "More than 1,900,000 circulation weekly" in December 1912 (at five cents per copy). In no small part, Cobb's rising fame and popular offerings brought a new dimension to the *Post.*[31]

With the success of *Cobb's Anatomy,* Doran published Cobb's second book, *Back Home: Being the Narrative of Judge Priest and His People,* in November 1912. In the preface Cobb told readers that he was trying to correct what he viewed as the northern penchant for depicting southerners in fiction as either "venerable and fiery colonels with frayed wrist bands and limp collars" or "snuff-dipping, ginseng-digging clay-eaters." He claimed that southerners were just like folks in Iowa or Indiana, with "the same blood in their veins, the same impulses and being prone under almost any conceivable condition to do the same thing in much the same way." He explained, "I wanted, if I could, to describe what I believed to be an average southern community so that others might see it as I had seen it. This book is the result of that desire." Cobb maintained that he based his characters on "real models," and "for some of the events themselves there was in the first place a fairly substantial basis of fact." In a review, the *Bookman* described the content of *Back Home* as "clever stories, and better than clever, they are delightfully, humorously and poignantly human," while praising their "southern" atmosphere.[32]

Although Cobb may have thought he was presenting a new side of southern life that northerners had not seen before, in effect, he was also creating and perpetuating a mythological yet plausible southland. The last story in *Back Home,* first published in the *Saturday Evening Post* as "Black and White," tells of two old Confederate soldiers, Judge Priest and Sergeant Bagby, who are the only ones healthy enough to attend a meeting of veterans in their community. "Uncle Ike Copeland" wanders into their meeting, which is taking place on a day that has been set aside for the black population to celebrate the annual "'Mancipation Day." In Cobb's youth in Paducah, addressing elderly African Americans as "Uncle" and "Aunt" was high praise. This sentimental story of old southern mores ends with Copeland being appointed "color sergeant" after recounting the melancholy story of returning his young Confederate master to his home for burial after he lost his life in a Civil War battle. This story and others highlighting Cobb's interpretation of southern reconciliation with its past found a ready audience who wanted to believe that all was well in the early-twentieth-century American South.[33]

Far more interesting than the early moneymakers compiled in *Cobb's Anatomy* and *Back Home* were two "grim" short stories, "The Belled Buzzard" and "Fishhead." Each demonstrated that Cobb could use his vivid imagination and attention to detail to create macabre fiction worthy of an Edgar Allan Poe. "The Belled Buzzard" represents one of Cobb's gothic southern stories. He first worked on it during his summer vacation in 1909. It is one of his most widely reprinted stories and is still worth reading today, if one can overlook Cobb's racism. The story is simple enough. An older man, Squire H. B. Gathers, suspects one "of these young dagoes, who come from nobody knew where," of consorting with his young wife, so Gathers lures him into "Little Niggerwool" swamp and kills him with a shotgun blast. "The gun, having served its purpose, was hidden again, in a place no mortal eye would ever discover. Face downward, with a hole between his shoulder blades, the dead man was lying where he might lie undiscovered for months or for years, or forever." However, Gathers's reverie about committing the perfect crime is interrupted by a buzzard, but not an ordinary one. This is a legendary buzzard with a bell tied around its neck. The distraught old man is sure he can hear the bell sounding, "tonk-tonk-tonk." "And he could see a bell too—that dangled at the creature's breast and jangled incessantly. All his life nearly Squire Gathers had been hearing about the Belled Buzzard. Now with his own eyes he was seeing him."[34]

Awakened early one morning by the belled buzzard, the squire trails it to the swamp and fires his old shotgun (the same one used in the murder) at the menacing bird. "Two long wing feathers drifted slowly down," as if to mock his marksmanship. The murderer begins to doubt his escape from justice, and "the little white worm that gnawed at his nerves had become a cold snake that was coiled about his heart, squeezing it tighter and tighter!" The next afternoon, the local constable comes to the squire's farm to announce that a body has been found in the swamp. A young man had been led to the unidentified corpse by "a buzzard with a cowbell on his neck." With the coroner "sick abed," the constable asks Squire Gathers, who is "the nearest justice of the peace," to preside over an inquest. Owing to the extremely hot weather and the body's deterioration, the inquest must be held immediately. Despite the squire's protests that he is ill, the constable takes him by buggy to a house where the coroner's panel is waiting for what should be a perfunctory meeting. But just as the first witness is about to begin his testimony, "the squire gave a great, screeching howl and sprang from his chair and staggered backward, his eyes popped and the pouch under his chin quivering as though it had a separate life all its own." He collides with the constable, and both men fall to the floor. Squire Gathers remains there and confesses:

"I done it!" They made out the shrieked words. "I done it! I own up—I killed him! He aimed fur to break up my home and I tolled him off into Niggerwool and killed him!" . . . "Oh, my lawdy! Don't you hear it? It's a-comin' clos'ter—it's a-comin' clos'ter—it's a-comin after me! Keep it away—." . . . And now they all heard what he had heard first—they heard the tonk-tonk-tonk of a cowbell, coming nearer and nearer toward them along the hallway without. . . . The sound came right to the door and Squire Gathers wallowed among the chair legs.

As the door opened, there "stood a negro child, . . . with all the strength of his two puny arms, proudly but solemnly tolling a small rusty cowbell he had found in the cowyard." That twist made the story memorable.[35]

"The Belled Buzzard" may be Cobb's most "widely celebrated" story for its use of the buzzard as a deus ex machina, but Wayne Chatterton called it one of Cobb's "least satisfactory from a technical point of view." Cobb continued to explore these types of stories for several years, explaining: "I find that when I have written something of a humorous order it gives me an appetite, so to speak, to turn out a nice, gruesome, gory, Edgar-Allan-Poeish kind of tale, and vice-versa." One of Cobb's contemporaries found his ability to portray both "the grotesque and the whimsical" to be his "most precious possession."[36]

Doran found that publishing small collections of Cobb's stories and articles was lucrative and allowed his works to reach the reading public quickly. *Cobb's Bill of Fare,* though not one of his better books, contained four pieces published by the *Saturday Evening Post* in 1912 and 1913: "Vittles," "Music," "Art," and "Sport." This book, which included fifteen humorous illustrations by Peter Newell and James Preston, presented a formulaic collection of Cobb's pieces characterized by his tongue-in-cheek, somewhat lower than middlebrow view of the world. He preferred old-fashioned food, nonclassical music, traditional art with no abstractions, and less than strenuous sports. About the latter topic, he got off a number of one-liners that his audience enjoyed. For example, "Golf and eating haggis in a state of original sin are the national pastimes of the Scotch, a hardy race." And, "The Irish are born club swingers, as witness any police force; and the Swiss, as is well known, have no equals at Alpine mountain climbing, chasing cuckoos into wooden clocks, and running hotels." While Cobb made "sport" of fishing and hunting, he quite enjoyed such pastimes. As the epitome of the "bemused Little Man," Cobb's persona fought against the pretentiousness of the world. *Cobb's Bill of Fare* received much notice in the English-speaking world and was also published by Hodder and Stoughton in Great Britain. A New Zealand publication declared in a review, "This little book banishes dull care on sight. The reader cannot keep to himself—he will either disperse his company or dispel their grumphs by doing his chuckles out loud in Cobbisms."[37]

With Cobb becoming a star in the publishing world, Doran published another collection of his stories later in 1913, *The Escape of Mr. Trimm: His*

Plight and Other Plights. In addition to the title story, it included several more from the *Post* as well as "Fishhead." First published by the *Cavalier* on January 11, 1913, its full title was "Fishhead: The Rejected Story," as it had been turned down by several editors. According to Cobb, one said: "This story is so strong that it is too strong," but if it were found to be a "forgotten story by Edgar Allan Poe, no doubt it would be gladly welcomed by everybody." Cobb told his friend John Wilson Townsend that "Fishhead" had "been refused by every reputable magazine in America" until being picked up by the *Cavalier.*[38]

"Fishhead" is macabre, to say the least. It is set on Reelfoot Lake on the Kentucky-Tennessee border, formed as "an afterthought of Creation" by an 1811 earthquake. Cobb knew the area well. "Reelfoot is, and has always been, a lake of mystery," Cobb wrote, drawing the reader deeper into the story. After highlighting its natural wonders, he described the more sinister denizens of the lake: the catfish. "Six or seven feet long they grow to be and to weigh two hundred pounds or more, and they have mouths wide enough to take in a man's foot or a man's fist. . . . Oh, but they are wicked things, and they tell wicked tales of them down there."[39]

"Fishhead" is the name of a man living on Reelfoot, "born there, of a Negro father and a half-breed Indian mother." Because she had been frightened by a monstrous catfish before her son's birth, "the child came into the world most hideously marked." Though he had the body of a man, Fishhead's face more closely resembled that of "a great fish." Even his mouth had a fishlike quality. Shunned by society, Fishhead was a loner who ventured to town only rarely. On one such occasion, he completely thrashed "two poor whites," Jake and Joel Baxter, after they baited him into a fight. Most of the onlookers accepted the outcome of the brawl, but the villainous Baxters vowed that "they were going to get the nigger." Sometime later they made their way by dugout canoe to where Fishhead lived, lying in wait for him to appear. When he emerged from his cabin, the brothers shot him at twenty yards and watched as he slid into the murky waters. Fittingly, they had no time to relish the success of their wickedness, as the recoil of the shotgun blast tipped their "cranky dugout," and it began to fill with water. The brothers fell into the lake, with Joel being the first to receive brutal Reelfoot justice. "Something gripped him—some great, sinewy, unseen thing gripped him fast by the thigh, crushing down on his flesh" and "steadily" pulling him down into the murky water. "His mouth went under, next his popping eyes, then his erect hair, and finally his clawing, clutching hand, and that was the end of him. Jake's fate was harder still, for he lived longer—long enough to see Joel's finish." A great fish took him under as well. When the bodies washed ashore, Fishhead's was identifiable, but those of the murderers "were so marred and mauled that the Reelfooters buried them together on the bank without ever knowing which might be Jake's and which might be Joel's."[40]

"Fishhead" enthralled readers, and it is still considered one of Cobb's great successes, long after Judge Priest has been mostly forgotten. Chatterton declared that there is nothing in Cobb's work approaching Poe's "broody supernatural madness." Cobb's "horror" stories (most of which are discussed later in this book), even "Fishhead," are plausible. "They are in this world and of this world, and their horrors are recognizable as the depths into which worldly affairs can plunge those who are susceptible to bizarre and outre circumstance. The result is a peculiar horror that belongs only to Cobb," Chatterton observed in 1986. A contemporary of Cobb, Grant Overton, wrote in the *Bookman* in 1927, "Nothing better can be found in Poe's collected works. One is impressed not only with the beauty and simplicity of his prose, but also with the tremendous power of his tragic conceptions and his art in dealing with terror."[41]

By 1913, Cobb had drawn the attention of literary maven Henry L. Mencken of *Baltimore Sun* and *Smart Set* fame. In an essay titled "The Burden of Humor" that appeared in the February issue of *Smart Set* that year, Mencken unleashed an attack on Cobb, dismissing him as having little talent and claiming that Mark Twain set the standard for American humor. He continued:

> Of the humor of Irvin S. Cobb, a newcomer upon the sawdust, I can give no such favorable account, though less a literary juryman than Hon. Robert H. Davis, whom I love and venerate extremely, puts him above Bret Harte, and has even ranked him with Mark Twain. . . . But all the same I am forced to raise a feeble voice in dissent, for a diligent reading of Mr. Cobb's *Anatomy* has failed to do more than gently tickle me. . . . I do not say that Mr. Cobb is not funny; what I do say is that his fun keeps to the surface, that its chief quality is its obviousness.

Mencken feebly praised *Back Home,* because Cobb "knows these people perfectly, and what is more, . . . he loves them well. The result is an excellent row of portraits, a bit old-fashioned but altogether attractive."[42]

Later that year, in correspondence with Theodore Dreiser about the latter's publishing plans, Mencken advised him, "Take the Doran offer, by all means. I hear only good of Doran, despite his publication of bad books by Irvin Cobb." Thomas L. Masson, writing about American humorists in 1922, exclaimed: "I was highly amused one day to pick up a book by Mr. H. L. Mencken, and read what he had to say about Cobb. He didn't like him. He said so. Mencken, so far as I have been able to discover in his writings, doesn't like anybody." Though Cobb never wrote about his disdain for Mencken, the feeling was mutual.[43]

Cobb often corresponded with his Lexington friend Townsend about his successes as well as his failures. In early 1913 Cobb told him, "Back Home is about to be translated into Swedish. As yet Japan has taken no steps," he quipped. A year later he reported to Townsend, "I'm working in fiction now—short story stuff mostly." Had he found his most effective mode of writing, his niche, his forte?[44]

Cobb continued to contribute short stories and commentaries to the *Saturday Evening Post.* In mid-1913 his articles about a trip out west, paid for by Lorimer, appeared in a five-part series titled "Roughing It De Luxe," published between June 7 and August 16. Doran and the Curtis Company copublished the immensely popular articles as five chapters in a book of the same name released just after the last installment appeared in the *Post.* Fifteen illustrations accompanied the text, and the cover depicted a humorous cartoon of a Cobb-like figure riding a miniature Santa Fe train with his hat wafting in the breeze.[45]

The first chapter, "A Pilgrim Canonized," chronicles Cobb's trip by train on the Santa Fe line from Chicago to the Grand Canyon (*Canon* in Spanish). With typical ironic understatement, Cobb began his commentary (which was also quoted in Ken Burns's PBS special *America's Best Idea*): "It is generally conceded that the Grand Canon of Arizona beggars description. I shall therefore endeavor to refrain from doing so." Undeterred, Cobb described the train trip and his assorted companions, whom he found to be somewhat ridiculous. A "distinguished surgeon" among the passengers was so famous that he "has had a rare and expensive disease named for him, which is as distinguished as a physician ever gets to be in this country." With their luxurious train and hotel accommodations, Cobb asserted, tongue in cheek: "We were a daring lot and resolute; each and every one of us was brave and resolute; each and every one of us was brave and blithe to endure the privations that such an expedition must inevitably entail. Let the worst come; we were prepared!" Cobb continued to make fun of himself and his fellow tourists as they descended the Bright Angel Trail (as mentioned in the introduction of this book). Besides the dazzling scenery, Cobb found his mule worthy of mention, noting that, though slipping and sliding occasionally, it "has no intention of getting himself hurt." Cobb was particularly pained to find so much graffiti where people had marked the rocks.[46]

The next chapter highlights a humorous tale about the "Hydrophobic Skunk" living at the bottom of the canyon where Cobb spent the night. After consuming all the steak he could eat, Cobb (with Twain-like exaggeration—a common ploy in American folk humor) repeated the tale told around the campfire by his cowboy guide about the "Hydrophoby Skunks" that often entered the visitors' tents at night. Cobb survived, he said, only by sleeping with his clothes and shoes on in case he had to run away.[47]

"How Do You Like the Climate?" is a tongue-in-cheek chapter about the boosterism of Californians, particularly those in Los Angeles. "Once upon a time a stranger went to Southern California; and when he was asked the customary question—to wit: 'How do you like the climate?' he said: 'No, I don't like it!' So they destroyed him on the spot. . . . Southern Californians brag of their climate just as New York brags of its wickedness and its skyscrapers, and Richmond brags of its cooking and its war memories." Of course, Cobb could not help but skewer the main varmints, noting, "Out from under a rock somewhere will crawl a real estate agent." Moreover, according to Cobb, the weather was not all that balmy, as "the all-wool sweater is the national garment of the West Coast." Here, as in much of his writing, Cobb created a composite character to illustrate his point. In this case, a young easterner tries to look comfortable in his all-white suit on a cool, blustery day in Coronado. "He was, in short, all white except his face, which was a pinched, wan blue, and his nose, which was a suffused and chilly red." The native Californians, knowing better, were wearing their heavy sweaters. Alarmingly, Cobb also found that Southern Californians expected to be tipped more for their services than New Yorkers.[48]

"In the Haunt of the Native Son" describes the virtues of San Francisco. Cobb praises the city's scenery, including the Golden Gate, its lack of concern about the weather, its recovery from the fire (although natives generally did not want to talk about the earthquake), and the upcoming Great Exposition of 1915. In keeping with the title of the chapter, the "Native Son" was "San Francisco's chief product" because "it counts in politics, and in society, and at the clubs."[49]

The last chapter, "Looking for Lo," takes a comical view of Cobb's search for Native Americans in the backcountry of the West. Though demeaning by modern standards, Cobb's comments about the Navajo and their handicrafts were considered humorous. "From Colorado to the Coast the Navajo blanket carpets the earth. I'll bet any amount within reason that in six weeks' time I saw ten million Navajo blankets if I saw one." Using comedic exaggeration, Cobb could find a laugh in almost every encounter, including his interactions with the Mormons of Utah, his last major stop before heading back eastward.[50]

In late 1913 and into 1914, Cobb began to explore the possibilities of moving to the country in "Life among the Abandoned Farmers," a rumination on the city man's gullibility before the wily farmer. He would eventually purchase such a place. He exercised not only his virtuosity but also his knowledge of the classics in "Shakespeare's Seven Ages and Mine." Moreover, he continued to write short stories.[51]

With the success of Cobb's trip to the American West, Lorimer decided to foot the bill and send him to Europe in the hopes of cashing in on his observations of life there. Out of Cobb's sojourn came a series of eleven *Saturday Evening Post* articles published between March 21 and July 4, 1914, entitled "An American Vandal." They were published in book form as *Europe Revised* in 1914, soon after the last article appeared; the book went into several editions.

Irvin and Laura Cobb sailed for England on the *Lusitania* on September 13, 1913. They stayed in London for about three weeks before moving on to tour the Continent and returned to the United States in December. In his articles, Cobb adopted an early-twentieth-century version of Twain's style of "writing a purely personal and subjective account of his travels." He never intended to write a real "travel book" that highlighted the wonders of Europe; rather, he wanted to provide readers with a somewhat idiosyncratic account. "So it occurred to me," he wrote, "that possibly there might be room for a guidebook on foreign travel which would not have a single indubitable fact concealed anywhere about its person." Cobb assumed the role of a typical middle-class American traveling abroad for the first time, for whom befuddlements occur at every turn.[52]

While in London, Cobb highlighted the lack of fog or other dreary English weather. Before leaving Paris for Rome, the unsuspecting American was confronted by every hotel employee expecting a healthy tip. Throughout the trip, Cobb emphasized his preference for American food over European food. In France he found the constant diet of chicken and veal particularly unappealing to his American palate. In his inimitable style he noted, "According to the French version of the story of the Flood only two animals emerged from the Ark when the waters receded—one was an immature hen and the other was an adolescent calf." Commenting on the sameness of the English diet, the American announced: "I know now why an Englishman dresses for dinner—it enables him to distinguish dinner from lunch." Cobb indulged in these barbs and one-liners throughout the book. However, he almost always countered such critiques with praise, highly recommending English mutton and English breakfast bacon, for example.[53]

Cobb satirized European fashion, lampooning German military styles, among others. One of the best illustrations in the book is of Cobb being fitted for pants in London. He later opined that English women did not know how to wear their hair or how to dress to advantage. Nightlife in London ended too soon, he complained, and the clubs of Paris were only slightly better. Beggars in Paris tended to be abusive, and Cobb concluded: "But then, what could you naturally expect from a population that thinks a fried cuttlefish is edible and a beefsteak is not?"[54]

The only blot on an otherwise humorous traipse through Europe was a deeply caustic racial comment. Cobb's southernness surfaced in Paris, where he observed the racial latitude allowed in cafés there. In one he found "a large, broad negro pugilist with a mouthful of gold and a shirt-front full of yellow diamonds. To an American—and especially an American who was reared below Mason and Dixon's justly popular Line—it is indeed edifying to behold a black heavyweight fourthrater from South Clark Street, Chicago, taking his ease in a smart café, entirely surrounded by worshipful boulevardiers, both male and female." This barely subdued racist diatribe apparently brought no flicker of condemnation from Cobb's editors and publishers or his adoring audience.[55]

Otherwise, Cobb's ingenuity in finding the humorous side of travel prevailed. Using a play on the words *guyed* (meaning "to satirize") and *guide,* Cobb wrote a hilarious chapter about the inept and disingenuous European guides, many of whom claimed to have led Samuel Clemens on his travels. Their main occupation appeared to be taking tourists to preferred shops, where the guides received commissions. Worn out by the end of his trip and the viewing of endless ruins in Rome and Pompeii, Cobb finally declared, "I saw ruins until I was one myself." By the end of his three months abroad, Cobb had more than enough material for his series of articles. On the homeward passage, Cobb observed that although the trip had been enlightening, "a chastened spirit pervades the traveler. . . . He had been broadened by travel but his pocketbook has been flattened. He wouldn't take anything for this trip, and as he feels at the moment [referring to seasickness] he wouldn't take it again for anything."[56]

Cobb ended the book with a typical comical flourish, sure to delight his readers. As the ship approached the Statue of Liberty, he wrote: "We slip past her and on past the Battery too: and nosing up the East River. What a picturesque stream it is, to be sure. And how full of delightful rubbish!" Once the ship docked and all the weary travelers congregated in the gangways, "someone raise[d] a voice in song." It was not any of the English, French, or German anthems, but: "Be it ever so humble, There's no place like HOME!"[57]

Although Laura accompanied Cobb on the European trip, he never mentioned her (although she would appear in some of his later articles and books). It was as if he were trying to re-create Twain's sojourn abroad but using his own persona. Cobb retold and recast many of the actual facts of the trip over the course of time. For example, although he visited with Rudyard Kipling in England, he did not include that visit in *Europe Revised.* Articles about their time together appeared in the *New York Evening Post* and *Book News Monthly.* Kipling had been a favorite of Cobb's for years. When the Cobbs arrived at the Kipling estate, the renowned author was reportedly out. While walking in Kipling's garden, "we had not gone far from the house when we heard a shout and saw a man jump over a hedge and run toward us." It was, of course, the irrepressible Kipling. The two men hit it off immediately, agreeing on their dislike of the current trends in modern literature. "He has a big jaw and he wears shiny glasses and shows his teeth like T.R. [Teddy Roosevelt] and he's a short man and blocky, with a big strong hand."[58]

Another incident not included in *Europe Revised* but noted in later writings was Cobb's comic encounter with high society in a Paris hotel. Whether true or not, Cobb embellished the story over the years, and it became a favorite in his after-dinner speeches. It seemed that the male secretary of Lady Randolph Churchill called the Cobbs' room by mistake, thinking that Cobb had called her. Cobb told him he had the wrong number, and when the secretary persisted, the American turned the tables. "When did Her Ladyship start doing this sort of thing?" The exasperated secretary replied: "Oh, God bless my soul! What a frightful bounder! What a frightful Yankee bounder! Oh, God bless my soul!" Sometime later Cobb told Lady Churchill of the incident and "she laughed her head off," according to Buff Cobb.[59]

After Irvin and Laura returned from Europe, they stayed at the Algonquin Hotel for the remainder of the winter and then moved into an apartment on West 110th Street, which was their home base through 1917. Cobb could once again converse with the Algonquin's assortment of intellectuals, actors, writers, and others. By mid-1914, Cobb had become nearly indispensable at the *Saturday Evening Post*. The *Post*'s readers could not get enough of Judge Priest. *Roughing It De Luxe* was well received, as were *Cobb's Anatomy* and *Europe Revised*. Images of Cobb that appeared in the press and in his books, whether illustrations or photographs, portrayed a corpulent man with a bemused expression on his face, one who looked at the world with a sense of irony. As the bewildered personification of the "born loser" of the corpulent variety, Cobb looked the part, and the public loved him all the more.[60]

5

World War I

Foreign Correspondent

During a much-needed lakeside vacation with his family in North Hadley, Quebec, Cobb wrote to old friend John Wilson Townsend in early June 1914 that after his hectic schedule, he was looking forward to getting some rest as well as having time to write. *Roughing It De Luxe* and *Europe Revised* were in press. A Swedish magazine had reprinted a Judge Priest story. *Back Home* was in production as a play, with his old *World* colleague Bozeman Bulger working on the stage version. Everything appeared to be quiet and productive, and Cobb undoubtedly hoped to enjoy some fishing too.[1]

However, in the summer of 1914 Cobb's world—and that of everyone else—changed abruptly. "One day the great European war will come out of some damned foolish thing in the Balkans," German chancellor Otto von Bismarck had predicted in 1888. The assassination of Austrian archduke Franz Ferdinand by a Serbian nationalist in Sarajevo, the "tinderbox of Europe," proved Bismarck's prophecy true. Between July 28 and August 4, the nations of Europe plunged into war. Austria invaded Serbia; more ominously, German armies invaded France en masse through tiny Belgium. At first, the German war machine appeared unstoppable. President Woodrow Wilson called on Americans to "be impartial in word as well as in action."[2]

"Seems like this here war has done busted out in our face," Lorimer telegraphed Cobb, using his columnist's affected "Kentucky-ese." "Your ship sails Thursday." The Boss had spoken. Cobb was going to Europe, where he would report exclusively for the *Saturday Evening Post* and the *Philadelphia Public Ledger.* Cobb received a forty-pound package that included a letter from Secretary of State William Jennings Bryan that accredited him as a representative of the American press to US diplomats and officials in Europe, clothes, an automatic pistol, a letter of credit on the *Post's* bank, travelers' checks, and $5,000 to $6,000 (depending on the source) in British gold sovereigns. With the coins strapped around his waist, Cobb reported that he arrived in Europe "jingling like a milk wagon."[3]

Richard Harding Davis, who had reported on the Spanish-American War for Hearst during the heyday of yellow journalism, left for Europe two days before Cobb, who set sail on the *St. Paul* on August 7, 1914. Traveling with him were several other well-known journalists, including Will Irwin representing *Collier's,* Arnot Dosch of *World's Work,* and illustrator John McCutcheon, who also reported for the *Chicago Tribune.* War correspondents had no official status, and France, England, and Germany had no plans to accredit independent reporters. These nations wanted to control the war news to their own advantage and feared that independent reporting would provide information to the enemy. Although President Wilson had declared strict neutrality on the part of his nation and its citizens, Germany suspected that most Americans would be sympathetic to the British and French.[4]

After the *St. Paul* landed at Liverpool, Cobb's group traveled by train to London, proceeded across the English Channel by ferry, continued to Brussels by train, and then moved on to the war zone. By the time Cobb and his cohorts got to Europe, Germany had overrun much of Belgium, driving back Belgian and French forces, as well as the few British troops that had arrived on the Continent. Owing to tight British control of cable transmissions, Cobb could not immediately send back reports from the war front. Between October 10, 1914, and January 30, 1915, the *Saturday Evening Post* published fifteen articles by Cobb about his experiences and observations in the early months of World War I. These articles also appeared in several American newspapers. Cobb's first commentary in the *Post* (and the first chapter in *Paths of Glory,* published in 1915), was a melancholy piece titled "A Little Town Called Montignies St. Christophe." Its destruction was a prime example of the effectiveness, at least initially, of the Schlieffen Plan to attack through Belgium and quickly encircle Paris. Cobb pointed out in a note at the beginning of *Paths of Glory* that the chapters, describing "some of my experiences and setting forth a few of my observations in Belgium, in Germany, in France and in England during the first three months of hostilities," were not written in chronological order. The title *Paths of Glory* came from a line in Thomas Gray's "Elegy Written in a Country Churchyard": "The paths of glory lead but to the grave." Cobb dedicated the book "To the Memory of Major Robert Cobb (Cobb's Kentucky Battery, C.S.A.)."[5]

In Montignies St. Christophe, a small Belgian town on the French border, Cobb directly observed the results of the German military juggernaut as it ground up its enemies. "I am going to try now to tell how it looked to us," he wrote, a day after "a dust-colored German column," mostly unopposed, swept through the town. He described what the town would have looked like before the invasion, similar to villages he had passed through the year before and described, humorously, in *Europe Revised*. He had made light of such places, noting "its small, ugly church, its wine shop, its drinking trough, its priest in black, and its one lone gendarme in his preposterous housings of saber and belt and shoulder straps."[6]

Now everything had changed forever in Montignies St. Christophe. "The war had come this way; and, coming so, had dealt it a side-slap," Cobb explained. The town had been shelled by both sides in a short skirmish. Afterward, Cobb and his friends found the remains of a French encampment, strewn with clothing and accoutrements. For the first time, Cobb observed German military efficiency. The only items of German origin were the beer bottles they left behind after their meals; they never left anything else to betray their strengths or weaknesses to the enemy. Here, Cobb saw the first of many war dead he would witness in the weeks ahead. Red Cross personnel brought two French soldiers by cart into the village for burial. Cobb described the face of one man: "It was a young face—we could tell that much, even through the mask of caked mud on the drab-white skin—and it might once have been a comely face. It was not comely now. Peering into the wagon we saw that the dead man's face had been partly shot or shorn away—the lower jaw was gone; so that it had become an abominable thing to look on."[7]

This vignette set the stage for the themes of his later *Post* articles. The material costs of war, the human carnage, the heroism, the destruction of property, and the displaced persons would be emphasized over and over again in his wartime writings. Cobb's three months in Europe proved to be the greatest adventure of his life, all colorfully reported with his eye for detail and in the style his readers had come to expect and appreciate.

Reporting on the war was a challenge. After obtaining credentials from Brand Whitlock, the American ambassador to Belgium, Cobb and his cohorts left the seemingly peaceful Belgian capital and made their way blindly toward the front. Just getting there proved to be difficult, owing to indistinct battle lines and unsure transportation. First, the small troop of journalists traveled by automobile, until a wise taxi driver put them out when he heard gunfire. They passed endless lines of refugees, proving that the German war machine was grinding forward. After a brief stay in the city of Louvain, they pressed on.[8]

After enjoying a meal and "good red wine" provided by some priests at the Church of St. Jacques, the American reporters ran into the war full bore. While walking down a street, they found themselves between a few Belgian troops and a German unit. When a German officer on horseback spied them, Cobb and his friends sought shelter. "I made for the half-open door of a shop. Just as I reached it a woman on the inside slammed it in my face and locked it. I never expect to see her again; but that does not mean that I ever expect to forgive her," Cobb noted with a hint of humor. Cobb described the young German cavalryman who rode past him with a reporter's keen eye for detail, declaring that if the young man's uniform were replaced with that of a cowboy, "he might have cantered bodily out of one of Remington's canvasses."[9]

Cobb attested that he never saw any German atrocities; however, he did witness civilians being summarily tried and shot—a "reprisal," as one German officer explained, against Belgian civilians who opposed the German invasion by firing weapons from their homes or acting as spies. Setting out on foot after losing their taxi ride, Cobb's group bought a horse and "dog cart" and two bicycles and proceeded toward the war front. Eventually, the inevitable happened. They encountered a large contingent of German soldiers and were detained, confined, and then placed on a train with both prisoners of war and wounded German soldiers. The journalists awaited their fate. American newspapers reported in early September 1914 that Cobb and his friends had been "detained by German military authorities." At least the Cobb family,

Lorimer, and the American public knew that the reporters were not in the combat zone.[10]

Cobb wrote two accounts of his detainment by the Germans and his transport into the German homeland for the *Post*. Eventually, American consul Robert J. Thompson "succeeded in convincing the military authorities that we were not dangerous. I still think that taking copious baths and getting ourselves shaved helped to clear us of suspicion." Ten years later, in an essay titled "The Funniest Thing that Ever Happened to Me," Cobb dealt more lightly with the drama. "It properly should have been a bit out a Viennese opera. . . . So far, we did not realize that we were cast to provide the low comic relief." Cobb's attire included a straw hat with the crown missing and a shirt he had purchased from a "wayside butcher" that was "so coated" with "suet and tallow and hog grease and other souvenirs of his calling, that had it caught fire I am sure it would have burned for at least half a day with a clear blue flame." To complete his costume, Cobb's worn-out shoes had been replaced by a pair of "homemade carpet slippers which I had acquired by barter from an elderly Belgian lady." When a German colonel told Cobb, "We have no correspondents with the German Army," Cobb replied, "Well you'll see that you now have five." Or at least that was his story in 1925. In the later piece, he also told of reaching his hand out a window of the train as it slowed and snatching a large sausage from a German meant for the wounded soldiers. Cobb was a good reporter, but he was also prone to the colorful retelling of stories, for even more comic effect, as time went on.[11]

In Aix-la-Chapelle, just over the German border, the detained Americans were allowed some freedom, as they were no longer considered an immediate threat. They attempted to get written permission to act as neutral correspondents surveying the war zone. Against the advice of a German who had befriended them, they wrote a letter to Kaiser Wilhelm. The boldness of the approach paid off when they received a pass that one of Cobb's associates doctored to allow them unlimited access to German forces. Apparently, the German high command finally understood that some good publicity could work to their benefit. In a letter published in the *New York Times* on September 7, 1914, Cobb, Roger Lewis of the Associated Press, Harry Hansen of the *Chicago Daily News,* and James O'Donnell Bennett and John T. McCutcheon of the *Chicago Tribune* testified that they had not witnessed any atrocities by the German army. Shortly thereafter, Cobb received a letter from German chancellor Bethmann-Hollweg, complimenting him on his favorable observations. For the remainder of Cobb's time in German hands, he had no serious problems—quite the opposite, in fact. On one occasion he watched a battle take place from a German observation balloon. Although one author passed this off as "a fascinating and humorous if trivial tale of personal experiences," it was hardly that. From that height, Cobb had the rare opportunity to see how a battle unfolded and how the observation balloon could be used to direct artillery bombardments and troop movements. After their initial reluctance to accommodate Cobb and his friends, German forces were now coddling them as part of their propaganda plan.[12]

While in German custody, Cobb observed "Prussian" confidence that Teutonic superiority would win the war, which was the ultimate destiny of the German people. Cobb reported several times that German officers touted their superiority in arms as well as in culture. They expressed the belief that German hegemony would bring harmony and prosperity to Europe, but first they had to subjugate the pesky French and English. "I tell you this: Forty-four years they have been wishing to fight us for what we did in 1870; and when the time comes they are not ready and we are ready," a young German lieutenant declared. "While they have been singing their Marseillaise Hymn, we have been thinking. While they have been talking, we have been working."[13]

In "Sherman Said It," published in the October 17, 1914, issue of the *Saturday Evening Post,* Cobb wrote that "a child's stuffed cloth doll" with a crushed head was a symbol of the terrible war. Later, in "Europe's Rag Doll," published on January 9, 1915, he again used the doll as a metaphor for the fate of Belgium, while praising the courage of its people. "That poor little rag doll, with its head crushed in the wheel tracks, does not furnish such a good comparison, after all, I think, as I finish this story about Belgium; for it had sawdust insides—and Belgium's vitals are the vitals of courage and patience."[14]

As a reporter, Cobb excelled at finding images that stood out on and near the battlefront. Nothing depressed him more than the thousands of dead, wounded, and dying. His reports to the American people spoke little of the glory of war. He emphasized the terrible sights and smells he witnessed. This example sums up his typical reaction: "When there has been fighting in France or Belgium, almost any thicket will give up hideous grisly secrets to the man who goes searching there. Men sorely wounded in the open share one trait at least with the lower animals. The dying creature—whether man or beast—dreads to lie and die in the naked field. It drags itself among the trees if it has the strength. I believe every woodland in northern France was a poison place, and remained so until the freezing of winter sealed up its abominations under ice and frost." Cobb wrote nothing to glorify this war, in contrast to his nostalgic view of the Lost Cause of the Confederacy.[15]

When Cobb and his colleagues left the war zone, they told the Germans they would be traveling directly to the United States. However, they intended to go to London first. The *New York Times* reported on October 14, 1914, that Cobb had arrived in Vaals, Netherlands. Three days later, the *Times* printed a piece in which Cobb reaffirmed his assertion that he had not witnessed any atrocities committed by the German forces. Cobb went directly from the Netherlands to London, and his first war story was cabled to America and published in the *Post* on October 14.[16]

Cobb scored more than one coup during his three months in Europe. While in London, Cobb received an invitation to interview Lord Kitchener. The meeting was arranged by Lord Northcliffe, an English newspaper magnate who controlled the *London Times, Daily Mail,* and other papers. In July, just before the outbreak of hostilities, Kitchener had been appointed secretary of state for war. He had achieved undying fame by winning the Battle of Omdurman and securing control of the Sudan in northeastern Africa in 1898. He had also taken part in the last phases of the Boer War and then served in India. Kitchener almost never talked to reporters; he disdained their trade and perhaps believed that Cobb would never write about their conversation. Field Marshal Kitchener probably agreed to meet with Cobb owing to the American's reputation for observation. In short, he wanted to know what Cobb had observed of the Germans' strengths and weaknesses. After the forty-minute interview, Cobb declared that Kitchener and German Field Marshal Von Heeringen, whom he had also interviewed, were comparable, in that "both men radiated the same quality of masterfulness." Each tried to impress the American with his grasp of the war, its causes, and its probable outcome from his own cultural perspective. Both men undoubtedly believed they were using Cobb. The *Post* published "An Interview with Lord Kitchener" on December 5, 1914, after Cobb had returned to America. "Who but Cobb could have secured an interview with the terrible and overawing Kitchener?" Doran declared. Lord Northcliffe went on to become the director of propaganda in the Lloyd George years.[17]

Cobb took no notes during the interview with the legendary Kitchener, and the old field marshal apparently thought the American would be awed into silence. However, he erred, and Cobb considered the interview a windfall. When he returned to his hotel, Cobb quickly made a "careful transcript" of the interview. He then asked Northcliffe if he should honestly report what he had learned from the Kitchener interview. Northcliffe gave his assent, as British censorship at the time would not have allowed him to publish the story in his own country. "When I reached America a fortnight later I wrote an honest and painstaking and, I am sure, an absolutely accurate account of the call upon Lord Kitchener," Cobb recalled in a memoir. Kitchener had been very candid with Cobb. Contrary to the opinion of most experts, who predicted that the war would be over in three months or so, the old general said it would take three years. He displayed his disdain for the German people and military and for the development of trench warfare, preferring movement instead. "He does not inspire confidence in you—he creates it in you," Cobb concluded.[18]

Kitchener denied the substance of Cobb's article, declaring that they had not talked at any length. Northcliffe apologized to Cobb. "Nothing has annoyed me lately more than the denial by the Censor of your interview with Lord Kitchener," he wrote in late December 1914. Thereafter, Northcliffe worked to allow American and British journalists to report on the war firsthand, rather than being limited to the information doled out by the British government censors. The efforts of Cobb and others in the early part of the war opened the way for more front-line reporting. Mary Roberts Rinehart and Samuel G. Blythe were among those who reported on the war for the *Saturday Evening Post* before American intervention.[19]

Cobb landed in New York City on November 1, 1914. Reporters met him at the ship and asked again about rumors of German atrocities, noting that some critics believed the American reporter to be pro-German. However, Cobb reported that the only "atrocity" he witnessed had been the devastation of poor Belgium itself. For the first time, photographs became more common in journals and newspapers. In one photograph accompanying Cobb's "European Rag Doll," he and other captured correspondents posed with friendly German officers. Doran rushed *Paths of*

Glory into print before the last of Cobb's war articles appeared in the *Post*. It was published in London as *The Red Glutton*, with only slight changes from the American version. On both sides of the Atlantic, Cobb's book received favorable reviews. The *New Republic* found it "odd perhaps that one of America's funniest men should write the best war correspondent's book, yet *Paths of Glory* is unsurpassed, not alone because of its rich material, but especially because of its moving style."[20]

Cobb's three months in Europe affected him in many ways. He had seen the young men of Europe at their worst and at their most heroic. He had seen thousands of men wounded and dying. He had even suffered what he called "a small umbilical hernia" while helping to carry wounded German soldiers in the northern city of Maubeuge "after the litter bearers on duty there dropped from utter exhaustion." Cobb also described how he and a companion had helped clean and dress the wounds of German soldiers until they were too exhausted to work. Daughter Buff noticed that on his return from Europe, Cobb was more impatient than ever. Several years later, Buff's daughter Pat revealed something more ominous. According to Buff, while she and her mother "were talking about Dad, . . . Pat absolutely flabbergasted us by remarking casually, 'Well, I guess he never did really get over his attack of shell shock.'" Pat told them that when she was a little girl, her grandfather had told her that the sound of a "thunderstorm, or any loud noise affected him very strangely." Cobb would sometimes go to sleep when he heard the sound of thunder. Buff lovingly wrote in her biography of her father: "And until he wrote this in his autobiography when he was an old man he never told any soul, not even his doctors, except a six-year-old child." Moreover, in 1914 he was thirty-eight years old and seriously overweight, and he had other health problems.[21]

The sights, the sounds, and even the unmistakable odor of the dead and dying had a great impact on Cobb. He had witnessed death before in his early reporting days in Paducah (he had even helped a convicted murderer die more quickly and mercifully from a botched hanging), but nothing on the scale of the Great War. In a chapter called "The Grapes of Wrath," Cobb recounted Germany's determination to obliterate its enemies. Visiting what remained of Fort Loncin, a Belgian fortress that had been obliterated by Krupp heavy artillery and internal explosions, he had a searing experience. Hundreds of Belgian soldiers had been buried in the rubble of the fort, and while speaking to a German officer, "a puff of wind brought to our nostrils a smell which, once a man gets it into his nose, he will never get the memory of it out again so long as he has a nose. Being sufficiently sick, we departed thence."[22]

Although Cobb had spoken to small groups in the past and enjoyed hobnobbing with his friends, some of whom were rich and famous, the war thrust a new role on him. As one of the few American reporters to have seen the war zone firsthand, the public demanded information. Part of Cobb's healing came from talking about what he had observed. At a banquet held at the Twilight Club on November 23, he gave a talk titled "What I Saw at the Front," which the *New York Times* headlined, "Cobb Tells Twilight Club of War Horrors." A few weeks later he gave a similar talk at the Greenroom Club and found a new vocation: lecturer. Cobb had become a celebrity.[23]

After his speech at the Greenroom Club, the Selwyn brothers, theatrical managers, persuaded him to go on a ten-week lecture tour that would cover much of the eastern United States. Cobb had some fear of lecturing about such a serious topic as war. Apparently, he even thought about taking some elocution lessons, but friends advised him to just be himself. True to the course he had followed throughout his life, he overcame his nerves and took up the task, delivering speech after speech without the use of notes.[24]

Cobb eventually came to enjoy this grind. And as with most experiences, he found something to write about, in this case, a humorous essay called "Unaccustomed As I Am—." He opened his tour in New York City and recalled that before his first speech, "I was perfectly calm and collected, except that I had already swallowed nine miles of Adam's apples and was still swallowing them at the rate of thirty or forty a minute. . . . But somehow I lived through it."[25]

Cobb's family and close friends wondered whether he could survive such an ordeal. When Cobb spoke to a packed audience in Carnegie Hall, a woman fainted near the stage when she heard the details of death and dying on the western front. Buff reported that her mother felt sorry for the woman, but she also feared that her husband's outward poise might be disrupted. Cobb paused, filled a glass with water, and signaled for an usher to take it to the stricken woman. After she regained her senses, Cobb resumed without missing a beat. Buff recalled: "I heard Laura let the air out of her lungs with a gasp, like someone who has been a long time under water. She had come near fainting herself." Cobb developed a rapport with his audiences. "They brought him to life. . . . They excited him, and nothing else did. Whether a man suffering from incipient or half-cured shell shock ought to be thus excited I don't know, but I doubt it," concluded Buff.[26]

Everywhere Cobb spoke, the press reported record crowds as he wound his way through New England, then the mid-Atlantic and southern circuits, and ending in the Midwest. One time, when a man in the audience berated Cobb during the question-and-answer period, the crowd "hissed and booed him into silence." He had great success in Kentucky, speaking before his own people. At the Ben Ali Theatre in Lexington, Townsend reported in the *Lexington Herald* that there was standing room only in the city's largest venue. After talking for nearly two hours, Cobb answered questions from the audience. He did not spare them the horrors he had seen, such as German soldiers suffering horrible pain caused by gangrene and lockjaw. He always repeated his belief that Germany had not committed any atrocities. "Often interrupted by applause," according to one newspaper account, Cobb told his audience, "I believe that the best thing to keep the United States out of war is preparedness." When asked, Cobb always replied that he was "neutral." Cobb also offered some comic relief by making fun of his own temerity at sending a letter to "Kaiser Bill." Two reels of film showing graphic war scenes usually followed each of his talks. After Lexington, he moved on to Louisville and Macauley's Theatre, then to Indianapolis, and finally to Chicago. Cobb also made a trip to his hometown of Paducah in mid-April 1915, where he was given a hero's welcome and a testimonial dinner. On the lecture circuit, he spoke in all kinds of venues, from theaters to opera houses to most kinds of arenas—everywhere "except vacant lots and circus tents." And, of importance to the entrepreneurial Kentuckian, his "tour made more money than any road show of the period except for the Ziegfeld Follies."[27]

Exhausted after nearly three months on the road, Cobb returned to New York. On the evening of Sunday, April 25, 1915, he received what was arguably the greatest honor of his life. At the Waldorf-Astoria Hotel, an elaborate testimonial took up most of the evening. Doran published a transcript of the event: *Dinner Tendered to Irvin S. Cobb.* Frank I. Cobb, editor of the *New York World,* opened the ceremonies by asking the audience to rise and drink a toast to President Woodrow Wilson while the band played "The Star-Spangled Banner." "This dinner to Mr. Irvin S. Cobb was planned originally by reporters as a tribute to a reporter who had measured up to the full opportunities and responsibilities of his occupation," said the toastmaster.[28]

The audience of more than 600 included Cobb's mother, wife, and daughter; Dorothy Dix; the Dorans; and other close friends. Following the custom of the times, women were seated in the balcony, while only men were among the dinner crowd on the main floor. Hedda Hopper, Mary Pickford, and the wives of several notable entertainers, journalists, and writers sat in the balcony. The menu for the evening included Cobb's favorites such as crabmeat cocktail, Creole gumbo, beef filet, squab, corn bread and biscuits, hearts of lettuce Paducah, and, for dessert, Savannah "au rhum." An African American band replaced the Europe Revised Orchestra, playing "My Old Kentucky Home" in honor of Cobb.[29]

A series of testimonials by friends and colleagues followed the music. "Irvin Cobb is one of our big men," quipped George McAnemy, president of the New York Board of Aldermen. In typical "roast" fashion, famed Broadway playwright Rennold Wolf proceeded to skewer Cobb: "Mr. Toastmaster, Mr. Cobb, Ladies and Gentleman: 'I come to bury Caesar, not to praise him.'" Wolf went on to humorously describe Cobb's rise to fame and his early days in New York, such as when he tried to escape paying fifteen cents for a meal at "Dolan's beef-and-beans joint on Park Row" ten years ago. "Tonight he sits here securely in all of the pomp of an evening suit of reasonably recent vintage (laughter), eating a dinner that cost seven and a half dollars a plate. (Laughter.) But he still runs true to form; he is not paying for this one either. (Laughter and applause.)" Wolf poked fun at Cobb's only failure so far—his inability to write a long-running play. "During the curt engagement of 'Funabashi,' the Casino Theatre became the favorite hiding place for crooks and fugitives who desired to avoid detection." Proclaiming Cobb's "Americanism," Wolf called *Europe Revised* "the greatest humorous book of travel since Mark Twain wrote 'Innocents Abroad.'" So the evening went, with praise for the transplanted Kentuckian along with well-placed humor.[30]

After Wolf's remarks, a short silent film, *From Paducah to Popularity or the Life of Irvin S. Cobb,* was shown. Humorous drawings of the honoree were also projected on a screen. Other luminaries spoke, including James Montgomery Flagg, artist and illustrator, who presented Cobb with an oil portrait. Included in the printed version of the proceedings were comments by Sinclair Lewis, Bob Davis, Rupert Hughes, and others. Recommending *Cobb's Anatomy*, William Johnson penned: "A big brain needs a big belly to balance it. Irvin Cobb has a well-balanced brain. He's never top-heavy and never will be."[31]

Responding at the end of the evening's festivities, Cobb began his remarks by claiming, "I never knew before that I knew so many people had seven dollars and a half." There followed a number of biographical or semibiographical asides. He could not help but tell "darky" stories to illustrate his points, which were well received by his all-white, predominantly male northern audience with laughter and applause. He concluded:

> If I told you that this was the proudest and happiest minute of my life, it would be a platitude, but it would be also true, and if I tried to tell you how much I have appreciated this evidence of your kindness, I should fail. There is a good deal here in my heart that calls for utterance, but there is a lump in my throat that keeps it from coming out, and all I can say to you is, coining or using a homely phrase of my own homely country, that I am mighty obliged to you all. Thank you. (Great applause.)[32]

After three months in Europe and nearly three months on a lecture tour, after being celebrated in his hometown by old friends and neighbors and then feted in New York City, Cobb intended to return to Europe to report on the Great War. However, his life would take an unexpected turn.

6

Midlife

1915 to Early 1918

On May 1, 1915, Cobb entered the Polyclinic Hospital in New York City for an emergency operation, ostensibly for a hernia suffered while in Europe. His exhaustive weeks covering the early months of World War I, followed by a lengthy lecture tour, had worn him down. Described as a "gastric hemorrhage" in the press, Cobb's condition turned out to be worse than his physicians had originally diagnosed. For two weeks Cobb could not even sit up in bed; nor was he allowed to read. Manie Cobb rushed from Paducah to be at her son's bedside. His condition improved slowly. "Mr. Cobb asked yesterday that the published report that he had been near death in the past few days be denied," the *New York Times* reported two weeks after his operation. Though this sounds like one of Cobb's usual comic lines, it was close to the truth.[1]

Daughter Buff knew that her father's health had declined during his long lecture tour. "His family began to catch onto the fact that perhaps Pa had been peaked (a southern colloquialism for ill) for quite a spell." After the apparently successful operation, Cobb recuperated at his apartment. Though he had planned to return to Europe to report on the war for the *Saturday Evening Post,* he would be out of action for at least two months. He did not improve as quickly or as completely as expected and realized he would not be going back to Europe anytime soon.[2]

In late June Cobb spent some time recuperating in Atlantic City. There he met up with a friend, Dr. Stanley Rinehart, the husband of *Post* contributor and novelist Mary Roberts Rinehart. Dr. Rinehart was recovering from an appendectomy, and he and Cobb commiserated about their experiences and began to see the humorous side of their hospital stays.[3]

With his return to the war front delayed indefinitely, Cobb published only a few pieces in mid-1915. He had a backlog of Judge Priest stories, beginning with "Judge Priest Comes Back." The *Post* also published an article about the foibles of American tourists that suited his reading public. As happened several times in his writing career, Cobb turned an incident in his personal life into a triumph of humor. He struck gold when he wrote the tongue-in-cheek "Speaking of Operations," published in early November 1915.[4]

"Speaking of Operations" became so popular that Cobb expanded it into a fifty-three-page booklet that also included four hilarious Tony Sarg illustrations. Doran rushed the book into print in late 1915. In the middle of his ordeal, Cobb exclaimed, "It dawned on me that I was not having any more privacy than a goldfish." This quip has been quoted numerous times. *Speaking of Operations* came out at a crucial time in the history of American humor. In *The American Humorist,* Norris Yates praised Cobb for expanding on the "Little Man" genre of humor, with which almost everyone could identify. As the "Little Man," Cobb even received notice by a national journal for nurses: "As an antidote to a long and continuous course of the serious side of nursing, nothing could surpass Irvin Cobb's 'perfectly painless' narrative of his own experience in the operating room and the hospital." A reviewer proclaimed that, at only fifty cents per copy, the book "will buck up timorous souls who have to face the experience which he has so delightfully turned to profit for himself and his publisher."[5]

By 1935, *Speaking of Operations* had sold more than a million copies. Publisher Doran recalled that Cobb "could laugh at surgeons and instruments and torture. And laugh he did. And the world laughed with him." About the same time the book was published, illustrator and artist James Montgomery Flagg, who had immortalized Cobb in dozens of humorous illustrations, completed a classic clay figure of the rotund writer with his hands in his pockets and the ever-present cigar in the side of his mouth. If Cobb was the early-twentieth-century personification of the "Little Man" in print, he was also widely known as a comic personality whose corpulent figure made him one of the most easily recognizable celebrities of the World War I era.[6]

In his entry on Cobb in the *Encyclopedia of American Humorists,* Gary Engle called *Speaking of Operations* the Kentuckian's "most successful work" because "the piece struck so resonant a chord with the public that it . . . remained in print long after Cobb's death. *Operations* represented Cobb's style of humor at its best. Conversational, witty, and well-focused, it offered the author's opinions about those minor details of a hospital stay that most patients overlook but all remember in the recounting." The year after Cobb's death in 1944, B. D. Zevin declared *Speaking of Operations* a "classic." "Just as Rome had its Gibbon, and Sam Johnson his Boswell, so the hospital bed of our time has its Cobb. . . . This account by the first great extrovert and historian of the operating-room has given millions of readers, the bed-ridden and the hale, cause for unrestrained laughter." According to Engle, Cobb was the first among humor and comedy writers and performers in the early twentieth century to portray the "Besieged Little Man" who, though faced with technological, medical, and industrial advances, kept his humanity by confronting change. Others such as Charlie Chaplin, Robert Benchley, A. A. Milne, James Thurber, and even comic-strip characters such as Dagwood Bumstead "are later examples of his besieged and bemused Little Man" who will not give up his individuality and sense of humor, concluded Engle.[7]

Although *Speaking of Operations* appealed to the American public at large, Cobb never strayed far from his southern disposition. Doran claimed in his memoirs, "If I have one prayer to offer for the preservation of Cobb it would be 'God keep him from becoming a professional Southerner,' for he is an atavist. His friends, well-wishers, and admirers would insist that he is of the nation, not of a part of it." Being "of the nation," Cobb's brand of "southern" racism was welcome almost everywhere because it fit the spirit of the age throughout the United States. In 1914 the *New York Times* asked seventeen writers of humor, "What is the best joke or anecdote that you ever heard?" Cobb replied with a belittling "darky" story that was completely acceptable to the *Times'* editors and its readers.[8]

Cobb's devotion to the Old South led him to attend the 1916 national meeting of the United Confederate Veterans (UCV) in Birmingham, Alabama. He was invited to appear as a special "orator" by the group's commander in chief General Bennett H. Young, a Kentuckian who had led the raid on St. Albans, Vermont, in 1864. Cobb accepted and apologized that he could spare only one day because of his commitments to a "theatrical production." As Cobb was being introduced by Young, a band began to play "My Old Kentucky Home," and the whole audience rose to join in singing the anthem. Cobb inserted some of his signature humor into the speech and spoke in favor of military preparedness before getting to the most important part of his address. He grandiloquently declared that when the last of the veterans died "and the army of the Confederacy is united in the whole and goes through the alabaster gates to pass in grand review before the Commander-in-Chief of the destinies of mankind, do you think that in the doomsday book of humanity your cause will be written as one that was lost? No! It will be written down as a cause that was won!" The band immediately struck up "Dixie," playing "in a frenzy" as the crowd rose, "smashing hats and crying like children. It was the greatest ovation ever paid to a speaker in Birmingham," reported the enthusiastic *Louisville Post* under the headline "Cobb Stirs up Dixie Veterans." By this date, the Lost Cause was well accepted throughout the United States. At the 1917 reunion of the UCV in Washington, DC— its first convention held outside a typically southern city—Virginia-born President Woodrow Wilson sat in the reviewing stand until the last veteran had passed. North and South now appeared reconciled as the United States entered World War I.[9]

Cobb had no intention of backing off from his sanctified and sanitized view of the Old South, the New South, and white racial superiority, and he also displayed a common, widely accepted form of American anti-Semitism. He might praise Confederate veteran Herman Felsburg and his brother as clothiers in his Judge Priest stories, but in the *Smart Set* he was just as likely to ridicule American Jewry. In "My Country, 't Is of Thee," Cobb distorted and mocked the life of American Jews: "My Cohen-try, 't is of thee, Sweet land of Levi-ty, Of thee I sing! Land where the Einsteins pour, Land where the Epsteins roar, From every auction store, Let Friedman ring!" Cobb and Mencken did not agree on much, but they did share a disdain for Jews in America. "The chief trouble with the Jew in this country is that he is not sufficiency lambasted, that he suffers a degenerating immunity from harsh criticism," Mencken charged. "The reason lies in his clannishness and his commercial consequence." Readers today are usually told that the *Smart Set* of Mencken's time stood out as a leading literary journal of the early twentieth century. It is indeed odd that such drivel would have been acceptable from an avant-garde journal that subtitled itself "A Magazine of Cleverness" and "The Magazine for Minds that Are Not Primitive."[10]

The normally affable Cobb resumed his usual frenetic pace after recovering from his operation. He introduced a new character, Fibble, D.D., a foolish minister that Cobb used to show his disdain for organized religion. As a teacher at "Fernbridge Seminary for Young Ladies, Lover's Leap, N.J.," Fibble is a comical, inept, rather stupid figure. Like most of Cobb's writings, if the public liked his characterizations, he fleshed them out into a book published by Doran. *Fibble, D.D.,* which came out in 1916, spoofed the life and times of the socially backward teacher and minister. Consisting of three long chapters, the book went into several printings. A *New York Times* reviewer gave *Fibble* a thumbs-up: Cobb "is a first-class caricaturist, but that has proved no hindrance when he chooses to create a real man or woman. On the whole, it appears that Mr. Cobb is doing a good big share of that interpretation of American life which should be the job of American authors, and that he is doing it remarkably." As the *Times* review implied, a growing number of Cobb's publications were intended as moneymakers, with little if any literary merit.[11]

Cobb could always find an outlet for his short pieces in other magazines. For instance, around the turn of the century, *McClure's* had a reputation for muckraking, publishing Progressive Era articles by Ida Tarbell, Lincoln Steffens, and others. But by the time Cobb's pieces reached *McClure's* readers, the magazine had turned into more of a general monthly, much like the *Saturday Evening Post,* with more emphasis on short stories and articles than on serious editorials. In 1915 *McClure's* published one of Cobb's Kentucky tales about an attempt to influence an election with whiskey. "Red likker, say about fourteen year old, is mighty deceivin' to a mountaineer. It tastes so smooth he forgets that its sting is strong enough to take off warts." However, those who were trying to get a mountain man so drunk that he could not vote discovered that he could hold his liquor better than they. In another piece for *McClure's,* "Big Moments of Big Trials," Cobb drew on his career as a reporter covering the Thaw trial in New York City and that of the assassins of William Goebel in Kentucky. Another monthly magazine, *Red Book,* appealed to the same audience as the *Post* and *McClure's,* and it often published works by many of the same authors, including Cobb. "The Gold Brick Twins" is one of his longish pieces, a "meandering" thirteen-page story about two scam artists with a Damon Runyon-esque theme.[12]

Throughout 1916 Cobb appeared to be suffering few if any ill effects from his possible war-related shell shock or his 1915 operation. He contributed several Judge Priest stories, along with other southern stories featuring Jeff Poindexter or Herman Felsberg, to the *Saturday Evening Post.* Most of his pieces that year, sixteen in all, were humorous, such as "Unaccustomed as I Am—," but there were attempts at drama as well. "The Eyes of the World" and "Field of Honor" fall flat to modern readers, but "And There Was Light" was a successful drama in the tradition of Cobb's "grim" tales. The lead piece for the October 14, 1916, issue of the *Post* proved to be Cobb's most hilarious of the year—a spoof of Cobb the sportsman called "The Battle Hen of the Republic." More and more it appeared that Cobb's southern humor was his bread and butter.[13]

Cobb's publication pattern had become well established by 1916: his published pieces in the *Post* and other journals became chapters in books. *Old Judge Priest,* consisting of nine formulaic stories about the Paducah judge and his cohorts, followed a familiar rubric: at the end of each story, Judge Priest has solved a problem and asserted his role as leader of the community. The stories are all set in a Paducah-like town during the horse-and-buggy days. By 1916, more and more Americans recalled these days with nostalgia, as the automobile and motion pictures began to change perceptions of life in the United States. They longed for the "good old days." Judge Priest appealed to Americans as a commonsense individual in an increasingly complicated world. In addition, Cobb could always dash off a humorous piece for a monthly such as *American Magazine,* where in mid-1916 he satirized his home state: "Four out of every five counties are so dry that often a stranger must travel nearly half a block to get a drink," he chortled. He admitted that "Kentuckians are belligerent by nature. We do not deny it. The crest of our state shows two gentlemen . . . holding each other firmly by the right hand. The intent of the picture is plain. So long as they both hold hands, neither can reach for his hardware."[14]

Cobb's short stories were often quite long—forty pages or more—owing to his habit of writing for "space rates" from his early newspaper days. He always built the story line rather slowly to achieve a solution or an unexpected twist at the end. The themes of North-South reconciliation and small-town neighborliness suited his audience; Confederates made peace with Yankees, or the average citizen found a way to assert his rights over the wealthy and the big banks. For example, in "A Chapter from the Life of an Ant," an assistant bank teller (the "ant"), with considerable help from Judge Priest, is able to clear his name from the predations of the "anteater," in this case, a con man–bank robber. The story is interesting owing to Cobb's knowledge gleaned from his days as a reporter covering such crimes. He knew the language of the criminal, which he interspersed with the usual western Kentucky dialect spoken by Judge Priest and his cohorts. Cobb ably presented Jewish, Catholic, Italian, and other minority citizens of Judge Priest's smaller world as typically American, but he could not do so with blacks. These stories are almost unreadable today because of Cobb's incessantly stereotypical dialect and characterization of African Americans. However, in 1916 these stories suited his clientele— average, middle-class white Americans—regardless of region.[15]

The *Nation* reviewed *Old Judge Priest* warmly if not enthusiastically. "Mr. Cobb may more fairly be called a unique figure among American magazinemen. At best, he is an accomplished journeyman in the direction of letters; at worst he is a vaudeville artist in print. He has a genuinely comic touch, and is always sure of his laughs. This writer has a true style, a way of saying things which expresses himself." The reviewer complained that the short stories were a bit long. "It may be slovenly often, but it seldom fails to go straight for the business at hand." Three years later, a reviewer in the *Literary Digest* highly praised Cobb's work as well as his ability to poke fun at himself. "Irvin S. Cobb is one of those fortunate mortals who are born humorists." Cobb, however, did not consider himself a humorist.[16]

While the stories in *Old Judge Priest* were predictable, in that the old jurist would always set things right in the end, *Local Color,* published the same year, contained some interesting variety. Seven of the ten stories had appeared in the *Saturday Evening Post,* but the opening story, "Local Color," and the closing one, "Smooth Crossing," had not been published before and formed excellent bookends. "Local Color" is about a successful novelist—well educated and well bred, though utterly colorless—who decides to write about the prison system. After dropping out of society, he arranges to be found guilty of petty theft and sent to Sing Sing prison. While incarcerated, he plans to gather material for his great American novel. After Felix Looms becomes convicted felon James Williams, his life changes abruptly and irretrievably. Cobb excelled at describing the New York prison system as dehumanizing, able to turn a perfectly decent man into a bumbling misfit. In the words of Looms/Williams: "The worst thing in our modern civilization is a prison. It is wrong and we know it is wrong; and yet we have devised nothing to take its place. A prison is crime's chemical laboratory; it is a great retort where virulent poisons are distilled . . . I know I could write about it, and so I am going to prison."[17]

Of course, Cobb wanted his readers to empathize with his protagonist, but our hopes for Looms/Williams are dashed. During his mind-numbing three years in Sing Sing, he learns how to commit violent crimes from a cellmate. Then he finds that society sees him as a released felon when he hits the streets of New York City. Forced to flee from his old Fifth Avenue neighborhood by a policeman, he takes up the way of life he learned in prison. In a powerful passage, Cobb explained how Looms forever became Williams: "It was precisely in that brief moment that Felix Looms, the well-known writer, died, he having been killed instantly by the very thing after which he had lusted." Williams picks up a piece of pipe; conceals it in a newspaper, as taught by his strong-arm cell mate; and attacks a man on his way home from work. He is sent back to Sing Sing for five years at hard labor. We know that when he is released again, he will commit another crime and return to prison.[18]

If Cobb had fleshed out this thirty-six-page story, he might have written his own great American novel. In any case, he proved that he could write something other than his southern stories. "Smooth Crossing" also had all the elements of a good novel, including plotting, characterizations, and suspenseful twists and turns.[19]

In addition to all his publishing activities, Cobb found time for politicking, campaigning for the reelection of President Woodrow Wilson in 1916. Between October 22 and November 3 he went on an all-expenses-paid speaking tour. "Got any good new ones (jokes) to spring in your speeches?" asked a reporter. "They aren't going to be that kind (of) speeches," Cobb replied, praising Wilson's efforts to keep the country out of war. "There's nothing funny about those Wilson notes, let me tell you. And watchful waiting to date has saved us a great many thousands of lives." Earlier, Cobb had advised Doran not to publish the so-called Peck letters, a considerable correspondence between Wilson, during the time he was president of Princeton University, and the wife of another professor. Many of the letters were not complimentary of politicians such as William Jennings Bryan. Doran intended to publish the letters after Wilson left office, but owing to the president's deteriorating health and early death, as well as subsequent legal challenges by the second Mrs. Wilson, they were never published. After Wilson's reelection in 1916, Cobb received a note from the president thanking him for his efforts and signed, "The Smooth-Faced Man." Earlier, at a supposedly nonpartisan dinner for Wilson at the New York Press Club, Cobb had not directly mentioned his support of Wilson but "in passing merely wished to state that my candidate happened to be kind of a smooth-faced man," which clearly was not the fully bearded Republican candidate Charles Evans Hughes. Both the audience and Wilson caught the humor, and the president never forgot Cobb's support in an extremely tight race that Wilson won in the Electoral College by a count of 277–254.[20]

Cobb did not give up his ambition of writing a successful, long-running New York play in the late 1910s. He also began to dabble in the movie industry, which at the time was centered primarily in New Jersey. Cobb even had a few bit parts in several movies. He appeared in one segment of *Our Mutual Girl,* a series of fifty-two one-reel films that featured celebrities such as Cobb on occasion. As it was a silent film with subtitles, Cobb's contribution was short and consisted of offering advice to "Margaret," a young woman visiting New York City, in "Reel No. 24." In this episode, he told the story of two Negro cooks who come in contact with a hungry white man. The story is so racist that it is unrepeatable today. In a *New York Times* piece, Cobb commented, tongue in cheek, on his experience as if he were a major movie star. "I began by demanding the centre of the picture. I believe this is customary among the veterans of the profession." Also, he insisted that his name be featured in all advertisements in red letters "not less than eighteen inches high and correspondingly broad." In short, Cobb mocked movie stars of the day.[21]

In one of those serendipitous turns that sometimes happen, Cobb also made a brief movie appearance in 1915 while in California. While on a lecture tour, he met one of the icons of moviemaking, Cecil B. DeMille. Up to that time, most motion pictures had been made in New Jersey, but the natural light and balmy climate of California had drawn DeMille to a barn at Hollywood and Vine in Los Angeles. "In the delightfully haphazard way of

1915, we persuaded him to play the American tourist," DeMille recalled in his autobiography. "He received no screen credit, but years afterward, when he launched upon a whole new career as an actor, he still gave me credit for his screen debut. I am not sure that 'debut,' which makes one think of willowy young girls in white, is quite the right word to apply to Irvin Cobb's rotund, rather pear-shaped appearance in *The Arab;* but I think he'd like it. . . . Casting him in *The Arab* was rather in the nature of a lark for both of us, and for the audience."[22]

Cobb's creative energy and eagerness to break into other fields seemed endless in the World War I era. Cobb's short story "Words and Music" was adapted by veteran playwright Bayard Veiller and came to the stage as *Back Home,* opening at Boston's Plymouth Theatre in early October 1915. Cobb told his Kentucky friend Townsend that he had refused an offer to play Judge Priest himself. At the play's opening, Cobb told the press he was not a dramatist but left that to others. While in Boston, the local press held a reception for him. "Any one here who has ever had a real old home town will like 'Back Home,' I think," Cobb said.[23]

Back Home opened at New York's George M. Cohan Theatre in mid-November 1915. Although the audience appeared to enjoy the play on opening night, it was not a resounding success. The *New York Times* reviewer declared the "mild and rambling melodrama at the Cohan Theatre is rich in tenderness and kindly humor" but not noteworthy. The reviewer found the actor cast as Judge Priest entirely out of character, while the actor playing Jeff turned in a more credible performance. "Indeed, the whole course of 'Back Home' is meandering and rather uncertain, but a great deal of warm sentiment and satisfying humor is found along the way." At the play's conclusion, when the "scattered cries for the author brought to the footlights not Mr. Veiller but Mr. Cobb, the latter hastened to explain with a perfectly straight face that he and his dramatist had matched quarters for the opportunity in the wings, and that Veiller had won."[24]

The *Chicago Tribune*'s review was no kinder: "It was not unexpected that 'Back Home' would fail to please New York. . . . 'Back Home' as simple comedy dramas go, was a fairly entertaining play made up of 75 per cent sentiment and 25 per cent stage hokum." Both the audience and reviewers considered character actor Willis P. Sweatnam, a white man in blackface playing Jeff Poindexter, the best part of the play. The Louisville newspapers offered some consolation to Cobb by noting that Bret Harte's stories did not translate well to the stage either.[25]

Cobb admitted in *Exit Laughing* a quarter century later that the staging of *Back Home* had been wrong, and "after a six weeks' struggle Heaven was its home." In the second act, an ill-conceived and expensive circus had been re-created. In his droll manner, Cobb explained: "They even hired a live elephant. The verdict of the newspapers was that the elephant had been badly supported." The *New York Times* reported, "So softly that it was not heard south of Forty-second Street, nor north of Forty-third, 'Back Home' tiptoed out of the Cohan Theatre Saturday night. When last seen it was not going anywhere in particular." But "that Irv Cobb is still a great short story writer," the *Times* concluded. The first major dramatization of a Judge Priest story ended in dismal failure, but Cobb was unfazed, telling Townsend he would just move on.[26]

The next year, Cobb and Roi Cooper Megrue, a successful New York playwright, collaborated on a play, *Under Sentence*. The script went through several rewrites, but basically the play was about a Wall Street financier who goes to Sing Sing prison for fraud. Ostensibly about prison reform, the play wandered too much for the reviewer from the *New York Times*. The writer described the first two acts about "frenzied finance" as "a bald, unvarnished and continuously interesting melodrama," but the third act fell flat. In fact, the reviewer compared the first two acts with Cobb's successful short story "The Escape of Mr. Trimm." Perhaps the only memorable thing about the play was that a young Edward G. Robinson, a Jewish immigrant from Romania, made his debut as a convict named Fagan. Cobb recalled that Robinson received a $10 prize for coming up with the title of the play. Thomas Mitchell, who later starred in *Gone with the Wind*, also had a minor role. This was Cobb's last attempt to write drama for the stage. In the twilight of his life, Cobb acknowledged, "So you see, it took me a distressingly long time of baiting and angling and praying for bites and spitting on the worm before I admitted to myself that I didn't have the dramatic touch." Even two decades earlier he had conceded to Townsend, "I thank God that none of my plays was ever published."[27]

Cobb participated in moviemaking whenever possible, along with his other varied activities. Though humor and comedy were his forte, he wanted to do serious work as well. In late 1916 Vitagraph Studios filmed

Cobb's script *The Dollar and the Law* in New Jersey. The film opens with footage of money being printed at the US Mint and then proceeds to dramatize "the influence of a dollar after it leaves the mint—for good or evil. It is a story of dramatic power, of interest and of suspense," claimed the *Louisville Courier-Journal*. But even though it starred Lillian Walker, a famed silent film actress, the movie was not a success.[28]

In mid-1917 Cobb explained in *Woman's Home Companion* the difficulty of writing a film script, as the movie industry did not use the same standards he was accustomed to as a magazine contributor. For magazine articles, he was offered a certain fee for his work and, if accepted, usually received a check within two weeks. "It is not thus in Filmland!" he grumbled. Movie producers wanted new scripts but did not want to commit to pay a guaranteed fee. "Mr. Whosiz," Cobb's fictional movie producer, wanted a script but would not settle on a fee when the author's hard work was delivered. Cobb believed, optimistically, that the "scalawags of the profession" were being weeded out by the success of the larger movie companies (the movie business was the sixth largest US industry at the time). "Lately I have met some big men and some square men in the moving picture business," he claimed. It could not happen soon enough for him, and Cobb still had hopes of achieving success in films one day.[29]

None of these activities kept Cobb from fulfilling his commitments to the *Saturday Evening Post*, writing for other magazines, or turning out books for Doran. As Cobb told Robert H. Davis—the barbs of Mencken notwithstanding—his drive for writing articles, movies, and books "so rapidly" came naturally to him. "My boy, the public is going to wake up some day and dismiss me. This is too good to be true. I propose to take it while they are not looking. It's now or never." He told Townsend he was "messing a bit with moving pictures stuff too." Moreover, he was trying to get each book reprinted as often as possible. Cobb's ability to write humor, fiction, and commentary appeared unceasing in 1916. The middlebrow public to which he appealed paid him well, and he intended to take advantage of their generosity. Cobb was one of the most recognized figures in America, and his pictures and caricatures appeared everywhere. For example, when a minor controversy erupted over the naming of Paducah and whether an American Indian named "Chief Paduke" had ever existed, well-known *Louisville Times* cartoonist Paul Plaschke solved the problem by anointing Cobb as "Chief Paducah" in a classic illustration with the Kentuckian in full Indian regalia. Cobb appeared on the national stage as well. At the 1916 annual dinner of the Authors' League of America in New York City, he attended as the "lead speaker" of the evening.[30]

Upon reaching the age of forty, Cobb engaged in some introspection. In a humorous essay in *American Magazine* in mid-1917, he compared in his inimitable way how life had changed since his birth in 1876. In his youth, farmers had been isolated, and a round-trip to the county seat by horse and wagon had taken more than a day. Now the automobile had changed all that. Amusement had changed as well, with the cinema replacing the shows of Buffalo Bill Cody. Cobb could recall seeing Geronimo as a sideshow figure "selling his autographs at a dollar a copy and wearing a pair of two-dollar overalls." During his eleven years in New York City, Cobb had witnessed modernization that only promised to continue. Cobb hoped to be part of that transformation. He believed that women would soon be able to vote and that Prohibition—an idea he detested—would soon sweep the land. Based on his war experiences in 1914, Cobb predicted that America's entry into the Great War would have a beneficent influence and that the United States was "preparing to become in truth and in deed a Big Brother to all the world. I've seen the starting of this great national impulse. I trust I shall be here to witness its complete enactment." Then, ending on a humorous note, he proposed that turning forty was not an end but merely a beginning.[31]

In the same issue, Robert H. Davis, editor of *Munsey's Magazine,* contributed a half-page laudatory piece on his friend. "It is safe to wager that there is not a man living to-day who has ever heard Irvin Cobb utter a disagreeable phrase about any human being, among either the quick or the dead. He is a kind of fat Pollyanna; at peace with all the world; full of friendly inclinations, cordial and kindly thoughts, and glad when everybody else is glad. . . . His shift from wool to silk socks hasn't made him proud," Davis exclaimed.[32]

At this point in Cobb's career, he had indeed witnessed great changes in America as it moved from the horse-and-buggy days into a new industrial age. Publishing was also changing as reading tastes modernized. Would Cobb's southern stories and southern orientation continue to win him readers and a good income? He had also demonstrated that he could write New York–style short stories and commentary. Would he be able to break through and produce a novel of appreciable length? Would he be able to keep up with the changing world as he entered midlife?

As the war in Europe dragged on, the United States was under increasing pressure to enter the conflict on the Allied side. Lorimer and the *Saturday Evening Post* became more supportive of the Allied cause and of President Wilson. Lorimer at first wanted the United States to remain totally neutral, but events moved too swiftly for the publisher, who thought of himself not only as a maker of public opinion but also as a leading proponent of his version of Americanism. The sinking of the *Lusitania* on May 7, 1915, did not take him off course in supporting Wilson. Germany's declaration that it was reopening its onslaught on neutral ships forced Lorimer to be a follower and not a maker of policy.[33]

Early in 1917, Cobb's pieces in the *Post* maintained their usual humorous pattern, but they became increasingly serious as tensions mounted. In January 1917 Cobb wrote an antiwar article, "The Garb of Men," in which he highlighted the growing shortage of men to fight on all sides in the war, after reading a news account that Germany would soon be calling up seventeen-year-olds. In effect, he was still espousing Lorimer's hope that the United States could stay out of the war. Other pieces early in the year followed Cobb's formula for the Judge Priest tales or other southern stories. He even gave his assent to women's suffrage.[34]

However, in "Thrice Is He Armed," published on April 21, 1917, Cobb gave his complete support to America's declaration of war. Whereas in *Paths of Glory* he had taken an evenhanded approach to describing the war front, going so far as to declare that Germany had committed no atrocities, he now excoriated that nation for its warmongering and brutality. "Having spread the gospel of force for so long, Prussianized Germany can understand but one counter-argument—force. We must give her back blow for blow—a harder blow in return for each blow she gives us," he wrote. Two weeks later Cobb contributed "The Prussian Paranoia," as Lorimer's editorials and the contributions of other *Post* writers joined the war effort. Cobb even published a Judge Priest story in the *Pictorial Review* that emphasized, rather romantically, the uniting of North and South after the Civil War. "With a single-minded war-inspired patriotism that entirely belied his earlier blunt and tough, though equally patriotic isolationism, Lorimer made the war his cause," explained biographer Cohn. "The United States declared war on April 6; the *Saturday Evening*

Post followed suit on April 21." By June 30, Lorimer was firmly in the war camp, writing editorials in each issue of the *Post*, pushing Liberty Loan drives, and advocating mobilization on all fronts. "Germany compelled us to choose whether we should, in effect, fight for her or against her," Lorimer explained. "We chose the latter, because our own rights were violated and because we profoundly believed the defeat of England and France by Germany would involve the very gravest menace to us and the cause of democracy throughout the world." Mary Roberts Rinehart and other *Post* regulars, as well as its cover illustrators, followed Lorimer's lead.[35]

Although the *Saturday Evening Post* continued to publish short stories and commentaries on other subjects, from early 1917 through 1918, the war in Europe took center stage. Cobb followed that lead wholeheartedly. Doran rushed into print Cobb's seventy-page screed to the war effort, *Speaking of Prussians—*, which was "Dedicated by Permission to Woodrow Wilson, President of the United States." Cobb excelled at quickly producing these single-themed books, but this one was not humorous in any way; it was part of the propaganda effort meant to unite the American people against a formidable enemy. "I believe it to be my patriotic duty as an American citizen to write what I am writing, and after it is written to endeavour to give it as wide a circulation in the United States as it is possible to find. In making this statement, though, I am not setting myself up as a teacher or a preacher; neither am I going upon the assumption that, because I am a fairly frequent contributor to American magazines, people will be the readier or should be the readier to read what I have to say." As Cobb's indictment against Germany continued, he became more bellicose. "We must hold it to be a holy war, we must preach a jihad, . . . we must risk our manhood." And later, "Without the shedding of blood there is no remission of sins." Cobb attacked German "Kultur" as the real villain by quoting several German intellectuals. "Germany eventually will be defeated as the Southern Confederacy was defeated—by being bled white and starved thin," Cobb predicted.[36]

Cobb wanted to rush to Europe to report on American participation firsthand, but he was forced to wait. Meanwhile, he churned out his usual short stories, commentaries, and articles for the *Post* and other magazines. He also returned to his old beat—newspapers. For the *Louisville Times* and other dailies, he occasionally reported on baseball in the 1917 season, and he even covered evangelist Billy Sunday. From his early days in Paducah, Cobb had considered himself "an innocent bystander" when it came to religion, and he had drifted from his Presbyterian moorings early in adulthood. Attending one of Billy Sunday's meetings in New York City in April 1917, Cobb observed: "It is vastly interesting to see twenty-odd thousand people swayed by one mind, . . . to be played on by this master musician of emotionalism, this harpist of the heart strings, this arch-performer upon human nature." Enjoying this rhetoric, Cobb declared that Sunday combined the gifts of Martin Luther, William Jennings Bryan, and P. T. Barnum. The evangelist's vigor and humor also impressed Cobb. Later, at a Richmond, Indiana, revival, Sunday returned the favor, stating, "I like everything Irvin ever wrote. He is a crackerjack."[37]

In time for the Christmas 1917 season, Doran published *Those Times and These,* a compilation of nine *Post* short stories and articles and one from the *Pictorial Review.* Like most of Cobb's longer books to date, this one had no central theme; it was an eclectic collection of his popular pieces. A. T. Robertson, a professor at Southern Baptist Theological Seminary in Louisville, praised Cobb's gifts. "His wit ripples along as usual and good nature pervades the book. Mr. Cobb is a tonic for the blues and his optimism is contagious. Hard times were the stock-in-trade in those days." Mindful of the war, Robertson concluded: "Let us be brave now."[38]

Far more interesting to modern readers is a series of five articles about life among the masses in New York City called "'Twixt the Bluff and the Sound." With his keen reporter's eye, Cobb described the wealthy, the poor, and the middle class, society high and low. He chortled at everyone with his distinctive brand of social commentary with an ironic, humorist twist. However, he could still turn out a serious crime story, such as "The Luck Piece." And one of his better Judge Priest tales, "Boys Will Be Boys," was the lead story in the October 17, 1917, issue of the *Post.* It was actually made into a stage play and then a silent film starring Will Rogers. However, because it had failed as a play, Cobb sold the movie rights "for a lump sum," he said. "Not a big lump. It didn't even suggest lumpiness."[39]

If Cobb still had ambitions of writing a full-length novel during this period, he did not appear to make the effort. It was simply easier and more financially rewarding to write and sell short pieces to the *Post* and other magazines and then compile several of them into a book. "The Thunders of Silence," a rather long story published just as American participation in World War I began to be fully felt in early 1918 (although Cobb had probably written it months before), may have been a book gone begging. It tells the tale of Congressman Jason Mallard, a great orator (at least in own estimation) who is opposed to American participation in a war and develops a large following (suggesting the oratorical skills of pacifist senator Robert LaFollette and his ability to command an obedient audience). Though many people consider Mallard to be a fraud, there seems to be no way to stop his affront against "Americanism." However, a young newspaperman persuades his colleagues across the country to simply ignore Mallard and not print anything he says or does. One night, Mallard speaks to an enthusiastic, overflow crowd at Madison Square Garden, but there is no press coverage of his oration. The next night, no one shows up to hear him speak. He is hounded by a conspiracy of "silence" and is ignored everywhere he goes. As the congressman's life deteriorates, he commits a crime to attract notice. While being chased by a policeman, Mallard stumbles into a river and drowns. "The body was never recovered. But at daylight a black soft hat was found on a half-rotted ice floe, where it had lodged against the bank. A name was stamped in the sweatband, and by this the identity of the suicide was established as that of Congressman Jason Mallard."[40]

"The Thunders of Silence," as well as some of his other writings during World War I, fit Cobb's role as part of the Vigilantes, a "secret" organization of writers who supported the British and Allied cause by late 1916. With generous contributions by Theodore Roosevelt and others, several members published their patriotic writings denouncing pacifism and extolling preparedness. Cobb joined this movement, as did Samuel Hopkins Adams, George Ade, Rex Beach, Booth Tarkington, and others.[41]

In February 1918 *All-Story Weekly,* a Frank A. Munsey property, published Cobb's story "The Gallowsmith," a southern tale reminiscent of Cobb's home region. It was the lead piece that week and was headlined as a "Novelette," running Cobb's favored length of fourteen pages. "Uncle Tobe," the hangman, is an otherwise unobtrusive middle-aged man who makes his living in an unusual but necessary profession for the time. For $75, he performs his service as the "Gallowsmith," carrying out his duty as efficiently and painlessly as possible for more than ten years without incident. Then the "Lone-Hand Kid" apparently places a curse on him. The story ends with a rather macabre twist, the type Cobb specialized in.

This was another of Cobb's popular, moneymaking stories. But would he ever produce a coherent, flowing novel? Was he even thinking about writing a novel?[42]

The future looked bright for Cobb as he entered midlife. He was prosperous and famous. Everything he wrote sold handily. As the United States entered World War I, Cobb became an outspoken voice for "Americanism" and victory against Germany.

7

Momentum

War and Peace,
Awards and Prosperity

By mid-1917, Cobb had become one of the best-known celebrities in America. Now in his early forties, he had proved himself as a newspaper reporter, humorist, short story writer, and author of best-selling books. His restlessness to prove his talents as a playwright and a movie script-writer revealed the inherent insecurities of a small-town Kentuckian who had achieved early success. In a dozen years he had risen to great heights and had found new ways to expand his talent. Would he be able to sustain this momentum?

Cobb's rise from near penury in his early life fed a desire to live the good life, as noted by his daughter. In a chapter entitled "A Long Ride Down Easy Street," Buff Cobb chronicled her family's increasingly pros-perous lifestyle. Cobb enjoyed good food and drink, and as long as he made a substantial income, he kept moving his wife and daughter to bet-ter and better accommodations. Well into his career, he was still provid-ing for his mother and two sisters, until sister Manie married Hewitt Howland, a literary adviser to Bobbs-Merrill and later editor of *Century* magazine.[1]

Moving from a New York City apartment to Yonkers during Buff's childhood proved fortuitous. There, Cobb met publisher George Doran. Subsequently, almost everything Cobb wrote for the *Saturday Evening*

Post and other magazines was turned into a best-selling book by Doran's publishing house.[2]

In fact, after he left Paducah, Cobb's life seemed to be one serendipitous event after another. As he became more successful and considered moving from the big city to a more relaxed atmosphere (as did many other New Yorkers), he wrote a hilarious piece called "Life among the Abandoned Farmers" for the *Post*. Ostensibly, it is about the gullibility of urban dwellers who have heard about "abandoned farms going for a song" just outside the city. When they embark on weekend jaunts in search of such places, the joke is on them: there are no abandoned farms—it is just a ploy used by real estate promoters. When one such city dweller (Cobb) confronts a Connecticut farmer about his "abandoned" farm, he is told in no uncertain terms that the land is not for sale.[3]

Although Cobb played the joke for all it was worth, he did indeed purchase an old sixty-acre estate outside of Ossining, New York, in 1916. The property had fallen into a state of disrepair, except for an old barn. "I am convinced that nothing is so easy to buy as a country place and nothing is so hard to sell," he observed. There were agents and workmen aplenty making suggestions about how to improve his "estate." Cobb kept his New York apartment, but he had the barn rebuilt into a residence that included servants' quarters, a furnace room, a kitchen, and a garage on the first floor. On the second floor, the living quarters for Irvin, Laura, and Buff consisted of three bedrooms, two baths, a dining room, and a large living room. Buff called it "our rakish barn." For the first time, photographs rather than illustrations accompanied Cobb's personal pieces in the *Post* describing his farm, known as "Rebel Ridge." His neighbors in the self-styled "Westchester County Despair Association" included the families of George Creel, Edgar Selwyn, and, a few years later, George Doran. Cobb also had a smaller lodge built, where he could work. Cobb wrote most of his work in longhand, and he incessantly made notes for future articles and stories. He could type, but he preferred to have a secretary get his writings into shape. Photographs of Cobb show him in a voluminous, full-length smock of his own design, which he wore while working in his lodge. While some might think this was intended to enhance his image, it merely served his purpose of being comfortable and allowing his growing girth its full freedom, particularly in private. In the country, Cobb asserted, you lived a simpler life. "You never forget to wind the alarm clock. The big red rooster winds himself."[4]

Cobb appeared to be a workaholic, yet he found time to relax with family and friends. A picture in *Collier's* magazine in 1916 shows him holding a sandwich in his right hand and a deep-sea fishing rod in his left, with, of course, a bemused smile on his face. He enjoyed the companionship of men on hunting and fishing trips, including one to Yellowstone and the Wyoming area in September 1921 with Lorimer. In the late 1920s he described these exploits humorously: "I have caused moose, deer, elk, caribou, antelope and black bear to bite the dust. I have slain coyotes, timber wolves, badger, woodchuck and polecats. As a boy I once took a pistol and shot a rat which was residing in the boat store at Paducah."[5]

Cobb joined the exclusive Wyandanch Club on Long Island and hobnobbed with wealthy businessmen as well as his close friend Bob Davis. He probably preferred the companionship of colleagues Bozeman Bulger, Damon Runyon, and a few other writers, however. Cobb, Bulger, and Runyon jointly bought a motorboat to use for fishing in the summer and bird hunting in the fall and winter months on Long Island Sound. Runyon enjoyed the companionship of the talkative Cobb, most of the time. Even though they shared cramped quarters on the boat, "Cobb was all the entertainment we needed," claimed Runyon. Cobb's stories, real and imagined, kept them amused. Western artist Charles Russell was also one of Cobb's favorite camping, fishing, and hunting partners; Cobb told Buff that his idea of heaven would be a "campfire in the woods . . . listening to Charley Russell tell stories." Cobb also enjoyed attending sporting events, particularly professional baseball, and he periodically wrote sports columns. The ever-active Cobb even tried his hand at golf when he moved out of the city and joined a country club. "I am all for golf. It has taught me patience, perseverance, determination, the futility of human effort, and several new but valued cuss words," the frustrated Cobb admitted.[6]

Despite his enjoyment of travel, Cobb never learned to drive an automobile—at least not successfully. According to Buff, her father gave up this concession to modernity after "he knocked down a new cement wall." When Buff came of age, she often drove him around; otherwise, Cobb hired a chauffeur to drive his personal automobile. Cobb's time in New York City taught him to use taxis, buses, the subway system, and trains connecting with the suburbs. Moreover, he relished rail and automobile travel with others in control, allowing him to fully observe his surroundings.[7]

There is no doubt that Cobb enjoyed his fame as well as the trappings of success. A lifelong Democrat, he supported Woodrow Wilson for president in 1912, as well as his reelection four years later. He even spent three weeks campaigning for Wilson in the close race with Republican Charles Evans Hughes in 1916. Given that his father, uncle, and other older friends were Confederate veterans, Irvin had a desire to join the military. Cobb claimed he had been rejected by the Second Georgia Infantry during the Spanish-American War "because of a set of flattened insteps." Apparently, he also wanted to return to the front in some military-style capacity after American entry into the war in 1917. At a private meeting in Wilson's office, the president told Cobb he could issue "one of those phony commissions," but as Cobb reported in *Exit Laughing,* Wilson insisted that if Cobb returned to Europe, he must write the type of stories he had in 1914, telling the truth about the American war effort. Whether before or after this meeting, Cobb dedicated his successful pro-war screed, *Speaking of Prussians—,* to Wilson.[8]

Cobb never lost the desire to return to Europe and practice his first love: journalism. After Russia withdrew from the war in March 1917, Germany immediately began to shift its war machine to the western front, planning to complete its mission in the west before American forces could arrive in substantial numbers. Eventually, 2 million American doughboys were sent to Europe. Cobb intended to see the battlefront firsthand.[9]

On Christmas Day 1917 the *Louisville Courier-Journal* published "Knocking 'Mania' out of Germania: God-Appointed Job of Boys in Khaki," by Cobb. "I am asked to send a message of Christmas cheer to the men in uniform at Camp Zachary Taylor," a US Army camp on the outskirts of Louisville that had opened in June 1917. Cobb praised the American spirit as these men embarked on their great crusade. "When did men, since first man was born of woman, ever have a cleaner, purer motive for taking up arms than the motive which has inspired you and your comrades all over the Union to take up your arms?" Cobb concluded his patriotic oration by asking God's blessing on these men and charged them with "the God-appointed, God-anointed job of knocking the 'mania' out of Germania."[10]

In early February 1918 Cobb boarded a ship for Europe. Now that a cable connection between England and the United States was available,

Cobb began to send his war reports to the *Saturday Evening Post* only one month after his arrival.[11]

As he had for *Paths of Glory* in 1914, Cobb collected thirteen *Post* articles and eleven others and published them in 1918 as *The Glory of the Coming: What Mine Eyes Have Seen of Americans in Action in the Year of Grace and Allied Endeavor,* his paean to the American war effort. Cobb declared in the foreword to *The Glory of the Coming* that he had not seen Germany in its true light in 1914. "Behind the perfection of the German fighting machine I did not see the hideous malignant brutality which was there." His observations from 1914 were fairly neutral compared with what he would write in 1918. The phrase "The Glory of the Coming" referred to the American forces' crusade to save Europe from itself with Wilson's declaration to "make the world safe for democracy." Believing the Germans to be without mercy, Cobb and his fellow American correspondents asked "that our leaders will make it a complete, not a conditional victory."[12]

"When the Sea-Asp Stings" appeared in the March 9, 1918, issue of the *Saturday Evening Post* and was the first chapter in *The Glory of the Coming,* In it, Cobb set the tone for his firsthand reporting on American entry into World War I. The "Sea-Asp" referred to a German submarine whose torpedo struck the *Tuscania,* a troopship full of Americans, on February 5. Of more than 2,000 on board, 210 Americans died. Cobb's article was published a month later, after it had passed censorship, and vividly detailed the incident. Cobb's ship the *Baltic,* a White Star liner, also carried more than 2,000 passengers, many of them Americans servicemen. Apparently, when the *Tuscania* sank, there was some fear (particularly on the part of his mother) that he had been on that ship.[13]

Cobb excelled at describing the ordinary and the extraordinary, the mundane as well as the terrifying hours of his voyage. He admitted to being seasick for three days upon leaving New York. "I missed only two meals, missing them, I might add, shortly after having eaten them." All the passengers sensed danger during the voyage, particularly when the ship was darkened at night. How frightened were Cobb and his fellow civilians? "For one thing, all of us made more jokes about submarines, mines and other perils of the deep than was natural. There was something a little forced, artificial, about this gaiety—the laughs came from the lips, but not from points farther south." Nearing the Irish coast, the passengers felt a bit safer. Some claimed that the torpedo that struck the *Tuscania* had actually been aimed at the *Baltic* and that they had heard something scrape the hull as it passed.[14]

Cobb followed his own natural inclinations as well as Lorimer's patriotic zeal in dramatizing the scene. As his ship sped away from the stricken *Tuscania*, "It made us feel like cowards. Near at hand a ship was in distress, a ship laden with a precious freightage of American soldier boys, and here were we legging it like a frightened rabbit, weaving in and out on sharp tacks." By the glare of rockets, "we had seen the last of that poor ship, stung to death by a Hunnish sea-asp." Cobb's last paragraph demonstrated his skill in not only telling a story but also setting the stage for more to come: "The first fruits of our national sacrifice in this war, went over the sides of the *Tuscania* to death: 'Where do we go from here, boys, where do we go from here?'"[15]

Always the consummate storyteller, in *Exit Laughing* Cobb told of a northern Baptist lay minister he had run into during this second trip to Europe. "Brother Broadus" may well have been a construct of all the things Cobb found distasteful about overzealous religiosity. He described the "short," unattractive American he met while being billeted at the "American Visitors' Chateau" before visiting the front. When German shells began to fall nearby, Cobb made light of the short-legged American outpacing everyone, shedding souvenirs he had collected on an old battlefield, as they ran to their waiting automobiles. At mess that evening, Cobb fully appreciated "forty bagpipes skirling and shrilling forth the opening bars of 'My Old Kentucky Home.'" So far from home, it was a great event for Cobb, who admitted using up "two pocket handkerchiefs and quite a quantity of Scotch."[16]

All of Cobb's pieces in *The Glory of the Coming* demonstrated the commonplace goings-on in an extraordinary time, which he personalized. This was personal journalism at its best, and his readers of 1918 expected nothing less from him. As described by Phillip Knightley in his history of war correspondents, by the time of Cobb's "second appearance" in Europe, he was already well known. "His appearance—melancholy expression, apple-red cheeks, alligator jaw, fierce eyebrows, and a permanent cigar—made him easily recognizable, and the American troops regularly mobbed him." Cobb's celebrity gave him almost unlimited access to American troops.[17]

Unlike Cobb's helter-skelter path to the front lines in 1914, when foreign correspondents were not welcomed by any of the warring nations, reporting was now somewhat organized, with a few exceptions. Bozeman Bulger, Cobb's old cohort on the *New York World* and a veteran of the Spanish-American War, reenlisted in the army and served as the chief liaison for American war correspondents, attaining the rank of lieutenant colonel. Cobb took advantage of their friendship to obtain access to just about anyone he wanted to see and anywhere he wanted to go. However, his writing still had to pass inspection through the Committee for Public Information headed by George Creel, a personal friend and neighbor in Westchester County.[18]

Cobb's ability as a wordsmith is evident in almost everything he wrote. For example, after arriving near the front, he described the rekindling of war with the spring offensives. "The constant sound of guns on ahead of us somewhere made one think of a half-dormant giant grunting as he aroused. Indeed it was what it seemed—War emerging from his hibernation and waking to kill again. But little more than a year ago before it had been their war; now it was our war too, and the realization of this difference invested the whole thing for us with a deeper meaning. No longer were we onlookers but part proprietors in the grimmest, ghastliest proceeding that ever was since conscious time began." For his American readers, Cobb pulled no punches; this was going to be a horrible if heroic experience for Americans. In an otherwise fine literary biography by Wayne Chatterton published in 1986 as part of Twayne's United States Authors Series, there is no discussion of either of Cobb's World War I books. I maintain that these two books are arguably the best of all his works, exhibiting the discerning eye of the reporter and the ability to combine human interest with humor while fully describing the horror and heroism of war.[19]

As he had during his first visit to Europe in 1914, Cobb got as close to the front as possible, but this time, there were more controls over his movements. However, he was able to get near enough to describe artillery explosions: "We were ringed about by detonations; by jars which impacted against the earth like blows of a mighty sledge on a yet mightier smithy; by demoniac screechings which tore the tortured welkin into still finer bits; by the fierce clangings of metal; by the thudding echoes floating back from where the charges had burst; by the distant voices of certain German guns replying to our salvo as our gunners dedicated the dusk to all this unloosened hellishness and offered up to the evening star their sulphurous benedictions." Though verbose, Cobb left no doubt in his readers' minds that it was hellish. During his second stint as a war correspondent, he lived "for five months, off and on," on the fourth floor of a Paris hotel, the lower two floors of which were used as a hospital. He was in Paris when Germany unleashed its long-range cannon called the "Paris Gun," which fired shells from nearly eighty miles away. "As I go to and fro in the land I sometimes wonder why the Germans keep a-picking on me," he mused rather lightheartedly. However, in "The Day of the Big Bertha," Cobb created a scene in which the kaiser, "His Imperial Majesty of Prussia," calmly returns to his headquarters for breakfast after the destruction of a busy Paris street. "The campaign for Kultur in the world has scored another triumph, the said score standing: seven dead; fifteen injured." Cobb left no doubt about his complete aversion to the German war machine and mentality.[20]

Cobb had the greatest regard and affection for the American soldier in the field:

> If there exists a more adaptable creature than the American soldier he has not yet been tagged, classified and marked Exhibit A for identification. . . . His native irreverence for things that are stately and traditional rises up within him, renewed and sharpened; and from that moment forward he goes into this business of making war against the Hun with an impudent grin upon his face, and in his soul an incurable cheerfulness that neither discomfort nor danger can alloy, and a joke forever on his lips. That is the real essence of the trenches—the humor that is being secreted there with the grimmest and ghastliest of all possible tragedies for a background.[21]

For "Young Black Joe," as Cobb referred to the typical African American soldier, he also had high regard, though it was an affection born of his thorough southernness and benevolent racism. This predilection showed through in his dispatches from the front. For one thing, Cobb enjoyed writing in the black dialect he had grown up with in western Kentucky. He had high praise for the black regiments he saw, interviewing several

men, but never shied away from using the word "darky." He freely admitted to his inheritance:

> I am of the opinion personally—and I make the assertion with
> all the better grace, I think, seeing that I am a Southerner with all
> the Southerner's inherited and acquired prejudices touching on
> the race question—that as a result of what our black soldiers are
> going to do in this war, a word that has been uttered billions of
> times in our country, sometimes in derision, sometimes in hate,
> sometimes in all kindliness—but which I am sure never fell on
> black ears but it left behind a sting for the heart—is going to have
> a new meaning for all of us, South and North too, and that here-
> after n-i-g-g-e-r will merely be another way of spelling the word
> American.

Did he really believe this? Was Cobb changing his fundamental views of
race? Perhaps even Cobb missed the poignancy of the story (most likely
apocryphal) he told of a young black American soldier who wrote home:
"'Mammy, these French people don't bother with no colour-line business.
They treat us so good that the only time I know I'm coloured is when I
looks in the glass.'" "Yes, most assuredly n-i-g-g-e-r is going to have a different meaning when this war ends," Cobb repeated.[22]

Cobb's comments about African American soldiers sound racist and
demeaning today, but at the time, he was the only well-known journalist
to write so much or so often about black soldiers. In particular, he praised
a black regiment commanded by a white New Yorker. "If ever proof were
needed, which it is not, that the colour of a man's skin has nothing to do
with the colour of his soul," the war was it, Cobb wrote in "Young Black
Joe" in 1918 and repeated in *Exit Laughing* in 1941. The *Post* gave permission for black journals to publish parts of Cobb's articles, and his fame
among African Americans spread. Cobb later shared the podium with
former president Theodore Roosevelt as the "chief speakers" at a meeting of the Circle for Negro War Relief at Carnegie Hall on November
2, 1918, which drew a crowd of more than 2,000. "The color of a man's
skin hasn't anything to do with the color of his soul," he declared. "The
value of your race has been proved over there and his value here at home
is unquestioned."[23]

As always, Cobb could find humor most anywhere, even in times of danger. Once, while on an automobile trip to the front with some of his cohorts, they got lost and nearly ran into a ditch. "By throwing on the brakes the chauffeur succeeded in halting the car before its front wheels went over and into the cut." Getting out of the vehicle to inspect it for damage, Cobb and his friends spotted an American sentry. After identifying themselves, they asked the young American, "'Can't we go any farther along this road?' Being an American this soldier had a sense of humour. 'Not unless you speak German, you can't,' he drawled. 'The Heinies are dead ahead of you, not two hundred yards from this here trench.'" Then Cobb added, in his inimitable style: "Without once suspecting it we had ridden clear through a sector held by us to the frontline defences alongside the beleaguered city of Verdun. It's just one paradox after another, in the thing we call war."[24]

During his time in Europe this time around, Cobb continued to be one of America's leading supporters of the war effort, and the vast majority of his countrymen felt the same way. The United States of America had done its share and deserved its place in naming the peace. Cobb sailed home on the *Leviathan,* a captured and renamed German ocean liner, in late June 1918. He had neglected to inform his wife of his impending arrival, so when he docked in New York harbor, he telephoned her and had the following confused conversation (as related by Buff):

"Hello Loll," he said, using his pet name for his wife.

She replied, "Hello, who is this?"

"Why it's me, Irvin."

"Irvin who?" she asked.

He replied, "Your husband."

"I'm sorry. I'm afraid I don't understand who you are."

"Look here woman, just how many Irvins are you married to anyhow?"

According to Buff, "She dropped the receiver and began to weep with excitement and they were cut off and Dad could not get her back, but just went on up to Grand Central and caught a train to Ossining, still not sure whether his wife knew that he was home or not."[25]

Speaking later that month in Philadelphia, Cobb declared that the German spring offensive would never break the Allied line of defenses now that the United States was playing an increasingly important role in the war effort. Both sides would have to listen to President Wilson when the war ended. "The difference between the spirit of our army and spirits of the fighting men of France and England is that the American boys are fresh. . . . The men of France and England are war weary." Cobb believed the Germans could not hold the initiative much longer.[26]

When Cobb visited his mother and sisters for Christmas 1918, he received a royal welcome in his hometown, including a tribute by Paducah's black population. After speaking at the Paducah Rotary Club, along with a British army major, on behalf of a Red Cross drive, Cobb and six other white leaders entered the Washington Street Colored Baptist Church on a Sunday afternoon, where a large crowd awaited. The event lasted well into the afternoon as several leaders of Paducah's black community lauded Cobb's efforts on their behalf. Cobb reported that he spoke a long time about the exploits of African Americans in wartime, particularly those of Paducah native Sergeant William Kivil, who had been decorated by the French government. As the crowd began singing "The Battle Hymn of the Republic," he claimed that he and the other white men in attendance "escaped through a back window." Exaggerated? Probably. Cobb alleged that it took him twelve hours to recover from his exertions and the excitement of the event.[27]

The Glory of the Coming is arguably Cobb's most successful book. In early 1919 the *New York Times* compared it with a book by Fullerton F. Waldo called *America at the Front*. The reviewer admitted that while both books had been written the previous spring, Cobb's had the advantage because of the way he presented his material. "Cobb's book is worth reading and worth keeping. . . . As news it is old; as description it treats of subjects which every war correspondent in the world has written about; but there is something new which will hold the reader, and it is something that Cobb has brought out of his head. He looks at the things which everybody else has looked at, he sees in them that which the others have not seen, and he makes the reader see it, too." In addition to describing the battle scenes, Cobb just as competently and comprehensively explained the massive movement of war material behind the lines. The reviewer also liked Cobb's treatment of black troops. "As to his foreword, it is a comment on the war and our part in it that Americans can read with profit long after the war is over."[28]

By 1919, Cobb was better known than ever and seemed to be at the top of his game. And there were honors for his efforts. In January, France

made him a chevalier of the Legion of Honor. Nearly all the Americans
on the list that year had contributed to the war effort. A writer for the *New
Orleans Picayune* declared that Cobb's second time in Europe, his "Come
Back," made up for his being fooled by the Germans' "stage setting" of
their invincibleness in 1914. Americans had been conditioned by their
own propaganda network of censorship, movies, and newspapers after US
intervention, particularly when American troops began to be killed and
wounded. So it is no surprise that Cobb was scolded for his evenhanded
treatment of the German war machine in *Paths of Glory*. Burton Rascoe, a
noted literary critic for the *Chicago Tribune,* was even more acerbic, sarcastically proposing "that after he had whitewashed the Germans [in 1914],
he so industriously smudged them with ink as to lessen their morale in
the Argonne and at Chateau-Thierry." And everything Cobb had included
on his *Post* expense account "was infinitely less in service value to his own
country or to France than that rendered by any single doughboy who gave
up his life in the Champagne, at the battle of S. Mihiel." Though there is
no evidence of Cobb's reaction to these critiques, I am sure he was only
briefly stung. He had never publicly answered such criticism in the past.
Given his pride, I suspect he bristled in private and told his close friends of
his anger. Otherwise, everything seemed to be going his way. On gradua-
tion day at Dartmouth College on June 26, 1919, Cobb received an honorary doctor of literature, a rather high honor for a man who had never
completed high school.[29]

Up to this point, Cobb had always been a wholehearted supporter
of President Wilson. But things soon changed. In contrast to their successful meeting before Cobb went to France in 1918, "A year later . . . I
couldn't have got into the White House with burglar's tools," Cobb wrote
in *Exit Laughing.* "For I had committed the unpardonable offense of daring to disagree with its chief occupant. There was this about Wilson and it
was ingrained in his inflexible and schoolmasterish ego: if you refused to
accept his judgments as true judgments then that would be proof of two
things: Either you were a besotted idiot or you were a deliberate traitor
and in either event you were ripe to be cast into outer darkness. For he had
become the viceroy of the Almighty; the fetish of infallibility enveloped
him like a mantle."[30]

First, the *Post* correspondent disagreed with Wilson's choice of the
representatives he sent to the Paris Peace Conference, "a commission

made up of men of the same political faith." Cobb believed the commission should have included a Catholic and even a "Confederate veteran and
a conservative Southerner," among others, including Republican senator
Henry Cabot Lodge. Second, he believed that Wilson never should have
gone to Paris because, "like the country boy headed for the city slickers'
poker game," the odds were against him. In any event, Cobb declared
with the benefit of hindsight, the Fourteen Points had been "whittled
down to shoe pegs," leading to more strife and the beginning of "this
Great War of 1939–1941. Whereas, had he bided at home, these others
must have come to him." Third, Cobb opposed American entry into the
League of Nations, not only in print but also during a brief speaking tour
in 1919–1920. In the last of his memoirs published in 1941, Cobb's scorn
for Wilson's postwar presidency was still white hot. He continued to think
of Wilson as an "intellectual bigot" with "the disdain of a book-taught
man who'd got his education off library shelves for men who got theirs
on street corners and in the back rooms of family liquor stores. He would
have been at home at a salon." Wilson's lack of political skill also frustrated Cobb, who had once admired the man. "I figure there never died
a lonesomer man than Woodrow Wilson, twice President of the United
States." If all this sounds like sour grapes from a high school dropout who
had once enjoyed a close relationship with the well-educated Wilson and
then been rejected for his opposition, it is also reminiscent of the views
shared by many learned commentators concerning the downfall of the
twenty-eighth president.[31]

Cobb's celebrity continued, despite his conflict with the postwar policies of President Wilson. However, he also rubbed up against the peevish-
ness of one of America's premier cultural mavens, Henry L. Mencken.
As mentioned in chapter 4, as early as 1913, Mencken had taken notice
of Cobb's growing reputation as a humorist, disparaging his accomplishments. At the time, Mencken had claimed that the "chief quality" of Cobb's
humor "is its obviousness"; it lacked the depth to make it worthy of comparison with the work of great humorists. In October 1914 Mencken paid
some attention to *Roughing It De Luxe,* calling it "a humorous account of
a journey to the Western show places, with capital illustrations by John T.
McCutcheon." Two years later, Mencken was vehemently critical of Cobb
and scourged *Speaking of Operations* as mediocre. "Snouting within, one
finds half a dozen genuinely clever and amusing observations hitched to

60-odd pages of ancient vaudeville patter and funny-column wheezes. . . . Such humor, to be sure, has its place, but is surely ridiculous to argue that it belongs to literature." A month later, Mencken sarcastically denounced comments from readers praising Cobb's abilities:

> I have not unfortunately, the honour of his acquaintance; but we have a great many friends in common [including Bob Davis] and the latter offer eloquent and constant testimony in his favour. Besides friends in common, we also have many interests, aspirations and vices in common. Both of us are too fat; both of us are anti-Carranzistas; both of us prefer malt liquor to the juice of the grape; both of us are old newspaper men; both of us are unlucky at all games of chance; both of us have written very bad books; each of us is the Original Joseph Conrad man. Nevertheless, despite these points of contact and amity, I cling tenaciously to the theory that "Speaking of Operations—" is a fifth class piece of writing and go before the jury maintaining firmly that I myself have never written anything worse.

Mencken's mind had been made up, and he was determined to disabuse all those who thought of Cobb as an outstanding American writer.[32]

Mencken probably noticed a piece in the *Bookman* in February 1918 in which Edward J. O'Brien repeated Bob Davis's praise of Cobb in 1913, with one grievance:

> Upon him (Cobb) the mantle of Mark Twain has descended, and with that mantle he has inherited the artistic virtues and the utter inability to criticize his own work that was so characteristic of Mr. Clemens. But the very gusto of his creative work has been shaping his style during the past two years to a point where he may now fairly claim to have mastered his material, and to have found the most effective human persuasiveness in its presentation. Our grandchildren will read these stories, and thank God that there was a man named Cobb once born in Paducah, Kentucky.[33]

In 1918 Mencken wrote to George Sterling, "My next critical book, if I ever do one, will exhibit the corpses, including Irvin Cobb, who was born dead. A good place for the monument is in front of the Curtis Building in Philadelphia." From 1919 through 1920 Mencken kept up a steady assault on Cobb, both privately and publicly. Thus, Cobb had no chance of joining Mencken's pantheon of great American writers.[34]

In chapter 7 of Mencken's *Prejudices: First Series,* published in 1919, he derisively dismissed Cobb's abilities as a humorist. "Nothing could be stranger than the current celebrity of Irvin S. Cobb, an author of whom almost as much is heard as if he were a new Thackeray or Moliere." Mencken excelled at overstatement and exaggeration, and the title of his book was apt. He blamed Cobb's fame not only on the writer himself but also on his friends like Bob Davis, as well as on George Doran. "Behind the scenes, of course, a highly dexterous publisher pulls the strings, but much of it is undoubtedly more or less sincere; men pledge their sacred honor to the doctrine that his existence honors the national literature." Nothing satisfied Mencken more than debunking individuals like Cobb. "In the actual books of the man I can find nothing that seems to justify so much enthusiasm, nor the hundredth part of it." Mencken went on for several pages, dismissing both Cobb's abilities and his publications. In *Speaking of Operations* he found nothing funny at all, but only a few "mildly clever observations . . . as flat to the taste as so many crystals of hyposulphite of soda." The indictment continued with Mencken sarcastically exclaiming, "This is the official masterpiece of the 'new Mark Twain.'"[35]

Mencken kept up the assault on Cobb in the early 1920s. In *Prejudices: Second Series* he cast Cobb along with O. Henry, James Whitcomb Riley, and Mary Roberts Rinehart, among others, into the "Literary Abattoir," damning their writing as, "in brief, the literature that pays like a bucket-shop or a soap-factory, and is thus thoroughly American." In a reprinting of Mencken's *Prejudices* series, he exulted in debilitating if not destroying the careers of Cobb, Hamlin Garland, and others. Mencken took pride in the fact that, owing to his criticism, Cobb was "never taken seriously after 1919." In the years ahead, Mencken, who was of German ancestry, must have relished the Schadenfreude of dismissing Cobb as an important American writer.[36]

Compounding Mencken's disdain for Cobb was the former's low regard for the South. And Cobb was foremost a transplanted southerner writing for an American audience, regardless of region. Claiming that the

South represented the "Sahara of the Bozart," Mencken demonstrated his predilection to be "an intellectual bombardier," according to southern journalist Gerald W. Johnson. "The title of his essay reflected a genuine opinion that the relation of the South to modern civilization roughly paralleled the relation of 'Bozart' to '*beaux arts*,' to wit, a crude and slightly comic distortion." According to Johnson, Mencken believed "that nothing else produces as smashing an effect as truth magnified by ten diameters." However insincere, it also sold copies of books and essays for the Baltimorean.[37]

Another reason for Mencken's attack on Cobb in 1919 was the latter's outspoken patriotism and anti-German writings in *The Glory of the Coming*. Cobb was utterly too patriotic for the pro-German Mencken. After the sinking of the *Lusitania* on May 7, 1915 (of the 1,198 passengers killed, 128 were American), Mencken exulted in a private letter: "The war is in its last stage! Deutschland uber Alles." He later defended himself rather disingenuously. "Not infrequently I am attacked unfairly, e.g., by fellows who accused me, during the war, of German propaganda, which was just as unfair as accusing a man, in Catholic Ireland, of being an Orangeman." He touted his criticism of everything. A smattering of his statements from one long paragraph provides ample evidence of his relentless iconoclasm: "I believe that nothing is unconditionally true, hence I am opposed to every statement of positive truth and to every man who states it." "To me democracy seems to be founded upon the inferior man's envy of his superior—of the man who is having a better time." "Hence my foreignness: most of the men I respect are foreigners. But this is not my fault. I'd be glad to respect Americans if they were respectable. George Washington was. I admire him greatly. It seems to me that, within our own time, Germany has produced more such men than any other country." Any American writer as patriotic as Cobb would have immediately been relegated to Mencken's list of literary mediocrities.[38]

Cobb never commented publicly or in print on Mencken's barbs, but he could not have taken them lightly. In mid-1919 Cobb contributed "I Admit I Am a Good Reporter" to *American Magazine* as a way of defending his career, but that was as close as he ever came to challenging Mencken directly. He wrote:

If anybody claims I am an authentic humorist I can show him a scrapbook full of clippings, signed by expert book reviewers, to prove the contrary. If anybody thinks me a rising young short-story writer—that is to say, young for my age, which is the only way a body is young or ever is old, either, for that matter—I repeat, if anybody chooses to regard me as one giving promise as a short-story writer, I can cure the obsession by producing another volume of criticisms done by men and women who freely concede that they know all there is to know about the short-story-writing game and who are equally frank and aboveboard in telling me what I do not know about it. But if anybody says I am not a good reporter, I'll bet him a million dollars he is a liar.

In the article—subtitled "And Here Are Some Stories to Prove It"—Cobb delineated his expertise in researching and reporting, which led to several important coups during his career, including the Thaw trial. Touting his ability to get the "inside story" that others missed, he explained that his success depended on using the direct approach in interviewing and getting to the sources. He also stressed his experiences in Europe in 1914 and 1918.[39]

John Wilson Townsend in Lexington kept up a lengthy correspondence with Cobb and an infrequent one with Mencken. In a small way, he acted as something of a go-between. Townsend recognized no great talent in Mencken, "surely not in his books or in The Smart Set." When Townsend inquired why the Smart Set did not review Cobb's book, Mencken told him that Doran no longer sent him copies. I am sure Doran knew that Cobb would never get a positive review from Mencken.[40]

In the case of Cobb and Mencken, the two could not even agree when it came to preparing the ubiquitous southern mint julep. While Mencken advocated using rye whiskey and crushed mint in his juleps, Cobb preferred Kentucky bourbon, of course. "Any guy who'd put rye in a mint julep and crush the leaves would put scorpions in a baby's bed," Cobb offered as a backhanded slap at Mencken and his Maryland ways. The November 1, 1919, issue of the Saturday Evening Post had a humorous cover illustration of a southern colonel replete with a julep cup hoisted in a toast—an example of how southern culture had been adopted throughout the United States as part of the post–Civil War reconciliation.[41]

Undeterred by Mencken's criticism, Cobb continued to frequent his usual watering and eating places after the war. At the Algonquin, he would have found the "stars" of the New York social, political, literary, and theatrical world, including such luminaries as author Rex Beach, columnist Dorothy Parker, actor John Barrymore, and Commander Evangeline Booth of the Salvation Army—"all the stimulating array of people that had already made the hotel famous," according to Margaret Case Harriman. Cobb probably would have avoided Mencken whenever the latter attended Algonquin events. Always good for a quip, Cobb once contributed an "epitaph for a beauty of notoriously general liaisons: 'Here lies Polly Simpkins: asleep—alone—at last.'"[42]

If anything, Cobb intensified his writing as he entered his forty-third year on June 23, 1919. Doran continued to publish Cobb's books through the beginning of the 1920s, but his contributions to the *Saturday Evening Post* lessened as he sought new styles and modes of writing. The entrepreneurial Cobb always found other outlets for his talents. As pointed out by his biographers, by this point in his life, Cobb knew what topics he could write about and what made money for him and his family; he also knew his limitations. His humor satisfied a large middling readership that appreciated his style, his presentation, and the length of his stories. Cobb continued to write nonoffensive, good-natured pieces (except for his obvious racial views) and did not engage in personal attacks. Moreover, he emphasized that he was laughing at himself even when writing about others.[43]

In a surge of momentum from 1917 through 1920, Cobb took every advantage, casting himself as the "little man" of the large variety who had to fight against the world, which always seemed to be against him. Cobb published four short stories and seven articles in the *Post* in 1919, including several hilarious humor pieces and an occasional serious story. The war was behind him now, and he contributed only one short story on that theme, "John J. Coincidence," about the heroism of First Sergeant Hyman Ginsburg.[44]

Cobb sensed that his readers needed a respite from the war and its continuing consequences, so he turned out more humorous pieces. "The Life of the Party" is about a well-heeled New York lawyer who goes to a costume party where the celebrants are dressed as children. Sometime after 3:00 a.m., Mr. Algernon Leary, still costumed as a baby, throws an overcoat over his scantily clad body and hails a cab. A comedy of errors ensues as the respectable lawyer runs into other people who think he is insane, dressed as he is. Like many of Cobb's stories, it suffers from being too long, at sixty-four pages.[45]

In one of his shortest stories of the year, Cobb turned again to a "grim" tale. Ethan A. Pratt, a copra buyer in the remote South Pacific, receives newspapers six months out of date. (Cobb's story ideas came from numerous sources, and he told a reader that he got this idea when he heard about an Englishman who lived in the "far North" and received the *London Times* in six-month lots twice a year.) Pratt, the victim of an April Fool's joke in his local newspaper, commits suicide before he can read the next day's item, explaining that the editor had mistakenly reported that Pratt's fiancée had married another suitor back home in Vermont.[46]

By far, the most humorous and successful of Cobb's writings in 1919–1920 were about his move to the country. Earlier, in 1913, he had written about searching for a county place in "Life among the Abandoned Farmers." Then in 1917, after buying a sixty-acre estate near Ossining, he had written "Back to the Land—Leading the Abandoned Life." Although he had renovated the barn into comfortable living quarters for his family and built a sizable lodge where he could write, the war had delayed construction of the real home Irvin and Laura had dreamed of building. Buff liked to refer to that time as their "barnyarder" years. "It was a long time before I understood what the building of a home could mean. In those days I used to watch my parents perched on a rock pile in the pouring rain, quite oblivious of the wet, weariness or weather, happily arguing about the proper place for the yet-to-be broom-closet," she recalled with more than a hint of her father's ironic sense of humor.[47]

In the *Post,* Cobb turned the construction of his and Laura's dream home into a series of humorous articles. He halfheartedly attempted to transform the land into a working farm by raising crops and animals, though clearly not for profit. A picture of Cobb standing in his cornfield in a May 1919 issue of the *Post* attested to his humorous attempt to help Herbert Hoover, director of the US Food Commission, provide more food for the American people and European relief. "In Which We Build a House" described the comedy of errors as the construction of the house actually began once materials finally became available after the war. Everything that could go wrong did so. Merciless builders, antiques dealers, architects, agents, and others took advantage of the Cobbs. As the house became more livable, Cobb wrote about his experiments in farming, adding different species of animals as "the bills kept piling up" and noting "the cussedness of hogs" and his "Plymouth rock loafers." Not a Kentucky farm boy, Cobb capitalized on his lack of knowledge of farming. Sadly, his hogs found ways to die, such as contacting hog cholera. "Our hogs have been observed in the act of standing in the pen with their snouts in the air, sniffing in unison until they attracted the germs of it right out of the air." He had no luck with chickens either. "We tried every known effort on those hens . . . to make them see the error of their ways and the advantages of eggs," including expensive feed, but they only "sat about in shady spots and brooded in a moody way as though they had heavy loads on their minds." However, the intrepid Cobb praised the farm life: "It's a great life if a fellow doesn't weaken—and we'll never weaken." The "lovable loser" or "little man" who came across in Cobb's writing about his farming experiences found a wide and appreciative audience.[48]

Once Cobb had actually moved to and improved his own farm, he changed his shtick from "Abandoned Farms" to "Abandoned Farmers." Cobb added new chapters to articles previously published in the *Post* and compiled a 247-page book called *The Abandoned Farmers* (subtitled *His Humorous Account of a Retreat from the City to the Farm*), chronicling the saga of Rebel Ridge from purchase to completion of the main house. Several humorous illustrations capitalizing on Cobb's physique and bewilderment accompanied the text, including one of Cobb feeding raucous chickens as frantic hogs scrambled for their feed in the background and a mild-mannered cow waited patiently to be milked.[49]

Upon completion, the house was a fine one—modern on the inside with a rustic look on the outside. Anyone who had ever built a house (or wanted to) could appreciate Cobb's wry sense of humor about all the foibles and problems associated with the enterprise. With a first and second mortgage, Irvin, like a typical male, thought "there would be ample time a decade or so thence to begin thinking of the furnishings." Laura had other ideas, sending her husband off to ruminate about the search for furniture and accessories.[50]

The main house at Rebel Ridge was a rather palatial two-and-a-half-story structure that fit the upper-class community. The old stone and brick exterior eventually became vine covered, giving it the look of a much older home. Formal dining and sitting rooms and a lovely library dominated the first floor. Irvin, Laura, and Buff inhabited the second floor.

Though Cobb joked about the furnishings, the house was well appointed, with both new fixtures and antiques. Laura oversaw the completion of the lawn and the extensive gardens. This was a house and a property befitting a man who had attained the height of worldly success. The Cobbs regularly entertained the members of the "Westchester County Despair Association" and others. With a maid, a cook, gardeners, and other servants, Cobb had to work hard to turn out articles and books to pay for his increasingly lavish lifestyle. Life was not always easy as he entered his mid-forties. On a visit in the early 1920s, Townsend found that Cobb had an abscessed tooth as well as "a budding carbuncle" on his neck that kept him from working at full tilt. In a letter some time later, Cobb assured Townsend that he would soon return to regular production.[51]

After comfortably settling into Rebel Ridge, Cobb told a visiting reporter about the difficulty of writing for a living. "It seems as if I were struggling more now than I did ever before!" Cobb said. "Writing is hard work. Hardest work there is, don't you think so?" The reporter praised Cobb for "how much you mean to the American people. How they talk about you, as if they had a kind of special claim. They say 'Have you read that last story of Cobb's? It was a corker!' They tell anecdotes about you." Obviously pleased, Cobb replied: "I like people and I like to write for the people—not the highbrows nor the lowbrows, but just the greatest number."[52]

For the next two decades, Irvin S. Cobb wrote and performed for that large middling audience. Few people read Cobb today, but his name occasionally turns up on the Internet. For example, in his November 5, 2010, blog entry, "Bottles, Booze, and Back Stories," Jack Sullivan highly praised Cobb for his humor, claiming he was "more celebrated in his time than Jay Leno or David Letterman in ours." This accolade would have suited Cobb just fine, as he continued to laugh at himself and with the world—not at it. For example, in "The Advantages of Being Homely," published in August 1918, Cobb wrote, "I contend that homeliness is a desirable asset for a man [referring to himself] to possess." Caricatures of Cobb were famous by this time, and the article included several by illustrator Tony Sarg. This made Cobb eminently recognizable in a crowd, but he found this comforting. As his life and that of the country entered another era, would he continue to find comfort in the persona he had created for himself?[53]

Cobb and his associates at the Paducah paper, 1896. Nineteen-year-old Cobb is seated on the left, holding a sword. Henry E. Thompson, part owner of the paper, is seated on the right, with the staff in the background. (McCracken County Public Library)

Cobb and fellow Paducahan George Goodman at the Pendennis Club in Louisville, 1942. (*Courier-Journal* photo by Brooks Honeycutt, courtesy of Gannett Company, Inc.)

Cobb seated at the radio controls with a dog named Fritz. (Courtesy of Todd Hatton, WKMS, Murray State University)

Comical promotion photo for a film. (Museum of Fine Arts, Houston)

Promotion photo for *Steamboat 'Round the Bend*. (Museum of Fine Arts, Houston)

Comical photo of Cobb, the inveterate hunter. (Museum of Fine Arts, Houston)

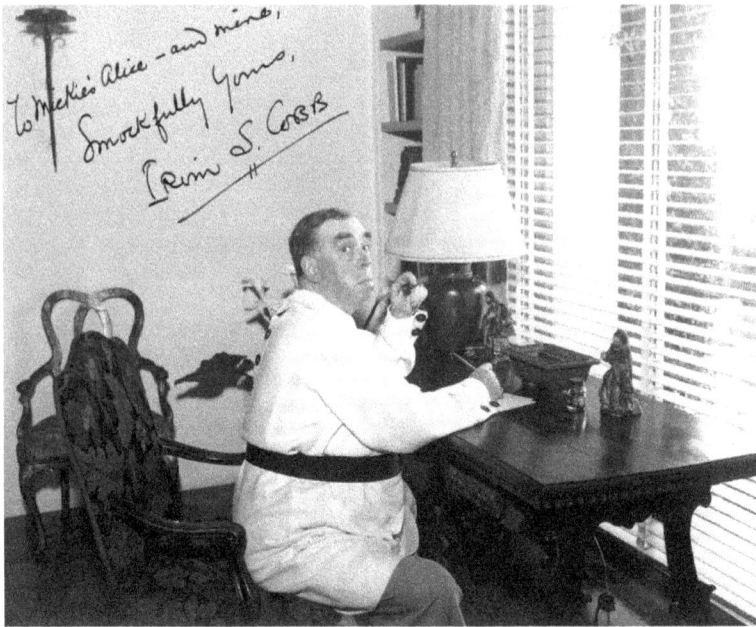

Cobb at his desk wearing his smock. (Museum of Fine Arts, Houston)

Cobb and Rogers, joking about Cobb's attire. (Will Rogers Memorial Museum Collections)

Rogers, Cobb, and John Ford on the set of *Judge Priest*. (Will Rogers Memorial Museum Collections)

Cobb at the funeral of Will Rogers. (Will Rogers Memorial Museum Collections)

Bronze statue of Cobb. It was cast from a caricature by James Montgomery Flagg, an artist and illustrator who worked on various magazines. (Eastern Kentucky University Special Collections and Archives)

Cobb's grave. The graves of Laura and Elisabeth are on either side. (William Ellis)

8

Accommodation

The Early Jazz Age

After his move to New York City in 1904, Cobb appeared to live a charmed life. However, he found himself at another crossroads when World War I ended. His life seemed much the same, with continued success writing for the *Saturday Evening Post* and other magazines and a steady flow of books from Doran, but had he reached his potential as an American writer? He had branched out into writing for movies, even appearing in some. His success included a handsome income and an escape from the city with his estate at Rebel Ridge. If concerned about critics such as Mencken, Cobb appeared not to take notice, at least publicly. Midlife brought new physical challenges as his lifestyle wore on his body. Was he also at the midpoint of his writing career? Moreover, media changed in the 1920s, with radio and "talkies" adding to the chatter and challenges of popular culture. Would Cobb be able to adapt to the new age?

A 1917 article in the *Forum,* one of the leading magazines for "thinking" Americans of the day, described the sources of Cobb's writings, as well as his working life up to that time. "Pendennis," the pen name of a *Forum* editor, acknowledged that Cobb was a great writer but found him somewhat conflicted over what he should write about. Pendennis maintained that Cobb's "types in fiction are among real people he has met. They are chiefly New Yorkers because he has lived in New York for twelve years." However, Pendennis feared that Cobb's Paducah characterizations were overwhelming his talent. In contrast, midwesterner Damon Runyon had established himself in New York literary circles and developed his lower-class hoodlum types and patois into an archetypal form that still resonates today in the musical *Guys and Dolls.* Could Cobb emulate Runyon and break from his old southern mold and fill a more modern niche?[1]

Cobb's circle of friends in New York included the best-known writers, producers, and editors of the day. These contacts stimulated his creativity. Interesting conversations with Runyon, columnist O. O. McIntyre, journalist Ring Lardner, and others filled his days at work and his evenings at clubs and dinner parties. Runyon and Cobb hunted ducks and geese together off Long Island, and Runyon allegedly sold "story plots" to Cobb on occasion. A baseball fanatic as well as a sportswriter for the Hearst newspapers, Runyon helped "cook up" an "All-American Table Stakes Eating Contest" in early 1920, pitting Babe Ruth and Cobb against all comers and spotting "any challenging team one Virginia ham per man and one porterhouse steak." Though the story got much press, there were no takers but lots of laughs.[2]

Other writers considered Cobb a friend or even a mentor. Oscar Odd McIntyre, called "Odd" by his friends, was another outsider from the Midwest who won fame as a syndicated columnist in America's largest city, writing a daily column called "New York Day by Day" for a quarter century. He also wrote for another Hearst property, *Cosmopolitan.* Though a dour workaholic, McIntyre shared a bond of friendship with Texas oilman and entrepreneur Will Hogg and Irvin Cobb. Even Ring Lardner, who often complained about Cobb's long discourses on Kentucky, still found him companionable. And then there was Bob Davis, the editor of *Munsey's Magazine,* who was Cobb's mentor as well as a close friend. Davis was one of Cobb's fiercest supporters during Mencken's ongoing disparagement of his writing accomplishments.[3]

Cobb's fame spread far and wide, based to a great extent on his war experiences and his writings. E. V. Lucas, an English humorist on the staff of *Punch* and the author of more than a hundred books, highly praised Cobb when he toured the United States in 1920. On a cross-country trip he met with Cobb, Don Marquis, and Oliver Herford—three humorists he believed were representative of American types. "Beneath Mr. Cobb's fun is a mass of ripe experience and sagacity. However, playful he may be on the surface, one is aware of an almost Johnsonian universality beneath. It would not be extravagant to call his humor the bloom on the fruit of the tree of knowledge." Though a bit flowery and overstated, Lucas's sentiments probably represented the thoughts of many English-speaking people worldwide. Cobb also expressed a high opinion of Lucas in his last memoir.[4]

In the immediate postwar years, Cobb kept up his hectic pace, writing articles for the *Post* and other magazines and compiling them into books published by Doran. All the while he was working on a novel that must have been lingering in the back of his mind, if not on his desk or in his typewriter. Out of his overseas experiences came another booklet, *Eating in Two or Three Languages,* published by Doran in early 1919. It was based on Cobb's "gustatory experiences" in Europe, and it turned out that the three languages were "English, bad French, and profane." Though Cobb expressed a general dislike for French restaurant cuisine, he claimed a fondness for provincial offerings where "the flavor of the delectable broth cured us of any inclinations to make investigations as to the former stations of life of its basic constituents." On his return to the States, Cobb exclaimed a longing for fried chicken, Virginia ham, trout, cantaloupes, "roasting ears, and—Oh, lots of things." A *New York Times* reviewer enjoyed Cobb's "chortlings." "It is to the credit of Mr. Cobb's talent as a humorist that he does make his comparison readable and amusing." At only sixty cents per copy, *Eating* was another addition to Cobb's string of successful short works.[5]

Though Cobb had already expressed his doubts about the necessity of American troops' wartime sacrifices and his opposition to the Versailles Treaty and the League of Nations, so far he had not adopted the postwar hyper-Americanism and antiforeign vigilance of many Americans. However, he did become part of a prestigious committee, whose members included Booth Tarkington, Hamlin Garland, and Ellen Glasgow, that judged a competition for the best version of "The American's Creed." William Tyler Page won this contest, and in late 1919 Page's creed was presented by former Speaker of the House Champ Clark and adopted by Congress. Cobb later got caught up in some of the postwar rhetoric while talking to a reporter in Houston in early February 1920. After giving a lecture titled "Made in America," he demeaned the lack of wartime service by boxing champion Jack Dempsey. "This fellow Dempsey is a slacker," Cobb declared. "Everybody's got his number. He is going to be railroaded clean out of the game." Later in the 1920s Cobb "eventually repented" his participation in The Vigilantes, who had attacked pacifism during the war years. He explained that he had succumbed "to the prevalent hysteria" of the time and that his writings had been "under the spell of that madness which we mistook for patriotism." No doubt Cobb would have taken back his call for a "jihad" against Germany.[6]

Cobb's celebrity gave him opportunities in almost any medium he chose to enter. He was so famous that everything he wrote was published. However, Cobb could falter on occasion. When paired with Mary Roberts Rinehart in *American Magazine* in October 1919, Cobb came off second best in a contest in which each described the opposite sex. Rinehart was a popular fiction writer for the *Saturday Evening Post* and other magazines and had made a name for herself as one of the few women to report from Europe during World War I. She was a formidable woman, the mother of three, and an excellent writer who was not afraid to voice her opinion on any subject. She was certainly as well known as Cobb. From her first published poem in 1904, she kept up a public presence into the late 1950s.[7]

Cobb's "Oh, Well, You Know How Women Are!" came off as clichéd compared with the sparkle of Rinehart's "Isn't that Just Like a Man!" The articles were turned into a double-sided book, with illustrations, published by Doran in 1920. Cobb explained how women shopped, how they exited street cars, how they dressed, and how they became devoted to causes in comical ways, without ever referring to Rinehart. In contrast, Rinehart addressed Cobb directly, making him the butt of the joke and even using words that reflected his writing style. Primarily, she maintained that men were just overgrown boys with an addiction to keeping old clothes, old shoes, and other mementoes. "The plain truth is that normal women need men all the time, but that normal men need women only a part of the time," owing to male solidarity. She found the fact that women outnumbered men humorous. "So, men hang together, and women don't. And men are the stronger sex because they are fewer!" "It is just possible that suffrage will bring women together," she "opined," borrowing the latter word from Cobb. Furthermore, Rinehart claimed that men were underworked, whereas women had to work long hours. "I wager I work more hours a day than you, Irvin!" she exclaimed. Because men were allowed to be little boys for a lifetime, it was important that women kept some control over the men in their lives. Renowned book reviewer Burton Rascoe wrote in the *Chicago Tribune* that Rinehart "reduces the

male of the species to the essentially sentimental, self-important, conven-
tion-ridden, infantile-minded, but rather necessary atom that he is." The
book sold well.[8]

Cobb never lost his love of reporting and his interest in politics. But
covering the 1920 Democratic National Convention in San Francisco and
the Republican National Convention in Chicago proved to be the last
time he would report on this type of event with much enthusiasm. A
badly divided Democratic Party, with an ailing president clinging to a
forlorn hope of power and no clear front-runner for the presidential nomination, was ripped asunder. Still clinging to the Democratic Party, Cobb
did not shy away from making editorial comments as a correspondent.
Writing a lead piece as the 1920 convention opened about the 1916 convention, he skewered the leaders of a party that he felt abandoned by. The
times had changed too abruptly for him. Prohibition, empowered by rati-
fication of the Eighteenth Amendment and passage of the Volstead Act,
went into effect nationwide on January 17, 1920. Cobb detested Prohibition and made no bones about it. Moreover, he disliked the "stage managers" who now controlled both parties' conventions, which lacked the
spontaneity of the old days.[9]

Writing for the *Louisville Post* and other newspapers of the Bell Syndicate, Cobb covered the 1920 Republican and Democratic conventions
with his usual jaundiced eye toward politics. His forte of observing the
ironies, ambiguities, and foolishness of life was reflected in these columns,
as were his prejudices. For example, he skewered William Jennings Bryan
as a possible Democratic candidate, noting that "Bryan eats so much he
wouldn't have room for a drink if he wanted it," taking a swipe at other
"dry" Democrats as well. "Constant wearing of a halo has worn his black
hair away somewhat," Cobb sneered. At the Republican convention in
Chicago, Cobb observed that the atmosphere was so dry that "a keg of
draught beer" would have started "a stampede." The Republicans nominated Senator Warren G. Harding, while the Democrats took forty-four
ballots to nominate Governor James M. Cox of Ohio. The voting and
maneuvering at the latter convention was so chaotic that Cobb actually
received one and one-half votes himself on the twenty-third ballot, to his
friend Ring Lardner's one-half vote. The *Nation* cynically editorialized
that Cobb was "the really dominating figure" in San Francisco. "Is he
not one of the heroes of the *Saturday Evening Post,* therefore of the great

American people? Is it not said of him among the multitude that he is the highest priced of the American literary fellers?" Ending on a note of tomfoolery, the *Nation* declared: "Our ticket is Irvin Cobb for President, and Ty Cobb for Vice-President—the American people's own."[10]

The native Kentuckian kept rolling out books in the early years of the Jazz Age. *From Place to Place,* another compilation of nine articles, hit the market in early 1920. It led off with "The Gallowsmith," a serious story about a man who makes his living as a hangman, and included a comedy, "The Bull Called Emily," about a gigantic circus elephant who runs "amok" in a small town, destroying any place harboring peanuts. This was another winner for Cobb, and it went into several editions. A *New York Times* reviewer of *From Place to Place* admired Cobb's ability to write both dramatic stories and farce. "I have witnessed a couple of thousand people of all classes who mingled tears with their laughter when Cobb wove a few bits of serious or somber sentiment and minor tragedy into a talk on his observations during the war," the reviewer concluded. In 1921 *A Plea for Old Cap Collier* and *One Third Off* followed Cobb's pattern of compiling previously printed stories along with a few new ones into books published by Doran.[11]

Cobb's schedule continued to be grueling, with lectures and speaking engagements increasingly taking up more of his time. Audiences loved to hear his stories, particularly when he spoke in an African American dialect. Though these stories grate on our modern sensibilities, in the 1920s they were well received in most American and international circles. Always the hero back home in Kentucky, Cobb was named an honorary "Colonel" on the staffs of several governors, which never failed to get press notices in Kentucky and elsewhere. Ever the popular native son, when Cobb was the guest of honor and speaker at a fete in Paducah, the organizers made sure he got a helping of his favorite Kentucky food—hog "jowl and greens." Wherever he spoke in the 1920s he usually made a comment about Prohibition, which he despised.[12]

Cobb did not follow a regular newspaper beat; he picked events that interested him and wrote about them. This included commenting on sports. During the playing of baseball's World Series, Cobb often contributed a syndicated column for several days. His commentary on the 1921 World Series, which pitted John McGraw's New York Giants against the New York Yankees, drew plaudits. Though the Giants won the series that year, the Yankees became the best team of the 1920s, with headliners such as Babe Ruth, Lou Gehrig, native Kentuckian Earle Combs, and other stars of "Murderer's Row."[13]

Cobb excelled at human-interest stories and observations of the mundane. He applied his unique reporting style to the famed heavyweight boxing match between champion Jack Dempsey and Frenchman Georges Carpentier in mid-1921 at Jersey City, New Jersey. Though Cobb had earlier accused Dempsey of being a "slacker" or draft dodger, in spite of the boxer's wartime charity work, the "Manassa Mauler" was a national hero. After taking the championship from Jess Willard in Toledo on July 4, 1919, Dempsey appeared to be invincible, and Cobb predicted that he would win the upcoming match. In a buildup to the Carpentier fight, Cobb maintained that in the Willard match, Dempsey had become "the proper ring fighter, cruel, relentless, cocksure and superbly competent; a cross between a wildcat and a mad bison bull." Cobb praised the Frenchman for being a decorated soldier in the war and for his undoubted skill as a boxer, "but he takes a gosh-awful chance when he climbs into the same roped inclosure with Jack Dempsey." Cobb ended ominously: "Let us pray!"[14]

In his *New York Times* piece, Cobb described the crowd as enormous and representing "the arts, sciences, drama, politics, commerce and bootlegging industry." They had all sent "their pick and their perfection to grace the great occasion. The names at ringside would sound like the reading of the first hundred pages of 'Who's Ballyhoo in America.'" The best ringside seats were filled with the likes of Bernard Baruch, John D. Rockefeller, Henry Ford, Teddy Roosevelt Jr., and other luminaries who had come to see the "first million dollar fight." Some of those in the boisterous crowd screamed "slacker" at Dempsey, but he ignored them. At 188 pounds, Dempsey outweighed the slender 175-pound Carpentier. Dempsey later said in his memoirs: "He looked like a graceful statue. I looked like a street fighter."[15]

Cobb's *New York Times* story about the Dempsey-Carpentier match is considered one of the best boxing pieces in history and is included in *At the Fights: American Writers on Boxing*, a compilation published in 2011. Other contributors include prestigious sportswriters such as Heywood Broun, Bob Considine, Red Smith, and Dick Schaap, as well as literary figures Sherwood Anderson, H. L. Mencken, Gay Talese, and Joyce Carol Oates.[16]

Cobb relied on his keen ability to observe the crowd as well as the ebb and flow of the match. His column the next day read like a minute-by-minute account, as if he were broadcasting the event. From his ringside station, he dashed off paragraphs on a typewriter. A messenger periodically took his copy to a telegraph operator, who relayed it to the *New York Times* office. The enormous crowd, estimated at nearly 100,000, filed into the bowl-shaped, hastily constructed temporary wooden stadium on "Boyle's Thirty Acres" as the preliminary matches wore on. At precisely three o'clock, the main bout began with the introductions. Cobb reported: "Carpentier comes first, slim, boyish, a trifle pale and drawn looking, to my way of thinking. He looks more like a college athlete than a professional bruiser. A brass band plays the 'Marseillaise': ninety-odd thousand men and women stand to greet him—or maybe the better to see him—and he gets a tremendous heartening ovation. Dempsey follows within two minutes. A mighty roar salutes him too," but "not so sincere or spontaneous as the applause which had been visited upon the Frenchman." Dempsey "grins—but it is a scowling, forbidding grin." The champion "makes me think of a smoke-stained Japanese war idol; Carpentier, by contrast, suggests an Olympian runner carved out of fine-grained white ivory." And so it went. Obviously, the Frenchman was Cobb's sentimental favorite.[17]

The fight developed into a brutal triumph for the American, who battered the Frenchman for the first three rounds before flooring him for the full count in the fourth round. Cobb and other observers, including Mencken, saw signs of life in Carpentier that were not really present. Cobb described the knockout:

For the hundredth part of a second—one of those flashes of time in which an event is photographed upon the memory to stay there forever, as though printed in indelible colors—I see the Frenchman staggering, slipping, sliding forward to his fate. His face is toward me and I am aware that on his face is no vestige of conscious intent. Then the image of him is blotted out by the intervening bulk of the winner. Dempsey's right arm swings upward with the flailing emphasis of an oak cudgel and the muffed fist at the end of it lands on its favorite target—the Frenchman's jaw.

In a matter of seconds, the bout was over. Cobb concluded that Carpentier never had a chance against the stronger and more aggressive Dempsey. For one of the few times in their lives, Cobb and Mencken agreed when the latter famously quipped: "Dempsey was never in any more danger of being knocked out than I was, sitting there in the stands with a pretty gal just behind me and five or six just in front."[18]

Meanwhile, Cobb continued to turn popular *Saturday Evening Post* articles into short books that sold well. For instance, *A Plea for Old Cap Collier* was a nostalgic piece in which Cobb challenged the relevance of "good" literature in the life of a growing boy. He recalled that many a time in his youth he had been caught and summarily punished for reading a book from the "nickul libraries, erroneously referred to by our elders as dime novels." He had often hid the adventures of "Nick Carter or Big-Foot Wallace or Frank Reade or bully Old Cap" behind a school text. Cobb opined that McGuffey's readers, with their moral lessons, were mostly ludicrous. He pointed out that it was, of course, impossible for a little Dutch boy to hold back the "entire North Atlantic" with one finger in a dike, and boys instinctively knew that. As for the boy who stood on the burning deck, "I deny that he was heroic. I insist that he merely was feeble-minded." However, Cobb admitted that *Huckleberry Finn* and *Treasure Island* were classics that any boy, or man, could read to advantage.[19]

He dedicated *A Plea for Old Cap Collier* to his wealthy friend "Will H. Hogg, Esquire." The reaction of the Texas entrepreneur's friends, to whom he sent copies, illustrated the reading public's varied opinion of Cobb's more frivolous books. John Lomax claimed, "Irvin Cobb never wrote a funnier story than the one dedicated to you unless it was his experiences in the Grand Canyon." However, in the opinion of fellow Houston resident Arthur LeFevre Jr., "In this high strung modern life, he is a false teacher who counsels—the artificiality of the whole theme is especially depraving to an undisciplined mind." These opposite reactions were typical: you either liked Cobb's nostalgic comedic work, accepting it as the short humorous read it was, or you dismissed it as tripe, unworthy of reading at all.[20]

Another longish book (147 pages) of Cobb's, *One Third Off,* came from two substantial *Saturday Evening Post* articles that appeared in 1921, highlighting his attempt to lose weight. Cobb emphasized that as a gangly six-foot-tall youth, he had been kidded about his lack of weight and had even been known as "Bonesy." But then the good life resulted in him piling on the weight. Cobb's girth was a prominent part of his persona, and the cover illustration showed him weighing himself, much to his disgust. In eleven chapters, Cobb described how he dieted, backslid, wrestled with various diets and physicians, and finally found success, going from a stout 236 pounds to a svelte 197. With a goal of 185, Cobb proclaimed, "I know exactly where I am going and I'm on my way. And I feel bully and I'm happy about it and boastfully proud. Three rousing cheers for lithesome grace regained." A picture of Cobb from about this time showed a rather fit-looking author in his white plus fours, bow tie, and jacket. Of course, Cobb eventually resumed his old eating and drinking habits and ballooned up again, but not before scoring another profitable hit with *One Third Off.* The *Times Literary Supplement* of London reviewed *One Third Off* briefly but positively: "In his own case the remedies he adopted must have been certainly reinforced by the exhausting character of his labours as a humorist."[21]

In the postwar years Cobb continued to experiment with moving pictures as an avenue for his talents, but he was not elated with his first efforts. When John Wilson Townsend was working on a biography of Cobb, the latter told his friend: "Personally I would prefer that you say nothing in detail of the work I have done for the movies other than to state that various persons have, from time to time, made screen versions of my short stories. My own stuff was so mangled in the adaptation that I feel no pride in the results as shown on the screen." Nevertheless, Cobb wrote the "titles" for such silent pictures as *Peck's Bad Boy,* starring child star Jackie Coogan, and *Pardon My French,* a farce. In a newspaper article, Cobb was more positive about his experiences in the movie business. "It is rather a wonderful experience—this movie game. Certainly to me it was an unusual one," referring to writing for a six-year-old star. Always looking to make a dollar, Cobb continued to dabble in the new Hollywood craze. Though it might have appeared that his career was meandering, Cobb had learned from an early age to take advantage of any profitable forum for his talents.[22]

In early 1922 Cobb's frenetic lifestyle caught up with him again. In his mid-forties, seriously overweight again, and drinking and eating to excess, his health broke down. While on a lecture tour he suffered a gastric hemorrhage. Though it was probably exaggerated in his self-revealing article written for *American Magazine*—nothing about his life was private—the situation was serious and reminiscent of his earlier health scare, which he had turned into *Speaking of Operations.*[23]

Always the showman, Cobb wrote about the near-fatal incident in his popular tongue-in-cheek style. While preparing for a lecture in Boston, he thought he was suffering from symptoms of the flu or possible "biliousness," which he treated with aspirin, whiskey, and other nostrums. Cobb suddenly felt quite ill and debilitated, and a friend found him prostrate and only half dressed for his nightly performance. The house doctor was called, and he proceeded to make a quick and accurate diagnosis. "As a matter of fact, a hemorrhage had started in my stomach," Cobb wrote. "I was bleeding to death and didn't know it."[24]

Cobb was confined to his bed in the hotel, and the doctor called in nurses for around-the-clock observation and ministrations, while he too kept a close watch on his famous patient. Initially Cobb did not believe the doctor's dire prognosis, but after receiving blood transfusions, he finally realized the gravity of his condition. During that first night of confinement, Cobb experienced what he described as sensations of "sinking" into darkness. For someone as nonreligious as Cobb, this was as close as he ever came to acknowledging the existence of something beyond life itself. Once he had recovered, he could make light of his situation: "The blackness had almost completely enveloped me. . . . After all, dying was about the most important thing a man could do in life." Even so, "At no time that night, neither then nor thereafter, did I appeal to any higher power for help. It did not appear seemly that I should do so." After his seventh struggle with the darkness, Cobb relaxed, talked to the nurse, and went to sleep. Cobb implied that his experience must be universal for those near death. Taking advantage of the misfortune of its popular correspondent, *American Magazine* sponsored a contest offering a first prize of $20 for the best letter on the subject "The Nearest I Ever Came to Death."[25]

When he was finally allowed to leave his Boston hotel, Cobb checked into St. Bartholomew's Hospital on Forty-Second Street in New York City for more "observation" and treatment. Unhappy about missing a duck hunting expedition in Louisiana with Will Hogg and others, Cobb complained, "My doctors will not let me go, but I am with you in spirit." It was six weeks before Cobb was able to return to his regular schedule. During his recovery, Townsend half-jokingly remarked that Cobb needed a "mess of smoked-hog-jowl and turnip greens, and a couple or three quarts of Old Pugh" to make him "quicker and clean!" Cobb often responded to Townsend by writing comments on the original letter and then returning it. "Right O!" Cobb replied.[26]

Like most Americans, Cobb reacted to the social, political, and economic changes of the 1920s, which included the rise of a resurgent Ku Klux Klan—and not just in the South this time. Paducah, the largest city in the Jackson Purchase, was in the most "southern" part of Kentucky, so it was only natural that the KKK had been prominent there just after the Civil War. Cobb romanticized race relations in his hometown, even though he must have known about the brutal suppression of blacks after the Civil War. Ex-slaves across the South often flooded into larger towns and cities like Paducah for protection. These were the blacks Cobb had come in contact with as a youth.[27]

African Americans were summarily lynched in Kentucky during the first heyday of the KKK, with the highest percentage of lynchings occurring in the western part of the state. In the 1890s eight states passed anti-lynching laws, and, at the insistence of Republican governor William O. Bradley, Kentucky was one of them. Nevertheless, summary executions of blacks were not always the result of Klan operations. One of the last and most spectacular in Kentucky demonstrated not only the continuity of Klan mentality, if not Klan organization, but also the impact of modern motion pictures. In 1911, just south of Owensboro at Livermore, one of the most brazen extralegal executions in American history took place. A white man entered a black pool hall, and a fight broke out. Will Porter, the proprietor, fired two shots at the white man, who was uninjured. The Livermore city marshal and his deputies arrested Porter and took him to the local movie theater. A crowd of about fifty white men paid admission to the theater and lynched Porter "on the stage of the local opera house" by firing more than 200 shots at his trussed-up body, half of which hit him. Filmed lynchings and other atrocities against African Americans had been shown in southern movies houses for several years. One press account declared that "the little Operahouse at Livermore . . . never witnessed such melodrama."[28]

The upheaval of World War I led to a resurgence of the organized Klan in the early 1920s. The former Confederate states once again became a center of Klan activity. However, other areas outside the old

KKK strongholds, particularly in the Midwest, also came under Klan influence in the Jazz Age. For example, Indianapolis had approximately 38,000 Klan members between 1915 and 1944, whereas Louisville had only 3,000; Indiana had a total of 240,000 Klan members, versus approximately 30,000 in Kentucky. The Hoosier State became a stronghold of Klan activity in local and state politics, while membership and influence apparently declined in the South. Although the revived Klan still ridiculed blacks, particularly in the South, the new emphasis is the Midwest included hostility against immigrants and Catholics.[29]

As it did elsewhere, the Klan attempted to make inroads into Kentucky local and state politics. Kentucky's Democratic leaders, particularly Senator A. O. Stanley, provided some leadership against the Klan. Cobb got involved when the Klan asserted itself into local Paducah politics. He had traveled to his hometown in late December 1922, ostensibly to celebrate Christmas with his mother. Owing to the resurgence of the Klan along the Ohio River, publisher Urey Woodson of the *Paducah News-Democrat* invited Cobb not only to write an anti-Klan piece but also to take over as editor of the paper for a day. This ensured that Cobb's December 30 editorial would draw national attention.[30]

"Praise God from Whom All Blessings Flow, for the Ku Klux Klan Has Failed in Paducah!" ran the headline of Cobb's front-page editorial. In no uncertain terms, Cobb praised the KKK's failure to organize in his hometown. "It is a damnable outrage that it should now exist in this country," he wrote. Referring to a Klan circular, Cobb claimed that he agreed with much of its agenda but adamantly opposed its methods. "As a Southern man, the son and grandson of Southerners, I believe with all my heart in White Supremacy. I do not believe in a campaign of terror and violence aimed against black men. . . . I believe in the protection of our pure womanhood. I do not believe though that men who ride in masks to perform their self-appointed functions are the proper guardians of womanhood." Despite Cobb's acceptance of much of the Klan's belief system, he insisted, "Real knights never were afraid to show their faces when they went forth a-crusading. . . . But by the admissions of its own organizers the Klan isn't doing very well in these parts, and for that vouchsafed blessing I say again as I said before Thank God!" Other writers in the Paducah paper praised Cobb's editorial, which he had written at his old desk from two decades ago. In a general history of the Klan, David Chalmers found that although it might have flourished briefly in the 1920s in Indiana, "it never felt quite at home in Kentucky" during that turbulent decade. Cobb played a vital role in denying the Klan a vital foothold in western Kentucky. However, his core beliefs about race, particularly his belief in white supremacy, had not changed.[31]

None too ironically, *One Clear Call,* a Louis B. Mayer production set in the postbellum South, was showing at a local Paducah theater during Cobb's visit. The movie was complete with a Klan-like set of night riders and a nurse played in blackface by a white actress. "Southern" movies were growing in popularity all over the United States, beginning with the release of Kentucky-born D. W. Griffith's *Birth of a Nation* in 1915. They suited the racial mores of Great Britain as well. All over the English-speaking world, Cobb was well received as a practitioner of what it meant to be a "southern" progressive on the race issue. "Dixiephilia" swept England as songwriters wrote ballads like "Headin' for Louisville" and "You're in Kentucky, Sure as You're Born," based on a romanticized view of race in America. The paternalism expressed by Georgian Johnny Mercer's lyrics was acceptable to an English audience in the 1930s. Both American and English musicians, songwriters, and entertainers took advantage of the longing for an idealized southland. That market also welcomed Cobb's evocations of the South in his Judge Priest stories.[32]

Though Cobb opposed the modern version of the Klan in the early 1920s, his views of race remained tied to his late-nineteenth-century southern heritage. The publication of *J. Poindexter, Colored,* his first full-length novel at 270 pages, and his interactions with African American author Walter White in 1922 illustrated his inherent conflict: a benign, paternalistic view of Negroes and a fear of change in American racial mores.[33]

Cobb's relationship with blacks evolved somewhat over time. He realized that he could never completely fathom the mind of African Americans owing to their inherent distrust of whites. Their sense of "agency" frightened most whites in both the North and the South. Cobb tried to interpret this interplay of blacks and whites in his stories about Judge Priest and Jeff Poindexter. While the white Priest was the leading character in the fiction, Jeff was his faithful black servant. Chatterton's mid-1980s literary analysis of Cobb's work found his views "somewhat more enlightened" than those of his fellow white southerners in the "first decades of the twentieth century." Biographer Lawson found Cobb to be more a creature of his culture and his time than Chatterton did. In a general discussion of recent writings by whites about African Americans, Benjamin Brawley's 1923 article in the *Bookman* found *J. Poindexter* interesting because of the main character. However, Brawley, an African American educator and author, believed that it did not approach reality. "The Negro himself as the irony of American civilization is the supreme challenge to American literature," casting "an irresistible spell over the American mind," Brawley declared. In short, Cobb's book did nothing to advance either race relations or the understanding of blacks in America.[34]

This was the first and only time that Jeff Poindexter served as a major character in a work by Cobb. The novel's intention was to portray Jeff as the quintessential black man: wise to the ways of the world; circumspect; a good, peaceful soul who always looks for the best in human nature even when faced with a segregated world. Narrated in the first person by Jeff, this fable is about his sojourn in New York City as the protector of young white Dallas Pulliam. As such, Cobb employs African American idiom extensively, which was popular with his readers in 1922 but comes across as excessively demeaning to today's readers. Though the novel is well plotted, modern readers would find much of it predictable and offensive. There is no doubt, however, that Cobb thought about and worked on this novel for some time, as it is well crafted.

While Judge Priest is off visiting "kinfolks" in Bermuda, Jeff finds himself at loose ends for a time. Jeff is persuaded by young Pulliam to travel from Paducah to New York, serving as his general servant, as the well-born young man seeks his success. As the story unfolds, Jeff becomes the voice of reason as Pulliam is continually fooled by the people and ways of the big city. Cobb interjects some of the cultural changes Jeff experiences. For example, after their passenger train crosses the Ohio River, Jeff is invited to sit with Pulliam, but he confesses he is more comfortable among his own people. One of the porters warns him that he should be careful using the word "nigger" among his own kind up north, which Jeff finds confusing, seeing as how the word is used so frequently in Paducah among his family and friends.[35]

The book is good social satire, and the city's white denizens, as well as some of the black folks, are fair game for Jeff's down-to-earth observations. Jeff outwits and outmaneuvers New York City blacks who try to

cheat him out of money. More importantly, he realizes that a white shy-
ster and Pulliam's girlfriend are trying to bilk him out of his meager estate
and push him into debt. He even negotiates a contract to become part
of a moviemaking company after wandering onto a film set in Harlem.
This comes about when Jeff informs the director that he knows Negro
language and actions better than any white man. In one of the best paro-
dies in the book, Jeff declares that the white director "must have studied
the business of acting like colored folks from watching nigger minstrel
shows." A white man in blackface playing the role of a waiter "is blackened up too much" and "keeps rolling his eyes up in his head and smack-
ing his lips" excessively, according to Jeff's authenticity meter. In Jeff's
inimitable style, he suggests that the movie director "mek the pitchers
comical. You kin do 'at an' still not hurt nobody's feelin's, w'ite nur black.
Ef you wants to perduce a piece showing a lot of niggers gittin' skinned,
let it be another nigger w'ich skins 'em," eliminating any racially charged
scenes. The conservative Jeff reminds the white movie director, as well as
the reader, of his racial views as a black man. "We gits mouty tired, sometimes, of bein' treated the way we of'en is. Tek my own case, I says. I ain't
no problem, I's a pusson. I craves to be reguarded." Jeff, as Cobb's inter-
preter, claims he is treated thusly "by my own kind of w'ite folks down
whar I comes frum." Cobb undoubtedly believed this to be true, but of
course, that was wishful thinking.[36]

While Jeff successfully adjusts to the ways of the big city, young Pulliam is beguiled by white thieves until he finds himself deeply in debt.
The end is predictable, as Jeff's services to Judge Priest have made him
more than a match for these city slickers. Jeff steps in to save the day. He
tricks Pulliam's money-grubbing fiancée by telling her that she can get
her hands on the rest of Pulliam's money only by producing "the most
chillen" in competition with his fictitious brother. She hastily releases Pulliam from their preliminary wedding contract. Pulliam's nefarious business partner is also scared into retreat, returning the young Kentuckian's
investments in an oil scam when Jeff persuades the meek Pulliam to pose
briefly as a cold-blooded Kentucky killer, complete with a large unloaded
pistol purchased from a black gangster.[37]

Reviews of Cobb's first full-length novel were generally positive. One
decidedly "southern" newspaper, the *Louisville Courier-Journal*, praised
J. Poindexter, Colored as "a revelation of Cobb's view of the race question;

and Mr. Cobb's attitude is that of a great many of his fellow Kentuck-ians." A *New York Times* reviewer apparently enjoyed Jeff's views of New Yorkers, as well as his guile and fortitude, yet concluded that the book was not one of Cobb's best. The most telling critique was an unsigned piece in the *Literary Review,* which noted that the book "is in reality little more than a padded short story." It continued, "If the native good sense of the negro appears exaggerated in this novel it may be well to remember that it has been too lightly regarded in most stories of the people of Jeff's race. Mr. Cobb could safely, however, have made Jeff's master a little less of a moron." Finally, it concluded, "Mr. Cobb the novelist is not Mr. Cobb of such shorter pieces as 'The Belled Buzzard.'"[38]

Cobb's benign, paternalistic view of African Americans clashed with the post–World War I movement for civil rights. In 1922 he became involved in a controversy over the publication of a manuscript by NAACP official Walter White (eventually published in 1924 as *The Fire in the Flint*). Mencken (who was just as racist as Cobb) suggested that White send the manuscript to Doran. Of course, owing to their successful pub-lishing relationship and personal friendship, Doran passed it on to Cobb for his opinion. Most individuals who have written about this incident maintain that Cobb read the manuscript and told Doran that its vola-tile nature would cause "riots" in the South. The story is about Dr. Ken-neth Harper, a black physician, and his family in Georgia. No matter what Harper does to obtain racial justice in a nonviolent way, including after his brother is killed by a mob of white supremacists, he is eventu-ally driven to violence himself. After attending to a white female patient, the thugs of "the Invisible Empire" ambush him, claiming that he abused the woman. The novel is graphic in depicting violence against African Americans in the South, of whom Dr. Kenneth Harper is only one in a long line.[39]

Mencken's reasons for recommending the publication of black novels were based largely on his disdain for the South, with its lack of culture, and the lack of "realism" in American fiction. To his credit, Mencken believed that only blacks could write about their lives with the neces-sary authenticity, and he held in disdain white writers such as Cobb who wrote books like *J. Poindexter, Colored.* Meanwhile, Doran had serious reservations about White's novel, based on "justifiable aesthetic reasons," and asked for revisions, according to Charles Scruggs in his book about the Harlem Renaissance in American literature. White refused. Mencken happily blamed Cobb for persuading Doran not to publish White's manuscript. In return, White told Mencken that "Irvin Cobb's influence on Doran was too strong for me!" and he unfairly lumped Cobb into a group of "southern" writers, including Thomas Dixon, who inflamed racial injustice. Cobb was not the sole influence on Doran's negative decision, but he undoubtedly carried some weight. Cobb commented negatively on the book in the *Savannah Press* after its publication by Knopf in 1924, but *The Fire in the Flint* turned into a nominal best seller. Although it did not cause race riots, the racial divide in the South and for much of America remained largely unchanged for the next two decades, as did Cobb's racial views.[40]

Cobb's life was about to change again. After his brush with death, he decided to give up the rural lifestyle of Rebel Ridge and move back to the city. He told Townsend that "largely on account of Mrs. Cobb's health I have put Rebel Ridge on the market," but one suspects he missed New York City. Perhaps the move was precipitated by the long commute by train or the fact that his daughter was an adult and about to set out on her own. Certainly the bloom was off the rose compared with his September 1921 letter to Townsend in which he had extolled the beauty of his estate. Living in an apartment at 830 Park Avenue in Manhattan gave Cobb easy access to his clubs and his friends. At twenty years of age, Buff would also be able to have a more fulfilling social life. Father and daughter often appeared together at large affairs and gatherings while Laura, who loved smaller parties, stayed home. Photographs of Irvin and Buff dressed in elaborate Arabian costumes for the Illustrator's Ball in early January 1923 appeared in the *New York Times* and other newspapers. At any rate, the Cobb family apparently eased back into life in New York City.[41]

All in all, Cobb's life as of late 1922 was one of continued success. He kept up his busy schedule of writing articles and turning out books; he ventured into more movie contracts and even entered the new medium of radio. *Sundry Accounts,* published in 1922, continued Cobb's successful string of anthologies. Dedicated to his Lexington friend and confidant John Wilson Townsend, the book appeared under the general title *The Works of Irvin S. Cobb,* testifying to his large and growing body of work. The volume contained two typical heart-warming Judge Priest stories, a

Jeff Poindexter story, a New York City tale, a humorous story about a movie director's problems, and a very short story about pre-Prohibition days and Kentucky politics.[42]

Leading off *Sundry Accounts* was "Darkness," which had first appeared in the *Saturday Evening Post.* One of his "grim" tales, it is "a psychological story" about a man who cannot face darkness. According to Hildegarde Hawthorne's review in the *New York Times,* it was one of Cobb's best efforts. It was also chosen for inclusion in *The Best Short Stories of 1921.* "Darkness" contained all the elements of his best writing: plot, character development, and a twist at the end. Nevertheless, Hawthorne added a qualification: "Mr. Cobb writes a great deal, writes perhaps too much. Something of the bubbling spirit that was his is missing from his later work, but he is a good and careful worker." An unsigned review in the *Boston Tribune* voiced a similar warning: "We wonder if Mr. Cobb is not spreading himself out a little thinly these days when his work is in such great demand." More importantly, a reviewer in the *New York Evening Post* touched on one of Cobb's shortcomings: "He writes with rare insight and with a warm sympathy" but with only a one-dimensional view of African Americans. "Mr. Cobb could, we feel, make a real contribution to his own reputation as a writer and to American fiction were he some time to write a series of stories of negroes as a serious undertaking, with sympathy and understanding."[43]

Cobb had reached his widest audience by the early 1920s, and he gave no indication that he intended to decrease his activities to concentrate on any one aspect of his art. He was a popular writer who was making a lot of money, and he intended to continue on that course. Never feeling overexposed, Cobb added a newspaper column to his chores, "My Favorite Stories," syndicated by the Central Press Association beginning in 1922. These brief columns, which ran nearly weekly or occasionally more often, had no more serious aspiration than to tell a humorous story.[44]

9

From the "Boss" to the "Chief"

Cobb at the Pinnacle of His Career

Cobb appeared to be at ease working for the *Saturday Evening Post* in the immediate postwar era. In December 1918 he contributed "George Horace Lorimer, Original Easy Boss," to the *Bookman*. "I have known him for seven years, about. I have been working for him for a slightly longer period. I have liked him—liked him unstintedly and without reservations of any sort—ever since I knew him. . . . Lorimer more nearly approximates the popular conception—and incidentally the proper one—of the typical American than any man I have known." Describing Lorimer as "the most brilliant figure on the editorial side of the magazine field," Cobb found him to be the perfect "Boss," which was why the *Post* was "the biggest weekly magazine in the world—the biggest in size, in circulation and in general influence." It seemed that Cobb would be writing for the *Post* well into the future.[1]

Into the early 1920s Lorimer's *Saturday Evening Post* boasted the finest popular fiction writers in America, including Kenneth Roberts, Thomas Costain, Sinclair Lewis, John P. Marquand, Theodore Dreiser, Mary Roberts Rinehart, and, of course, Irvin S. Cobb. Since moving to the *Post* full time in the second decade of the twentieth century, Cobb averaged ten or more pieces per year through 1921. However, in 1922 this pace slowed perceptively, with only two published fiction pieces: "J. Poindexter, Colored" on June 10 and "—That Shall He Also Reap" on July 15. The latter was Cobb's final Judge Priest story to appear in the *Post*.[2]

In a letter dated August 14, 1922, Cobb reported to his Kentucky friend Townsend: "Beginning September first, I take on a contract to write practically exclusively for two of the Hearst magazines—the Cosmopolitan and the International—for a period of three years. For them I hope to do at least one novel-length yarn and a considerable number of short stories and special articles. The connection means a larger financial return for my work than I have had from other sources and I believe in all regards will prove attractive and agreeable."[3]

In short, Cobb had sold his services to the highest bidder and joined the publication empire of William Randolph Hearst. Hearst, known as the "Chief" to his innermost staff, had inherited his wealth and power from his father. He moved to New York City from California and began a rivalry with Joseph Pulitzer at the height of yellow journalism toward the end of the nineteenth century. A man of overwhelming ambition and talent, Hearst was a "progressive" crusader in the early twentieth century and had vast political ambitions. He served two terms in the US House of Representatives but overreached when he yearned for the White House. He remained a powerful voice for whatever cause he chose to champion and used his newspaper and magazine empire not only to make himself a fortune but also to push his agenda of reform.[4]

Hearst bought *Cosmopolitan* for $400,000 in 1905, and Ray Long became its editor in 1918. Long eventually earned "over $180,000 a year in salary and bonuses at his peak," making him the highest paid editor in the nation. After Long took the helm, the magazine made great strides, increasing its sales. With no limits on spending, Long "set out to raid the *Saturday Evening Post*," according to one of Lorimer's biographers. "Offering high prices, he bagged not only Cobb but also Peter B. Kyne. . . . Both men had been close friends of Lorimer's as well as frequent contributors." Long also went after some of the biggest names in contemporary fiction, including W. Somerset Maugham, Edna Ferber, Sinclair Lewis, Booth Tarkington, Theodore Dreiser, and Ring Lardner. The break with Lorimer and the *Post* was purely a matter of finances for Cobb, who hailed the "Boss" for vastly improving "an elderly and indisposed magazine" and turning it into the leading weekly magazine of its day. However, Lorimer held a personal grudge against those writers who left the *Post*. When Cobb offered to return after his three-year contract with *Cosmopolitan* expired, Lorimer refused. Moreover, in a memo to his staff, Lorimer reminded them that the *Post* "never makes contracts with authors."[5]

When Cobb moved to *Cosmopolitan* in late 1922, he joined a cadre of successful writers. Lardner, Kyne, Maugham, George Ade, O. O. McIntyre, Rex Beach, P. G. Wodehouse, Kathleen Norris, Stephen Vincent Benet, and Winston S. Churchill, the future prime minister of Great Britain, wrote occasionally for *Cosmopolitan.* George Ade, whom even Mencken credited as "inescapably national," wrote two-page humorous asides for *Cosmopolitan,* as well as longer pieces. Called a "literary Rotarian" by one of his biographers, the Indiana native returned home after a brief newspaper career in Chicago and became quite wealthy. Ade was famous for writing "fables" that, like Cobb's writings, have not withstood the test of time. Identified by another biographer as "a good, simple man with a magnificent gift that he packaged for the market place," Ade wrote about the foibles of his fellow midwesterners in a nonoffensive way. In 1934 Ade praised Cobb "with reservation," which he did not explain, and noted that Cobb and Damon Runyon were among his favorite writers "when they are hitting on all cylinders."[6]

Cobb's story "Snake Doctor," first published in the November 1922 issue of *Cosmopolitan,* won the O. Henry Memorial Award Prize for short stories that year. Cobb received $500 in gold and served as toastmaster of the ceremonies held by the Society of Arts and Sciences at the Hotel Astor in late March 1923. Though some critics were already devaluing this award in 1923, it is still presented every year.[7]

"Snake Doctor" is one of Cobb's "grim" tales based on his experiences growing up in western Kentucky. All these stories contain elements of "horror," "terror," and "the grotesque." "Snake doctor" is a southern name for the common dragonfly, which, according to African American folklore and superstition, has a mesmerizing and beneficial effect on sick water moccasins. The story is simple enough. A low-life farmer named Japhet Morner, who abuses his wife and others, dreams of riches. He believes that his neighbor, the swamp-dwelling Rives, keeps a large sum of money in a secret place in his cabin, so Morner plots to kill Rives and steal his money. He tells his wife that he is going hunting, and although he kills a couple of squirrels, his real plan is to circle around to Rives's cabin, lie in wait, kill him, and pillage the money. By mistake, Morner shoots and kills his own wife, who had gone to the cabin to bring Rives some folk medicine. Morner runs away and wanders around in the swamp until he hears that a posse is after him, so he returns to the cabin to collect the money and make his getaway. In the darkened cabin, he sees a hole near the fireplace, reaches in (expecting to find the money), and receives what he believes to be a snakebite. Morner dies a horrible death, writing in pain, but when his body is found by the local physician and others, there is no swelling to indicate a snakebite. Investigating the cabin, they find that the hole is lined with barbed wire, which merely pricked Morner's hand. So, fittingly, Morner died of fright after murdering his own wife and trying to steal a paltry $95.[8]

This story was republished for the first time in *Snake Doctor and Other Stories,* brought out by Doran in 1923 and dedicated to Cobb's new editor, Ray Long; it also appeared in several later anthologies. This book solidified Cobb's break with Lorimer, as none of the pieces had appeared in the *Saturday Evening Post.* "One Block from Fifth Avenue" is the tale of Letty Ember, a young woman from "Whippoorwillville" who goes to New York City seeking fame and fortune as an artist. In fact, she is not very talented and is eventually rescued by her hometown sweetheart from her deteriorating life in the big city. Of course, Cobb always had a couple of Judge Priest stories in his repertoire: "—That Shall He Also Reap" is a melancholy story of an old maid who is wooed by a villain, and "His Mother's Apron Strings" proves once again that Priest is adept at settling problems outside of court. "Red-Handed" is one of Cobb's occasional crime stories, "Otherwise Sweet William" is one of his "darky" stories, and "The Eminent Dr. Deeves" is an underrated psychological thriller. "The Second Coming of a First Husband" is actually a "short" short story by Cobb's standards, being only fourteen pages long; it reveals how the ghost of a first husband solves the problem of a second husband. To date, this was Cobb's best and most diverse anthology of his short fiction, and it sold well.[9]

Critics' reaction to *Snake Doctor and Other Stories* varied. The *Louisville Courier-Journal* compared Cobb to Bret Harte and even declared that the Kentuckian's stories had "more red meat, and more to remember long after the reading," than did O. Henry's. In the "Literary Review" section of Cobb's old haunt, the *New York Evening Post,* H. L. Pangborn took a more strident view of not only Cobb's story but also American short stories in general. Pangborn declared that "such awards as the O. Henry Memorial have become the worst enemy of creative literature of our day" by applying "processes of standardization." Pangborn claimed that other authors tried to conform to a style without "the writer's free search for expression," but nothing was further from Cobb's mind when he wrote "Snake Doctor," as that story was not typical of American short stories of the time. Edward Francis Edgett in the *Boston Evening Transcript* praised Cobb's ability to write a "humorous sketch" but declared that "Snake Doctor" was "not a good story in any sense of the term. It is, however, an excellent pen picture of scenes in a Southern swamp, and with its trick ending, it is perhaps perfectly logical that it should be awarded a prize bearing the name of the master of that peculiar form of story." A *New York Times* reviewer was a bit more charitable when critiquing the book and its lead story. First and foremost, Cobb was a storyteller, and writing overly long stories was his forte. "Our personal idea of entertainment is to sit on one end of a log and to have Irvin Cobb at the other, telling stories," the *Times* reviewer noted. "He must have been born telling stories. If not, he has acquired an amazing aptitude."[10]

I believe Cobb would have been satisfied with the appellation of storyteller. He apparently ignored critical reviews, having already written off the critiques of Mencken and other mavens. A contemporary of Cobb's, editor and humorist Thomas L. Masson, praised Cobb in 1922 for being his own man and dismissed Mencken's sour views of Cobb as unimportant. "Mencken, so far as I have been able to discover in his writings, doesn't like anybody." Moreover, "when I say I would rather listen to Cobb talk than anybody else I know, I mean it in the right sense." Another commentator found Cobb's Judge Priest character to be a benign if stereotypical evocation "of the kindly old Southerner." The admonition to "write what you know" is an axiom, sometimes tritely expressed, among American writers. Cobb did precisely that.[11]

If critical acclaim eluded Cobb, his short stories had wide popular appeal. All in all, Cobb had five entries in *The Best Short Stories* series edited by Edward J. O'Brien, which began in 1915 and continues today as *The Best American Short Stories,* published annually. Cobb's "The Great American Auk" was published in the 1916 edition, "Boys Will Be Boys" in 1917, "Darkness" in 1921, "The Chocolate Hyena" in 1923, and "No Dam' Yankee" in 1928. Cobb was in good company, as works by Sherwood Anderson, Theodore Dreiser, Ellen Glasgow, Edna Ferber, Ernest Hemingway (misspelled "Hemenway" in the 1923 anthology), and Louis Bromfield appeared in various 1920s editions.[12]

In 1923 Cobb added to his substantial list of publications by producing his first autobiography: *The Works of Irvin S. Cobb: Stickfuls (Myself to Date)*, published by Doran. A *stickful* is an old newspaper and publishing term denoting "as much type as a composing stick will hold, usually two inch columns." Though Cobb embellished his life a bit, *Stickfuls* was mostly truthful and certainly insightful. Cobb's publisher believed his life story would be of interest to a general audience, and he was correct, as the book sold well.[13]

It appeared that everything Cobb did was newsworthy in the early 1920s. One day, the newspapers reported, Cobb hired a taxi to take him to his apartment at 830 Park Avenue, "where all the rich authors live," and the driver drove recklessly. "Mr. Cobb, who is not as stout as he once was, bounced terribly, but when he tapped on the glass and ordered the driver to slow up, he did not." Cobb reported to "Magistrate Marsh he never had such a ride in his life," and hack driver Albert J. Kimbecker received fifteen days in a workhouse for his crime. "The ride shook fully a dozen short stories out of his system," Cobb told the press, never at a loss for words and never averse to a little publicity. Cobb made the news again when he was accused of violating Texas game laws by purchasing a resident license for $2 instead of a nonresident license for $15. One assumes his multimillionaire friend Will Hogg remedied the problem, as at the time, they were on a fishing trip off Aransas Pass, Texas, in the Gulf of Mexico. Whether a photograph of Cobb on horseback at a ranch in Pendleton, Oregon (unsmiling and looking none too comfortable), or an announcement that a modern 200-room hotel in Paducah would be named in his honor, the reading public enjoyed Cobb's adventures and misadventures. Late in 1924, when several newspapers mistakenly reported Cobb's death, he answered much as Mark Twain had in the same circumstances: "I hate to disappoint anyone, but the Chicago report that I am dead is, as far as I can learn, entirely unfounded."[14]

Cobb was continually being interviewed, asked for his opinions about current affairs. Cobb's picks for "the ten books I have enjoyed most" were newsworthy in 1923; they included *The Book of Job, Robinson Crusoe, Huck Finn, Treasure Island, Hamlet,* and *Barrack Room Ballads* by Rud-

yard Kipling. In mid-1923 several writers expressed their views of censorship in the *Literary Digest*. "The reason why we are threatened with
censorship is because we have too much *sensualship*," Cobb explained,
rather adamantly. "I am against both. I believe in free speech, but I don't
believe in it being free and easy. As for the notion of censorship, it merely
is another expression of the desire to destroy individual liberty by sump-
tuary legislation which, made fat and greedy by the adoption of the Eighteenth Amendment, now would assault our rights again." Cobb rarely
missed a chance to rail against Prohibition. "If Prohibition is a Noble
Experiment then the San Francisco Fire and the Galveston Flood should
be listed among the noble experiments of our national history," Cobb
said offhandedly. However, there was something deeper in his critique of
some modern writers, particularly the so-called Chicago School. "They
are so busy discovering sex and garbage they have forgotten beauty exists
in the world." Cobb's attitude represented a generational divide. "They
try so pitifully hard to be up-to-the-minute, and it can't be done. You
set down to write a novel of today—and by the time you have finished
it is a novel of yesterday. Already old fashioned. You have to wait until
today has crystallized into yesterday before you can describe it accurately."
Speaking at the Paducah Rotary Club in early 1925, Cobb assailed "the
literary bad boys" of the East for being out of step with the majority of
Americans. Clearly, Cobb favored old-fashioned American literature as
opposed to the new school of writing developed after World War I. Moreover, Cobb criticized young college-trained writers who wanted to break
into the newspaper trade. In a piece for *American Mercury* titled "How to
Begin at the Top and Work Down," he contrasted his career path—that
is, coming up the hard way—with the one taken by the better-educated
but overly ambitious new crowd. "They don't want to work for success,"
he railed. "They want somebody to hand it to them, like John the Baptist's
head, on a golden platter." Though most people thought writing was easy,
he maintained that it was hard manual as well as mental labor. "I envy
those who dash off these priceless gems. You should see me some morning
when I'm in the mood for dashing off the stuff. There I sit, dashing it off
at the rate of about an inch and a half an hour, and using drops of sweat
for punctuations."[15]

　　Cobb, a man of great pride in his accomplishments, increasingly
appeared not to care for critical approval but only for that of his reading

public, the vast middle class that read poplar magazines and novels. In 1924 Ray Long edited a compilation called *My Story I Like Best,* which included the works of Cobb, Edna Ferber, Peter B. Kyne, James Oliver Curwood, Meredith Nicholson, and H. C. Witner—all of whom had gravitated to *Cosmopolitan* owing to the higher pay. Cobb maintained that his favorite story gave him the opportunity to use his imagination to write about how to "defeat the will" of a real-life financier who had thwarted justice. "Maybe I like 'The Escape of Mr. Trimm' best of all my stories because it was this story which opened the door for me into magazine work," Cobb admitted. At this point in his career, nothing he wrote seemed outdated or out of step with popular trends.[16]

With a grown daughter in the household, the Cobbs' lifestyle grew more complicated. After moving back to the city, Buff became the center of attention. She and her father took a trip to Bermuda, apparently to rebuild her health after an illness. But they both found the island terribly boring. "We have been two weeks on this silly island now and the most exciting thing that has happened was a ride on a bicycle—we started out in a platoon formation and came home limping," Cobb wrote to Will Hogg. Apparently, Buff had difficulty controlling her vehicle, and Cobb, of course, made it sound hilariously funny.[17]

Buff was now in her early twenties, and "she dazzled Manhattan as she had Westchester County." Margaret Case Harriman, the daughter of Algonquin hotelier Frank Case, recalled, "My chief concern was whether I would be cut in on as often as Connie Bennett or Buff Cobb" at dances. Cobb commissioned Wayman Adams to paint a portrait of him and his daughter, and it was reproduced in several newspapers and magazines, including *Hearst's International.* The painting showed an unmistakable facial likeness between the two, although he was rather chubby while she was petite. The photograph of Irvin and Buff in their Arabian costumes at the Illustrator's Ball, titled "The Beauty and the Bedouin," was also reprinted several times.[18]

Buff was indeed her father's daughter, and she began a writing career despite having no university or college degree; she had, however, attended Mme. Skerton's School. She soon found a job as an editorial assistant at the *Bookman.* Cobb sent his daughter's first effort at short fiction to Bob Davis, who critiqued it seriously, suggested revisions, and promised to pay $100 for it after an adequate rewrite, which he did. In mid-1923 Buff became engaged to Frank Michler Chapman Jr. of Englewood, New Jersey, son of the curator of the Department of Ornithology at the Museum of Natural History in New York City. The wedding was held at the Cobb home at 830 Park Avenue on February 12, 1924. Her father joked in his remarks at the wedding that he had often read Chapman Sr.'s *American Birds* while carrying "Buff as a colicky baby." Chapman Jr. was a budding opera singer who studied in the United States as well as in Florence, Italy. Meanwhile, Buff continued to write her fiction.[19]

Cobb's career in the early 1920s took a decided turn toward comedy rather than straight humor. Earlier in his career he had been encouraged to go into vaudeville, either performing in a comedy act or playing Judge Priest on the stage, for what he claimed were high salaries. He had already dabbled in silent movies as both an actor and a screenwriter. He also adapted his style for radio, which moved him even further toward comedy. His syndicated column "My Favorite Stories" ran throughout the decade, its only purpose being to get a laugh. He also kept up his monthly contributions to *Cosmopolitan* and other magazines, as well as working on novels. If he ran short of story ideas, he was not above paying for one. Buff reported in *Liberty Magazine* that her father was more than just a humorist. "In spite of his amazing gift, fundamentally he is an intensely serious, even a sad man. No one can be such a prolific and versatile writer and fail to be. . . . His work is dreamed over and worked on for months before a word of it is written." Money was always a concern for Cobb, as his lifestyle required a large income. The press reported that he received between $3,500 and $4,000 for each "tale." If the 1920s was "the prosperity decade," Cobb spent lavishly, and he depended on wealthy friends like Will Hogg for financial advice. After buying some property in Houston at Hogg's suggestion, Cobb took a trip to California and reported in mid-1925: "I left New York with my balance reduced to moderate proportions and I probably won't have any considerable sums coming in from any source until I get back. Savvy?" Cobb also praised California for its "lovely climate, splendid scenery and no closed season on fur-bearing Jews."[20]

By the mid-1920s, Cobb had convinced himself that his future lay in Hollywood. He was still churning out "My Favorite Stories" up to six days a week and turned 366 of those columns into *A Laugh a Day Keeps the Doctor Away*. The stories were typical of Cobb and included his usual spate of tales about African Americans and their childlike simplicity, although he mockingly conceded in the book's foreword, "There is not a single story in it in which a colored character is referred to as 'Rastus.'" The table of contents included more stories under the title "Negro" than any other. Two years later, Cobb compiled another 365 columns into *Many Laughs for Many Days,* which had a similar format and basically the same style of humor.[21]

The year 1924 became one of Cobb's most productive, as he kept up a steady flow of magazine articles and books. From January through September 1924 Cobb contributed long stories to *Cosmopolitan* about the adventures and misadventures of John C. Calhoun "Juney" Custer Jr. in a river town much like Paducah in the 1890s. He rewrote and reorganized these stories into nineteen chapters for *Goin' on Fourteen: Being Cross-Sections out of a Year in the Life of an Average Boy,* his paean to a childhood spent on the river.[22]

Goin' on Fourteen can still be read today for Cobb's interesting views about how the world was changing for a hyperactive thirteen-year-old at the turn of the twentieth century. The book is worthy of comparison to both Mark Twain's *Tom Sawyer* and Booth Tarkington's *Penrod* series, as it combines some of the same elements. Adulthood was just around the corner for Juney and his cohorts, whose activities included treasure seeking, confronting a bully, and running away from home. Being able to replace his short pants with long ones was a coming-of-age ritual that Cobb turned to hilarity in "Little Lord Pantsleroy." This satire was based on the Little Lord Fauntleroy costume, wherein a mother made her son grow his hair long and wear a large lace collar and a black velvet suit just before the advent of puberty, as inspired by English writer Frances Hodgson Burnett's novel.[23]

Juney and his friends roam the town and the countryside at will. What today would be called cruelty to animals provides ribald hilarity when a cat's head gets stuck in an empty salmon can. Out of that incident, Juney and his buddies form the SDKA, or Society for Dumb Kindness to Animals. Finally, at the end of the book, Juney's father promises his son "a reg'lar long pants with a vest and all," including "suspenders." Though his mother protests, knowing it means she is losing her baby to adulthood, "Pop" also promises "some shoe-nuff men's shirts."[24]

Reviewers of *Goin' on Fourteen* were quite laudatory. The *New York*

Times reviewer called the young protagonist Johnny rather than Juney but otherwise got the story straight, writing that it "abounds in humorous and ironic comment mingled often with deep feeling. Many of the telling scenes are full of real pathos." *New York Evening Post* reviewer Clement Wood caught the Sawyer-Penrod connection but declared that Cobb's creation was more believable. "For one thing Juney is a more average boy than they. When he fights he gets licked often enough. He is neither a young Noah Webster, nor a young Jack Dempsey—he is a regular boy."[25]

Cobb's repertoire of stories was wide and deep. The remainder of those that appeared in *Cosmopolitan* in 1924 provide some interesting contrasts. The October story was full of pathos without straying into bathos. "Standing Room Only" is the tale of Reuben Oldham, a retired druggist from a small town who goes to live with his daughter and her husband in Manhattan. Though well taken care of by his family, he seeks companionship by walking around the city, particularly in the parks. Though he finds Central Park interesting, he fails to make any lasting friends in the busy city. The ending of the story is among Cobb's finest. After Reuben's death, his daughter and her husband delay taking his cremated remains back to his hometown. Finally, his urn is pushed further back on the closet shelf, because "you know how odds and ends accumulate in an apartment. There just was standing room only."[26]

Cobb also found time to appear in the movie *The Great White Way*, released in early 1924 (the "Great White Way" refers to Broadway's theater district). Reviewers today pan the film, finding its three interlocking stories confusing. Dozens of celebrities appeared in cameo scenes, including Damon Runyon and Tex Rickard. In an advertisement, Cobb is shown in a still photograph wearing his trademark clothing for such occasions. "The rotund gentleman to the left of this group, attired in his nifty knickers and leaning on a stick is Irvin S. Cobb, of Kentucky, who makes his debut as a movie actor in 'The Great White Way,' the Alamo feature for this week," ran an advertisement in a Louisville paper. Actually, this was Cobb's second movie, his first being a walk-on appearance as an Arab in a DeMille picture. The *New York Times* humorously reported, "Mr. Cobb took the occasion in a sporting way, possibly a bit nervous because of his plus fours and his light-hued golf hose, filled with rounded calves and quite small around the ankles."[27]

In the 1920s Cobb played his role as a celebrity to the hilt. His pictures and caricatures appeared regularly in newspapers and magazines, and biographer Chatterton claims that Cobb was the most caricatured individual of his lifetime. Cobb's weight, heavy eyebrows, and general appearance were an illustrator's and photographer's dream. Everyone knew Cobb, either by his appearance in press photos or through his writing.[28]

Despite his well-known physical persona, Cobb seemed a natural for radio. On December 4, 1923, he made his first appearance on the *Everready Hour,* a variety show sponsored by the National Battery Company. It was broadcast on WEAF in New York City; the station was begun by AT&T and became the basis for the formation of the National Broadcasting Company in 1927. As a periodic guest on the program, Cobb joined such personalities as Eddie Cantor, Pablo Casals, and Will Rogers. Cobb played the "comic fat man and the southerner," to the delight of the radio audience. Cobb was becoming typecast, which he was perfectly willing to do as long as he made money from the performance. "Incursions into radio have lasted longer and have paid better than various of my shoppings," Cobb declared in his last memoir. He loved performing on radio, but only if there was a small audience with which he could interact.[29]

Cobb continued to write furiously. In 1924 he also published the *Kentucky* installment of his *America Guyed Books* series.[30] By this time in his life, Cobb had traveled extensively, and his reporter's eye for detail led to many witty asides in his descriptions of Kentucky, New York, Kansas, Indiana, Maine, and North Carolina in the series. Consisting of about fifty pages of text and illustrations, each volume demonstrated Cobb's view of the ridiculousness of Americans, no matter where they lived. In the case of Kentucky, he capitalized on the typical citizen's overweening sense of pride, though always with tongue in cheek, so as not to offend anyone. For example, Cobb interpreted the state seal, which shows two gentlemen shaking hands—to mean that "so long as they hold hands, neither can reach for his hardware." The motto accompanying the seal should be, according to Cobb, "United We Stand, Divided We Fall To" (he added the last word). He also pleaded his case for Kentucky cooks to omit sugar from their corn bread recipes. Using an aphorism he had developed years before, he claimed a Kentuckian "will tell you that it is better to be born an anonymous orphan in Kentucky than to come into the world as duly authenticated twins in Kansas." He even made fun of Kentuckians who wept whenever "My Old Kentucky Home" was sung.

One of the book's funniest illustrations, by John T. McCutcheon, is of the state's trio of "Fine Whiskey," "Fast Horses," and "Good Looking Women." Prohibition had closed Kentucky's distilleries, but it was still possible to find good whiskey in the state, although "a thirsty stranger may have to walk all of half a block to find a place where he can get a drink," Cobb averred. Reviews of the *America Guyed Books* varied—from merely acceptable to far inferior to Cobb's best work. However, like all of Cobb's writings, each volume went into multiple editions. In 1929, for example, the combined Doubleday, Doran, and Company reissued *Irvin Cobb at His Best* for the fifth time.[31]

Cobb's second attempt at a novel, *Alias Ben Alibi*, published in 1925, turned out to be more of a series of connected stories than a novel. The main character, Ben Ali Crisp, is reminiscent of the hard-driving *Evening World* editor Charles Chapin, with human sensibilities added. Crisp is the managing editor of the fictitious *New York Star*, located on Park Row at the turn of the century. Nicknamed "Ben Alibi" by his staff, Crisp always finds a way to reform politicians, right wrongs, or solve crimes. Many of the book's twenty-five chapters are based on Cobb's experiences during his days at the *Evening World*. Crisp controls the newspaper like a dictator until the *Star* is bought by a wealthy man who desires a more sedate publication. In the last chapter, Crisp faces dismissal if he does not change his editorial style. "Where, along the Row, was there room for a man within hailing distance of his fifty-fifth birthday?" he asks. Crisp decides that the only way out is suicide, and after writing his own obituary, he shoots himself in the head at his bachelor apartment. His loyal staff decides to print the piece exactly as written by their boss as a final tribute to him.[32]

The book received good reviews in the New York City press. Noting Cobb's knowledge of the newspaper trade, the *Saturday Review of Literature* concluded that "the present fiction gives the impression of being a rewrite of truth." Despite finding Crisp to be a practitioner of old-fashioned yellow journalism, the *New York Evening Post* also lauded the book. "Boss Crisp, a mosaic pieced together from many lives, as most good fictional characters are, leaves a vivid impression after most of his remarkable adventures are forgotten." Likewise, the *Boston Transcript* declared: "Not only will you not set it down when you start it, but you will not soon forget it, having finished it." Only the *New York Times* took a lighter tone, finding that "Crisp is not so well-rounded and likable a character as Mr.

Cobb's 'Old Judge Priest,' but he is a splendid addition to the Cobb gallery." Although biographer Lawson did not comment on *Alias Ben Alibi,* Chatterton wrote that it "deserves better than the almost total obscurity into which it has fallen." I agree with Chatterton; it was probably Cobb's finest long work of fiction to date and was certainly the best of his New York City pieces, proving again that he could master material outside the context of his native Kentucky.[33]

The mid-1920s proved to be one of Cobb's most productive periods. *"Here Comes the Bride—"and so Forth,* following on the heels of *Alias Ben Alibi,* contains seventeen articles, stories, and observations that had previously been published in *Hearst's International Magazine,* the *Saturday Evening Post, American Magazine, Country Gentleman, Red Book,* and *Hampton's Magazine.* The book is a compendium of humor and commentary that spans much of Cobb's career. From childhood memories to his experiences in Europe during World War I to observations at a zoo to "Our National Holidays," Cobb had a story or an anecdote for all things. In the lead piece he comments, "Marriage used to be a contract; now so many seem to regard it as a ninety-day option." Revisiting "The Advantage of Being Homely," he counts himself lucky because men like him are unspoiled and "leading the world's armies and shaping the world's commerce."[34]

Critics were generally positive. The *Boston Transcript* and *New York Post* concentrated on describing the content of the book in detail, without offering critical reviews. The *Saturday Review of Literature* quibbled a bit while praising Cobb for following the common American style of humor that emphasized "exaggeration." Cobb "has learned his trade so disastrously well the effort appears now to have become mechanical, and the reader often feels that he is not reading spontaneous humor so much as the forced and designed paragraphs of a process." In effect, Cobb's wit had become stale, "only revealing in part the true evidence of a really genial personality."[35]

Always eager to cash in on Cobb's popularity with the reading public, Doran came out with *Prose and Cons* in early 1926, another repackaging of older material. Cobb and his editors liked to devise catchy titles—in this case, a play on "pros and cons." By this time, Cobb's list of Doran publications included fourteen "fiction" titles, twenty "wit and humor" titles, and five "miscellany" titles, which was quite an accomplishment in less than two decades. The pieces in *Prose and Cons* came from *Good Housekeeping, Cosmopolitan,* and even the *Saturday Evening Post.* They included a couple of mildly racist stories, "The Chocolate Hyena" and "The Parker House Roll"; a couple of Judge Priest stories; some other mysteries; and a rehash of coming-of-age in "Long Pants."[36]

The most interesting story in *Prose and Cons* is "The Thrill of a Lifetime," which is reminiscent of Twain's adventures involving Tom and Huck. In Cobb's rendition, a young boy "between eleven and twelve" years old and his "partner and confederate" become embroiled in a scheme with some older boys to perpetrate a "dog-canning." After capturing a stray hound, the boys tie an old coffee pot filled with pebbles by a length of cord to the poor canine's tail. When let loose, the dog, of course, is panicked by the noise and discomfort and races off, providing amusement for the boys. Eventually, the event turns into typical Cobbian hilarity. The dog runs through a funeral procession for "Old Doc Wheeler," who is encased in an old-fashioned "glass-walled hearse" pulled by horses. During the ensuing chaos, the casket falls off the hearse. It "struck with tremendous emphasis upon one end. And then—oh, dire and gruesome stroke!—the top of it came off, and in his funeral habiliments, wearing a large white tie and with his long side-whiskers neatly combed back, Old Doc Wheeler emerged full view before us—or so it seemed to us—of chagrin not unmixed with surprise." Scared out of their wits, the boys beat a hasty retreat. The narrator confesses that it took ten years "before I quit dreaming of a grievously interrupted funeral; and I was nearing my thirtieth birthday before I began to perceive any humor in the event which I have narrated. . . . I know that the greatest thrill I ever had was when for the first, last, and only time in my life I met Old Doc Wheeler face to face."[37]

In Chatterton's opinion, "The Thrill of a Lifetime" was "one of Cobb's most endurable anecdotes." At the time of *Prose and Cons'* release, the *New York Times* reviewer praised Cobb's ability to write serious short stories as well as humorous ones. "As every one knows, Cobb is a natural story teller" with the versatility to do it all. The *Boston Transcript* was not quite as complimentary but declared the book "good reading. And good reading for the summer is good reading for spring, autumn or winter."[38]

The reviewer of *Prose and Cons* in the *New York Herald Tribune* accepted Cobb's "Jewish turn yclept 'The Silent Partner'" as being a worthy effort to write about that community. "It would seem to be one of the few certainties here below that what Irvin S. Cobb says to-day George H. Doran will publish tomorrow—or words to that effect." However, this would be Cobb's last book published by his old friend Doran. They appeared to be going in different directions. Cobb told his friend Townsend in early 1927, "I have left Doran for Cosmopolitan temporarily. I have made a three year contract with Hearst." However, he would never return to Doran, and the business evolved into Doubleday, Doran, and Company in 1927. Was Cobb getting stale? The *New York Post* thought so. "Cobb is almost three years behindhand. . . . Can one keep on writing stories indefinitely, without laying oneself open to the charge of triteness?"[39]

Cobb turned fifty years old on June 23, 1926. Paducah's native son received a hero's welcome in his hometown and a dinner in his honor on May 5 with more than 300 people in attendance. Old friend Bob Davis was there, as were folks Cobb had known since his days in short pants. The "Duke of Paducah" and his family had special accommodations at the new Hotel Irvin Cobb.[40]

At fifty, Cobb appeared to be at the top of his career, and he now turned his talents toward movies, which seemed to be a natural fit. He made periodic trips to Hollywood to work on films during the 1920s. The scripts he wrote for *Fields of Glory, Pardon My French*, and *Five Dollar Baby* expanded into several cameo roles in *The Great White Way* and other silent films.[41]

One of Cobb's early scriptwriting ventures did not turn out well, however. Following on the success of King Vidor's 1925 classic *The Big Parade*, a World War I drama, MGM studios hired Cobb to write a scenario and then a script for a movie tentatively titled "The Big Ditch," a drama about the building of the Panama Canal. He traveled to Hollywood in 1926 to begin work on the project; for example, he wrote dramatic scenes about a navy commander who did not have the best interests of the United States at heart. Cobb was lavishly paid for his time on the West Coast, and by this time, Hollywood was becoming well known for its excesses of wealth, pride, and partying. "I had invaded the picture colony during perhaps the crowning cycle of Babylonian excesses and almost childish cutting-up amongst the inmates," explained Cobb.[42]

Owing to the impending birth of Buff's child, Irvin and Laura traveled to Italy in the fall of 1926. Granddaughter Patrizia Cobb Chapman was born on October 19, 1926, in Florence. Upon Cobb's return to the States, he received an unpleasant surprise. Because of Irving Thalberg's attention to the "Big Ditch" project, Cobb had believed it would surely be produced. But when he arrived in New York City, the anticipated emissary from the movie studio did not appear, and a friend of Cobb's at the studio could not get a response from the bigwigs. It turned out that MGM had decided not to make the movie and was developing another major project instead. "So R.I.P., says I," Cobb concluded. At least he had been well paid in advance for his efforts.[43]

While in Italy, Cobb had a brief audience with Benito Mussolini. Cobb seemed to be favorably impressed, at least by the apparent efficiency the dictator had brought to his nation. When Buff and her husband argued that all was not well under the dictator and that the soldiers at the Chigi Palace "were merely a bunch of well-dressed mobsters," Cobb seemed oblivious. Upon returning to the United States, Cobb observed that the Italian dictator "has a remarkably vivid personality. Mussolini has done wonders in Italy." By 1941, Cobb failed to mention this event as a highlight of his life in *Exit Laughing*, in which he dropped many a name. He did comment, however, that William Goebel, the gubernatorial candidate murdered in early 1900, was "a Mussolini of politics if there ever one lived."[44]

With Cobb's celebrity came public attention to almost every aspect of his life, including his opposition to Prohibition. That position was based on his lifelong love of distilled spirits and his sense that Americans should not be denied their right to tipple. It was just that simple. Like most Americans of the time who were so inclined, he found a ready supply of liquor, despite the inconveniences.[45]

Opposed to the machinations of the Ku Klux Klan, Cobb was also opposed to the anti-evolutionism movement sweeping the South. From his early days to his death, he kept his distance from organized religion, preferring to be "an innocent bystander." He was neither puritanical nor prudish, but he opposed what he viewed as some Broadway productions that were "just dirt for dirt's sake," with no redeeming qualities, as he told a Louisville reporter in 1926.[46]

In what might be described as the Earl Carroll incident of 1926, Cobb played a minor role in the continuing drama of the Prohibition enforcement in New York City. Carroll had created a Broadway show with the backing of Will Hogg and others, and the highlight of the opening-night party was supposed to be a nude model seated in bathtub onstage filled with liquid from which the partygoers would be invited to slake their thirst. While seated in the tub, Joyce Hawley became distraught for some reason, and a furious Carroll had the tub moved offstage, refusing to pay the young woman the agreed-on $1,000 fee for her services. A vindictive Hawley informed the authorities that Carroll had served alcohol. Cobb, who had attended the party and was a friend of both Carroll and Hogg, told a reporter before his court testimony that he had "arrived early and left early," and "measured by the accepted standards of Broadway, the party seemed to be perfectly proper." Perhaps only columnist Walter Winchell got in a better quip when he was asked if Carroll's affair had been "a regular Broadway party?" Winchell replied, "It wasn't. There were too many Senators present." Cobb told the court he had imbibed two glasses of near beer and one glass of "White Rock" wine. "I drink a cocktail when I am reasonably certain that the effect will not be immediately fatal," Cobb added at the end of his testimony, which likely garnered a laugh from the audience. Carroll was convicted of perjury, and after several appeals he served a year and a day at the federal penitentiary in Atlanta for violating the Volstead Act.[47]

Seemingly at the top of his form as well as his career, Cobb's comments about life in general were still interesting to the public, despite the insistence of some critics that he was wasting his talent. Three magazine pieces from the mid-1920s offer insight into that talent. "The Convict Who Made a Garden on the Road to Hell," which appeared in the March 1925 issue of *Hearst's International and Cosmopolitan,* could be dismissed as a throwaway piece written just to make a deadline. However, it is a sensitive story about Cobb's old *Evening World* editor Charles Chapin. After killing his wife in 1918, Chapin served a life sentence as inmate number 69,690 at Sing Sing prison. Chapin maintained he had killed his wife as an act of kindness because of her ill health. Cobb took him at his word, but the rest of the world condemned Chapin for not following through and killing himself as well. Chapin was not a typical prisoner, and Cobb praised him for refusing "to cease to exist," shut off from society. Chapin edited a prison newspaper, wrote his memoirs, and planted a prison garden not only to beautify his surroundings but also to make his life worth living. Eventually, Chapin planted and tended 3,000 rosebushes leading to the death house. Cobb, who had earlier cowritten an ill-fated play about prison life, insisted that if he wrote such a play now, "I'd try to show that a prison—even a prison—may serve as a place for the rebirth of a twisted and tortured soul." Chapin died at Sing Sing in 1930.[48]

In many of his writings, Cobb stood up for the little guy against the power of either machine politicians or big business. In "The Principle of the Thing," a miserly New York City bank president, aptly named Mr. Bleke, discovers that one of his employees, Harry Treve, has been stealing money. As a means of wearing him down, Bleke takes Treve on an apparently endless chauffeured automobile ride through New York City, always passing by the city jail known as the Tombs. Eventually, the culprit cannot stand this torture any longer and admits his guilt. "You've sinned, young man, and under the law you've got to pay and I'm going to see that you pay," Bleke exults. "That's what laws and jails are made for—for people like you. It's not so much the money that's involved. It's the principle of the thing." On the way to jail, Treve reveals that he and Bleke's daughter are engaged to be married and that he stole the money to pay for their wedding and to escape from her father. A furious Bleke insists that Treve be quickly jailed and that the newspapers print his story. But only an hour later, Bleke returns to the Tombs a changed man and forces his way into the cell block. Though we are never told the complete story, it seems that the banker's daughter is pregnant by someone other than Treve, who was going to marry her anyway and give her a respectable life. When Bleke tries to right the sorry mess he has made, Treve tells him that his life is already ruined because the newspapers are already printing the story of his thievery. As Treve is being shoved along with another prisoner, Bleke shouts out that he will "withdraw this charge, let me go bail for you." "No," Treve replies, rather sardonically. "As you were saying, Mr. Bleke, it's not so much the money. With me it's the principle of the thing." This story works well, with its O. Henry–like ending, even for the modern reader.[49]

On another level and more problematic is Cobb's story called "The Unbroken Chain." The theme is race, but this is not the usual type of story one would expect from Cobb, and it is unclear exactly what he is trying to say. There is nothing of Kentuckian J. Poindexter or even Cobb's typical New York City African American story line. The tale begins with a coffle of slaves being brutally moved to an East African port, led by Arab slavers. On the way, most of them are killed by a rampaging rhinoceros. Beginning with man's inhumanity to man, Cobb carefully describes the pain and suffering of the slaves as they are transported to America by a sanctimonious ship captain. Then the story flashes forward 100 years to Long Island in 1920. There, "Mr. G. Claybourne Brissot was living the life of a gentleman." A mysterious recluse, Brissot attends a dinner at the estate of George Blackburn, where he meets a "southerner," Judge Martin Sylvester. During a conversation with Blackburn, Sylvester expresses his thoughts about race. "I think about the cruelest tragedy we've got in this country today is the man with a tincture of negro blood in his veins—the infinitesimal trace which according to our laws on consanguinity nevertheless brands him a negro—and who still has education, good taste, refinement, even may have in him sometimes the seed of genius which makes him an artist or a creator." Sylvester goes on to say that although he sympathizes with such a person, "one drop of black ink in a pint of water discolors the whole cupful."[50]

The southerner senses that Brissot is hiding something, and he eventually tells Blackburn that Brissot is undoubtedly from the South. But why is he reticent about admitting it? Sylvester has looked for all the telltale signs of Brissot being part Negro and has found none, but he wants to inspect his backbone for the "negro smudge," a dark area on the spine. This, of course, does not happen, and Sylvester returns home. Meanwhile, Brissot dies in an automobile accident when his car is struck by a train. Cobb then ends the story with a preposterous finale. Riding in the auto with Brissot and his chauffeur was the only survivor, Colonel Bate-Farnaro, an English explorer with vast knowledge of Africa. The colonel asks Brissot's lawyer about the dead man's experiences in Africa, but the lawyer insists that Brissot had never been to Africa. The colonel replies that he must have because, just before being struck by the locomotive, Brissot "cried out" in "Mbama" the words for "great animal." Cobb chose this ludicrous ending, passing up the opportunity to say something important about race in America.[51]

Cobb continued to do what he did best: turning out popular and predictable articles and stories for Hearst publications. The *Saturday Review* summed up Cobb's quandary in its review of *On an Island that Cost $24.00:* "The career of Mr. Irvin Cobb is not an encouraging phenomenon. . . . He has never lacked, apparently, for something to say and some-

one to print what he has said. He has been successful and syndicated."
Though some of his stories made for good reading as magazine pieces, "in
the end nothing counts but the cheapness of the whole." Then came the
damnation as a hack writer. "It is all a trifle depressing, because one suspects that Mr. Cobb with the most laudable intentions in the world has
written in spite of himself just another syndication standard book."[52]

Nevertheless, Cobb continued to make money on his trademark writings and apparently took no notice of his critics. Moreover, he was ready
for another shot at country living. This time, the Cobbs moved into a spa-
cious house in East Hampton on Long Island in 1927. They named the
place "Back Home." The property was large enough to accommodate Laura's gardening skills, but there was no foolishness about farming, as there
had been at Rebel Ridge. At age fifty, Cobb "had not become a second
Mark Twain after all," explained biographer Lawson. But more important
to Cobb, "he was still one of the highest paid writers in the country."[53]

10

From Prosperity to Depression

In 1928 Cobb was asked if he liked being famous. By this time, he was the author of dozens of books and was one of the most recognizable Americans. He had a substantial income (he was probably a millionaire) and hobnobbed with the rich and famous. "Don't be silly!" he answered quite honestly in a *Smart Set* article. "It is a curious thing, this business of being a so-called celebrity. In the hope of achieving what, among us, passes for fame you work your head off. If you fail to win it you die disappointed. If you win it, you find that the taste of it isn't exactly what you thought its taste would be. Also, you find that it's as hard to keep as it was to gain—maybe harder." Moreover, "in this country particularly we have a way of putting an individual on a pedestal one day and knocking him off the next. As a race we're affectionate and fickle. And the higher the pedestal the farther the fall. . . . I want to cling fast to my little share of the thing you call notoriety."[1]

About this same time, Cobb's friend Townsend expressed his own ambitions of breaking into the New York City literary scene. Cobb warned him to stay away "if you value your peace of mind and happiness. New York is as hard to break into as a steel safe. It's cold, over-crowded, fickle, and selfish. I starved to death here for three years before I really got a foothold and at that I was luckier than most." For the remainder of his life, Cobb hung on the precipice of fame as he attempted to keep his place among American writers while venturing into radio and movies.[2]

Books published in 1927 and 1928 made money but did not bring

critical acclaim. For the first book, Cobb followed his old process of compiling articles published in *Cosmopolitan* and other magazines and quickly
turning them into a book, which apparently sold well. *Ladies and Gentlemen, Chivalry Peak,* and *All Aboard* fulfilled Cobb's contract with Hearst
for three books in rapid succession.

Some of the chapters in *Ladies and Gentlemen,* published by the Cosmopolitan Book Corporation in 1927, were stories from as far back as
1924. Most were predictable. Cobb even used the old tale of an overbear-
ing and haughty Englishman who dismisses terrapin stew, based on his
real-life encounter with Arnold Bennett back in 1911. This compilation
does not include a Judge Priest story, but it does have "We of the Old
South," about a Confederate veteran who goes to Hollywood to appear in
a film as an extra and, in the process, aids the career of a young actress.
Cobb proved again that he could write a New York City tale (similar to
Damon Runyon's) in "Three Wise Men of the East Side." He also added
to his growing collection of western stories with "The Cowboy and the
Lady—And Her Pa" and even included his close friend Charles Russell
in one story.[3]

However, the major reviewers panned *Ladies and Gentlemen.* "We
now rise to the occasion to remark pointedly that Mr. Cobb in 'Ladies
and Gentlemen' is not quite so pleasant" as he had been in his earlier
work, claimed the *New York Times.* The *Saturday Review* was even more
scathing in a very brief review: "There is no perceptive reason for getting excited over Irvin Cobb's latest collection of short stories. In 'Ladies
and Gentlemen' he has gathered eleven lightweight tales that will perhaps
amuse a placid reader. . . . In short, 'Ladies and Gentlemen' is seldom of
interest and never important."[4]

Biographer Lawson summarily dismissed Cobb's later books. "By
1927 Cobb was no longer one of Doran's distinguished authors; he was a
popular writer for a low-brow magazine and its equally low-brow book-
publishing arm." Chatterton, in another earlier biography, was a bit
kinder, claiming that Cobb's "'big' years extended roughly from the end
of World War I to the financial 'crash' of 1929." My view is that Cobb's
writing did not change much at all and that *Cosmopolitan* was not quite
as "low-brow" as Lawson claimed. Contributors to the magazine in 1929
alone were Theodore Dreiser, Edgar Lee Masters, P. G. Wodehouse, Sinclair Lewis, Ring Lardner, Peter B. Kyne, Damon Runyon, Amelia Ear-

hart, and Somerset Maugham. Each issue contained more than 200 pages and variety enough for the general reader.[5]

Cobb's second attempt at a full-length novel, *Chivalry Peak,* is a "western" piece. It is as close as Cobb ever came to writing a love story. He deals with sex in a somewhat old-fashioned way, but one that was satisfying to his readers. It is an interesting yarn that includes Cobb's disdain for wealthy swindlers, his love of the outdoors, and his propensity to lead the reader up false alleyways before revealing all at the end. *Chivalry Peak* can be read today as an example of what middle-class readers of the late 1920s enjoyed. Critics were not impressed by the novel, however. The *New York Times* found it episodic, and even the *Louisville Courier-Journal* noted that "at times Mr. Cobb is somewhat self-conscious, his writing lacking something of that freedom and joyous spirit so characteristic of his short stories."[6]

All Aboard, a collection of loosely connected stories about the people of the Tennessee River, failed as a novel. In "Chapter I—A Prelude— But Mercifully a Short One," Cobb explains that river life has continued unchanged for many years, and although there is still a remnant of the old steamboat trade on the Tennessee, it is fast disappearing on other rivers. "The Romantic River, as such, is on its last legs," he laments. Cobb relies on knowledge from his youth, when steamboats came down the Tennessee River and docked in Paducah to exchange their wares. His characters are based on men and women he could have met as a boy. And, of course, he uses his inventive mind to fill in the details. There are some interesting stories in this disjointed book, which would have appealed to an older generation looking for nostalgia in tales about bygone days. The *Louisville Courier-Journal* commented, "What 'Mark Twain' did for the Mississippi River and its environs, Irvin Cobb has done for the beautiful Tennessee with it romantic stretches of winding blue water where something of the old South still lingers." The more urbane *New York Times* reviewer groaned a bit, noting that "some of the episodes are humorous, some are mournful, and several are chiefly meritorious because they kept a linotyper gainfully employed in a Presidential [election] year." That reviewer later claimed the "best pages of the book are those that chronicle the views of Tip January," Cobb's chief protagonist who dominates parts of the book.[7]

Cobb only occasionally commented on politics, primarily to make fun of politicians and the whole political process, but he took a strong interest in the 1928 presidential election. Cobb stuck by his old Democratic Party heritage, particularly after its nominee for president, former New York governor Al Smith, spoke against the continuation of national Prohibition. Cobb made a few personal appearances on behalf of the Democratic ticket, including in his hometown. Cobb's mother supported Smith, as did the rest of Paducah, narrowly. As Cobb said, "When Al Smith ran in 1928, it [Paducah] did have a rather close call from going Baptist," referring to that denomination's devotion to the antiliquor cause. Though Smith lost by a wide margin to Herbert Hoover, Cobb kept up his public opposition to Prohibition. In mid-1929 he became chairman of the Authors and Artists Committee of the Association against the Prohibition Amendment. Other committee members included Stephen Vincent Benet, Rex Beach, Richard Halliburton, Nunnally Johnson, and Emily Post. Cobb argued that time had proved that the "Noble Experiment" did not work, given a rise of criminality as well as the loss of tax revenue.[8]

Cobb found another way to publicly display his opposition to Prohibition: a novel, *Red Likker*. He spent more time researching, writing, and producing *Red Likker* than any other book he had published up to this time. It can best be described as a "southern romance" about the Bird family of Kentucky from the earliest pioneer days through the imposition of Prohibition. No doubt, Cobb wanted to continue his demonstration against the Eighteenth Amendment and the Volstead Act in fiction, telling Townsend, "I aim to write a novel having for a background the making and selling of Bourbon whiskey, beginning with its beginnings and bringing it down to present times." He took trips to Kentucky to do research and consulted with several Kentuckians to make his novel as authentic as possible. Cobb corresponded with Otto Rothert, secretary of the prestigious Filson Historical Society in Louisville, about knowledgeable men he could interview. He visited Louisville, Frankfort, and Paducah to gather information about the making of bourbon, now that the distilleries were shuttered.[9]

Though *Red Likker* turned out to be a novel, it began by what Cobb called "shadow-boxing," first writing an introduction and then allowing the story to fall into place, at least as explained in the *Bookman*. *Red Likker* ran as a serial in *Cosmopolitan* from March through July 1929. Editor Ray Long touted the beginning of the series in February: "When Irvin Cobb lived in Kentucky, the state had three boasts—Its Fair Women. Its Fast Horses. Its Fine Whisky. Today only two remain. . . . A novel which takes no sides but which puts on paper the story of a phase of this country's life that has gone." Cobb's sentiments are never in doubt, as the characters who support the production of bourbon are the forward-thinking heroes of the novel, and there are villains aplenty on the other side. He dedicated *Red Likker* to his fast friends "Bill Hogg and His Brother Mike."[10]

Biographers Lawson and Chatterton, whose works were published in the mid-1980s, found that *Red Likker* was the end, or at least the beginning of the end, of Cobb's string of successful writings. Times were changing, and according to Chatterton, Cobb's "leisurely, rambling, anecdotal style of which he had become an acknowledged master was yielding to that of young writers like Ernest Hemingway. . . . Cobb had to face the changing times, and his reluctant acceptance of the change was devastating to everything he had made his own." Lawson was less charitable: "Like *All Aboard*, [*Red Likker*] is flawed by the sentimental haze that had settled over Cobb's memories of Kentucky." Though I agree with them for the most part, I will save my final analysis for later in this book. Amazingly, Cobb faced adversity and declining popularity with a sense of humor, albeit bitter at times, and continued to work every day on whatever his next project was well into the 1930s. He had to make a living, and he knew it.[11]

There were still occasional high points to cheer him up. "An Episode at Pintail Lake," a psychological thriller masked as a hunting story, was chosen as one of the seventeen best stories of 1928 by the O. Henry Memorial Award Committee. A photograph of Cobb posing for a painting by a Norwegian artist, with a cigar in hand and spats on his feet, was newsworthy in that pre-Depression year. When he expressed sympathy for "Our Revolting Youth," even citing his daughter as an example of "a terrible flapper," he was not joking. "She is now a fine type of American wife and mother." For all the publicity and fame, Irvin S. Cobb was a very conventional husband and father.[12]

This Man's World, a collection of stories from *Cosmopolitan*, *Good Housekeeping*, and *Golden Book Magazine*, follows Cobb's tried-and-true pattern. These thirteen stories offer a variety of scenes and characters: eastern, western, and Kentucky locations; big-city mobsters, a man who goes mad, and another man driven to suicide. Cobb even puts in a good word for evangelical religion when a minister forces a scoundrel to treat his young wife properly. Another story revolves around one of Cobb's favorite hobbies, collecting Native American relics, which he had started as a lad in McCracken County.[13]

One story stands out: the title story in which Cobb confronts the inequality women faced in his day. In "This Man's World," two sisters, Annie and Anita, work in a big-city department store "for considerably less" than their male counterparts. Because they are unable to support themselves, they must depend on men. Annie marries a manual laborer, who tries to control her every action and instinct. Anita, the younger sister, lives with a well-to-do dandy who does the same. "Annie got herself a husband, Anita got herself a man," Cobb remarks. Both end up being cast out by their men: Annie is falsely accused of adultery, and Anita is thrown out when she develops a goiter. The sisters get back together and attempt to eke out a living. Anita tells her sister, "You go straight and I go crooked and the best either one of us gets is the worst of it. Sis, what the hell's wrong with this rotten world, anyway?" Cobb concludes this modern theme by arguing, "Brute force ruled and the man, being physically the stronger," dominated society and women.[14]

Biographer Lawson gave Cobb credit for dealing with a modern theme, while Chatterton praised him for telling a story that was "surprisingly modern." Writing at the height of the Equal Rights Amendment controversy, Chatterton argued that this story "could be used as a case-study of pre-ERA attitudes toward the role of women in a society dominated by men." Chatterton viewed Anita's question as a serious comment on the world. Moreover, "Cobb pushes humor to the edge of a narrow line that divides the comic from the serious" in a more European than American vein. This is not recognized because, "in America, only the sophisticated reader has achieved the old-world perspective that allows him to perceive bitter ironies as a form of humor." Chatterton agreed with author Vardis Fisher that "we have not yet learned to recognize humor as at bottom 'a defense against life and an admission of partial defeat.'" In Cobb's story, "fate" or "life" appear to trump the protagonists, behaving "like some cosmic practical joker that enjoys perpetuating a cruel trick upon Annie and Anita. But it is nonetheless a joke and therefore a legitimate form of humor," according to Chatterton. This is high praise for a writer who is generally forgotten today.[15]

Although *This Man's World* apparently sold well, it took a beating from the critics. The authoritative *Saturday Review* gave it a fifteen-line scolding: "Of the thirteen short stories in this volume, one is excellent, four others are passable, and the remainder are best forgotten. . . . The volume as a whole hardly justifies Mr. Cobb's reputation as capable journalist-humorist for the literary middle-classes." The *Louisville Herald-Post* declared that the stories had been written "with a sledge-hammer. . . . One is tempted too often to skip or even to send for the old friend (Cobb) and tell him, next time he feels tempted to gather together work not worthy of himself, to think twice." The *Louisville Times* found only one story, "The Wooden Decoy," worth reading. The *New York Times* agreed that this story was the only one worthy of attention; the others contained too much "philosophical commentary." One wonders whether Cobb read these reviews or simply ignored them. Surely he must have felt the sting of such denunciation. However, everything he wrote ended up in print and made money, so why change?[16]

In April 1929 Cobb attended the dedication of the Hotel Irvin Cobb in Paducah, built by local businessman Adolph Weil. The eight-story, 200-room structure included a roof garden. Hundreds came to the opening to hear Cobb give a brief speech and present a portrait painted by Jams Montgomery Flagg to be hung in the lobby. With Governor Flem D. Sampson in attendance, the state of Kentucky was well represented. The *New York Times* reported that Cobb already had "a cigar, a dahlia, a Missouri corncob pipe, a race horse, a bass bait, a hunting shirt, an Oregon canyon, a Texas street, and a pointer dog" named for him. A bridge connecting Paducah with Illinois would later be named for Cobb.[17]

Cobb enjoyed traveling and writing about his adventures in the company of his friends, whether fishing, hunting, or just sitting around a campfire. With famous sportswriter Grantland Rice, Cobb pursued swordfish off Montauk, on eastern Long Island. Today, their method—the swordfish was harpooned by the captain of the boat—would be considered not only unsporting but also illegal. "The swordfish is the sole survivor of the real harpooning dynasty—the one magnet that draws the old guard out to sea," Rice wrote. "Within a few hours we had come upon one of the few dramas of the sea still left. And it was a drama worth seeing!" Another time, while on a Texas hunting trip with Will Hogg, Cobb wired Laura, "HAVING A BULLY TIME."[18]

When western artist Charley Russell died, Cobb mourned deeply, writing in *Exit Laughing*, "So another one was gone who made a hole in the world when he left it." Russell had introduced Cobb to many of the wonders of the West and Native American history and lore. Cobb even included Russell in some of his fiction. After the deaths of Russell, Cobb, and Will Rogers, John Wilson Townsend published a paean to the lives and interconnections of the three men that included a famous but apparently unpublished story by Russell, "Piano Jim," as retold by Cobb. Jim, who led a rough-and-tumble life before settling down with a retired prostitute, wants to re-create the old farm life of his youth, which includes growing pumpkins. When the pumpkin vines produce no fruit, he "rounded up a German, a practical dirt-farmer," who informs him that he has only female vines and needs to plant a male vine. Jim refuses, saying, "All my l-l-life I've been a r-r-rotten, no-good, l-l-low-down s-s-son-of-a-bitch, but I'll be t-t-teetotally God-dam' if at the age of s-s-sixty-four I'm goin' to start p-p-pimpin' for a p-p-pumpkin!" Will Rogers added in a postscript, "I can't write anything in a book following Irv Cobb. Why that old rascal can take the 10 Commandments and make 'em funny. All I know is just what I read in the papers."[19]

Cobb loved the outdoor life and contributed fiction and nonfiction on the subject, even writing a piece about the unusual intelligence of "Bob," a bird dog, in *Smart Set* after Mencken had left the magazine. In a well-publicized photograph, Cobb looked somewhat out of place wearing a western kit and sitting astride a cow pony, apparently helping to round up cattle with Bob Davis on the ranch of Frazier Hunt, the European editor of *Cosmopolitan,* in Alberta, Canada. However, it was all part of Cobb's celebrity life. In one of his syndicated columns, "Manhattan Days and Nights," Herbert Corey even took notice, stating that, according to Hunt, "Mr. Cobb is more than a complete loss as a cowboy. So is Mr. Davis." Corey claimed to know the reason: "Both Mr. Cobb and Mr. Davis have well-rounded contours," though "they are chatty boys to have around a ranch." Cobb always seemed to be in the news, one way or another.[20]

Cobb was fascinated by the West and by Native American life. In 1925 a band of South Peigans (Blackfeet) in Montana adopted him "and humorously named the roly-poly Kentuckian 'Piitaohpikis,' or 'Eagle Ribs.'" In January 1928 Cobb met Chief Buffalo Child Long Lance, who had risen to fame in the 1920s as a hero in World War I, a movie actor, and a proponent of Indian rights. They were introduced by Ray Long, who had published an article by Long Lance in *Cosmopolitan*. Long Lance was working on a book at the time, and Ray Long encouraged him to ask Cobb to write an introduction for it. At their first meeting during a luncheon at the Ritz Hotel in New York, the native Kentuckian and the Native American seemed to hit it off immediately. As described in a biography of Long Lance, "Cobb puffed on his cigar. 'I'd be delighted [to write the introduction],' he said."[21]

Some weeks later, Long Lance attended a "glittering cocktail party at Cobb's Park Avenue apartment." He epitomized Cobb's image of the noble red man, a heroic he-man who was well educated and had fought valiantly in a white man's war. But as it turned out, Long Lance was only part American Indian; he was also part African American and part Caucasian and had been born in Winston-Salem, North Carolina, as Sylvester Long. Some of the stories he told about himself were true, but many had been fabricated to gain an advantage in white America. When Cobb learned of this, he allegedly said: "We're so ashamed! We entertained a nigger!" When the truth of his mixed heritage became known, Long Lance apparently took his own life, shooting himself with a handgun at a female friend's estate in California on March 20, 1932. Though his death was ruled a suicide, there was some controversy; many of his friends believed it was murder. In the most complete biography of Long Lance to date, Cobb expressed his own doubts, writing to a friend that he did not "'believe so gallant a man as he was ever deliberately took his own life.'" Moreover, Cobb heard there had never been a complete investigation of the incident. Would Cobb have made such a statement if he had totally disavowed Long Lance? Was he ashamed of his earlier racial denunciation? There is no mention of Long Lance in *Exit Laughing*.[22]

Having been born and raised in small-town America, Cobb indulged his wanderlust as an adult. In late 1928 and early 1929 he traveled to several South American countries. With typical tongue-in-cheek verbiage, Cobb related that "our party of three created a distinct impression. Dean Palmer was thirty pounds heavier than Bill Hogg and Bill Hogg was fifteen pounds heavier than I was, and I was—and am—no tricksy sprite myself." Beginning their adventure at the port of New Orleans, they transshipped through the Panama Canal after a stopover in Cuba. Then they crisscrossed the major South American nations on something of a goodwill and fact-finding trip. A press release was referring to Cobb when it reported, "A Well Known American Writer Stopped Yesterday in Lima," Peru, in early January 1929, and he gave a talk to the "American Club" in Buenos Aires, Argentina, in early March 1929. "Of all the cities—and I have seen my share of them—Rio is incomparably the most beautiful," Cobb stated in the *Brazilian American* while visiting that country. Cobb, of course, wrote extensively about his travels upon his return, adopting a folksy style to describe the highlights of a wide-eyed tourist visiting South America for the first time. Cobb wrote a series of seven pieces for *Cosmopolitan* that later became the first seven chapters (collectively titled "The Folks Next Door") in *Both Sides of the Street,* published in early 1930.[23]

The apparent purpose of this extended trip was to visit several countries and then report back to newly elected president Herbert Hoover, who had also made a trip to Latin America. It was all part of the "boosterism" that was so common in the 1920s as prosperity seemed endless and South America was seen as a prime source of both exports and imports. Cobb concluded his last piece in the magazine with a plea for more trade and closer relations. "It behooves us as it never behooved us before to cultivate the friendship of South America, not only for the sake of the dollars rolling in, but for the infinitely greater cause of a hemispheric solidarity against all the rest of creation." Like many Americans of this era, Cobb had apparently turned against Europe, becoming more conservative and isolationist.[24]

Cobb and Hogg returned to the United States and then spent several weeks in Europe. This trip led to three more chapters (collectively titled "The Folks across the Way") in *Both Sides of the Street.* These pieces were pedestrian in nature, but they did include a very humorous one about Cobb's experiences gambling in Monte Carlo, "I'm the Man Who Broke the Bunk at Monte Carlo." In the last section of the book, titled "The Folks Here at Home," Cobb rambled on about "Golfitis; Its Curse and Cure," which included some great lines; for instance, he credited the Scots with "reorganizing golf and getting it on a straight Calvinistic basis," which "in America has been—and still and consistently is being—restored to its ancient model of direct kinship with the dogmas of predestination and a physical Hell." In "Wall Street's Leap Year," Cobb took a slap at the stock market, which had developed into a predatory beast that had not yet recovered from the crash when this article was first printed.[25]

Around this time, just after the election of Hoover, Cobb apparently began to take a political turn to the right. Or at least he enjoyed being able to talk directly to the president for the first time since the Wilson administration about areas of concern for the United States, such as foreign policy and trade with South American nations. Charles Cason, a vice president of Chemical National Bank in New York City, invited Cobb to an exclusive luncheon to talk about his observations of South and Central America. Those invited to attend included Will Hogg, Norman Davis, Adolph Ochs, Grantland Rice, and Will Rogers. In May 1929 Cobb told Hogg he was going to Washington to talk to President Hoover about his trip. "Irvin Cobb busier in Hell," he wrote to the Texan.[26]

By 1929, Cobb's radio career was blossoming, and his photographs and caricatures often turned up in the press, such as a somewhat pensive one of him in profile, cigar in hand, that appeared in the January 20 issue of the *New York Times* and in the *Bookman* as well. Cobb could report to Townsend by late 1929, just a few months after its publication, that *Red Likker* had sold 20,000 copies. Back in early 1928, Cobb had been making jokes about the stock market: "When it comes to being nervous, Wall Street is the rabbit's nose. If, as has been alleged, it's the barometer of our national business, then the windflower of the wide prairies is the national emblem."[27] But for Cobb and his family, the crash took its toll. He reported humorously, if bitterly, in his memoirs that he had got caught up in the speculation frenzy:

For, as I have said, this was in the forepart of 1929, when brokers and the bankers were doing so beautifully well for all the lads and lassies, and the only way to lose money in Wall Street was to stay out of Wall Street, and speculation wasn't really speculation, but merely investment against the future blossoming of a prosperity which could never wane; and we could take Uncle Andy Mellon's word for it, with Charley Mitchell and Wiggin and all the other true prophets of high finance to back it up; and such Happiness Boys as Roger Babson and General Hell-and-Maria Dawes coming in strong on the chorus. President Hoover likewise caught the contagion of joyous optimism.[28]

Cobb lost heavily. Buff reported in 1945 that her father, who may have been contemplating semiretirement, reacted gloomily to the inevitable call from his banker. "He walked silently for many miles. Finally he turned to me and said, 'Well this year I pay no income tax. . . . Thank you, Mr. Goldman—Thank you, Mr. Saks!' And then suddenly he could not write any more short stories. That was all there was to it. He did not have any more short stories in his system." Though not quite true, it was clear that Cobb's creativity was nearing an end.[29]

Buff remained a confidante of her father's as she matured into an accomplished writer herself. Her budding career was no doubt helped along by her father's guidance and connections. One of her short stories, "With Glory and Honour," appeared in the 1927 "O. Henry Memorial Award Prize Stories." In 1929 Doubleday, Doran, and Company published her first novel, *Minstrels in Satin*. The next year Selwyn and Blount of London issued *Children of Glamour*. *She Was a Lady* followed a few years later.[30]

However, after nearly six years, Buff's marriage foundered, and she was granted a divorce from Frank Chapman in Reno, Nevada, on March 10, 1930. She received custody of their daughter Patrizia. In September that same year she married Alton A. Brody, a native New Yorker who was involved in the real estate business. Cobb informed Will Hogg, "Buff is fixing to marry again—a nice kid named 'Steve' Brody being the nominee. We like him. This time she's got a real man." Brody, a pilot in World War I, had been a prisoner of war. "And—thanks be to God—he can't sing a note," Cobb exclaimed (in reference to Chapman the opera singer). Buff also told Will Hogg about "My Steve": "He's a grand guy too. A real person. Intelligent (highly) sweet, successful and a personality. I am very happy and I do think that this try I've got a real chance at making a go of it."[31]

While traveling in Europe with his sister, Ima, Will Hogg died suddenly on September 12, 1930. This devastated all the Cobbs. Irvin was on a hunting trip in North Carolina at the time. He immediately returned to New York City and, according to O. O. McIntyre, encouraged his friends not to mourn excessively. "'You know what old Bill would say to this? He'd say I don't want any of you so-and-so's sniveling over me.'" McIntyre continued: "Bleeding inwardly, he made us laugh and he laughed himself. We somehow began to feel like Bill was right along with us." Cobb had depended on Hogg for much of his information about western politics, and it is possible that Hogg led Cobb into some risky financial ventures before the stock market crash, but this did not diminish Cobb's regard for him. He praised Hogg's zest for life, his business acumen, and his philanthropy, especially his generosity to the University of Texas. "For courage, for spontaneous generosity, for measured thoughtfulness, I never saw his equal. . . . He was the most lovable human being I ever knew and I shall go on missing him until the time comes for me to follow along where he went." (Hogg had been even larger than Cobb and only a year older, so his death must have caused Cobb to fear for his own health.) Cobb had lost one of his boon hunting and fishing friends, whom he called "the most perfect of all possible traveling companions."[32]

One of the more curious—almost bizarre—incidents in Cobb's life occurred at dinner at the Metropolitan Club on March 19, 1931, organized by his friend Ray Long. The afternoon before the dinner, Sinclair Lewis had delivered a speech on "American Literature Comes of Age," praising "the novels of Theodore Dreiser above all others." Lewis, a recent winner of the Nobel Prize for literature, and Dreiser—two of the literary giants among American writers—were invited to the dinner, along with Boris Pilnyak, a visiting Russian novelist. Lewis, like Cobb, first became "a master of light fiction for the mass-circulation magazines." *Saturday Evening Post* editor George Horace Lorimer had kindled Lewis's early career writing and once wrote to him, "Now that you have made a start with us I hope you will follow the example of Irvin Cobb, Bob Fitzsimmons [the boxer] and Miss Phoebe Snow [a fictional character promoting a railroad] and start to become a household word." He did, with the publication of *Main Street*. Cobb humorously described Lewis's *Main Street* as necessary reading for all Americans: "People in the cities are sure to like it because it makes fun of rural places, and the folks that live in villages and little towns have to read it just to find out what Sinclair Lewis is saying about them." Dreiser, the more avant-garde of the two and the author of *Sister Carrie* and *An American Tragedy*, took to liberal causes and even flirted with communism. Cobb, who was more of a "popular" writer but not without social, political, and economic concerns, would find himself shackled with these two prima donnas at Ray Long's big event.[33]

The details of the dinner party are a bit blurred, and some in attendance drank to excess, which "no doubt contributed to the events that followed." When Dreiser arrived late, having been confused about the address, he attempted to shake hands with Lewis and was rebuffed. Feel-

ing the effects of "eating little sausages, drinking, drinking and drinking," Lewis "replied by puckering his face and emitting a Bronx cheer."
Later, according to one attendee, "Lewis swung a bottle under the table
while he muttered threats about breaking it over Dreiser's head." After
dinner, Long called on his guests for speeches. "Lewis, invited to speak
first, rose slowly, bowed and said in a lackadaisical fashion, 'I am very
happy to welcome Mr. Pilnyak to this country. But I do not care to speak
in the presence of a man who has stolen three thousand words from my
wife's book [on Russia], and before two sage critics [Heywood Broun and
Arthur Brisbane] who have lamented the action of the Nobel prize committee in selecting me as America's representative writer.'" Everyone recognized the insult to Dreiser, whose face "reddened." Long stood up and
quickly called on Cobb to calm the waters. Cobb told some Paducah tales
to lighten the mood. In her biography of Cobb, Lawson insisted that "the
situation was a humiliating one for Cobb; he had known both Dreiser
and Lewis when he was more famous than they, and now he was serving
as comic relief to their struggle for recognition as the best writer in America." Frankly, I do not see it that way. Cobb only did what came naturally
to him—entertaining a crowd—and it happened to come at just the right
time for Long and his partygoers. The conflict between Dreiser and Lewis
continued after the dinner broke up, with the former slapping the latter
several times amid a mincing of harsh words. The New York dailies had
a field day, and one even proposed that the two meet in a boxing match.
Cobb did not mention this incident in *Exit Laughing*, but I am confident
that when he arrived home that evening, he and Laura had a good chuckle
over the comical dustup between America's two premier literati—one ine-
briated, the other incensed, and both full of themselves.[34]

In the early 1930s Cobb was just as industrious as ever and continued
to turn out articles and books, perhaps in an effort to rebuild his wealth
after the stock market crash and the beginning of the Great Depression.
He tried to take the crash, which he called "the recent unpleasantness" (a
phrase used by polite society in the South in reference to the Civil War),
in stride and get on with the business of making a living. Visiting his ailing mother in the fall of 1930, Cobb told the Paducah Lions Club that
the present economic downturn "is the first business depression I know
anything about which can't be traced to the existence of a Democratic
Administration and a Democratic President then in office, or proclaimed

a hangover from a previous Democratic Administration." More than two years before the inauguration of Franklin D. Roosevelt, Cobb presciently observed: "I think the best remedy for this depression is confidence."[35]

In the coming years, Cobb would move into movies and comedy as his career turned toward whatever was popular and lucrative. It is important to remember that Cobb did not have the extensive educational background of many of his peers, but he did have a strong work ethic. Cobb also expressed great hopes for radio: "'I look to see it broaden and develop into the greatest force in the world, not only as a medium for entertainment, but also as a means for dissemination of information, intelligence and advertisement.'" He predicted, "'I believe the day is not far distant when every schoolroom in America, and perhaps in the habitable globe, will be equipped with apparatus for radio and television.'" Ending with a comment on "mike-fright," Cobb explained how revolutionary the medium had been in its early days: "'I recall that I was dizzy when I listened in only a few years ago on the first broadcast that I ever heard. And wasn't I dizzy the first time I tremblingly faced a microphone and tried to be comic!'"[36]

New York City became a center of radio broadcasting, and Cobb found work on programs such as the *Armour Hour* on NBC and the *Coca Cola Program* in the early 1930s. His performances usually consisted of telling Kentucky stories, giving an occasional interview, or delivering short talks on humorous topics. He wrote his own material. "If I must take to the air, I prefer this method," Cobb said, referring to a new series of radio programs. "It is the most convenient way I know of going places and staying home." The Kentuckian enjoyed the *Amos 'n' Andy* radio program, in which two white men—Charles J. Correll and Freeman F. Gosden—played two black men. He called their book, *Here They Are—Amos 'n' Andy*, "the finest expression of the Negro character in literature."[37]

In the early 1930s Cobb continued to write a monthly column for *Cosmopolitan*. He turned one of them, "To Be Taken before Sailing," into a forty-five-page book about the problems of traveling abroad. His advice to travelers was full of typical Cobbian humor. For example, during one's first voyage to Europe, one should "send souvenir postcards to envious stay-at-homers" and then "brag on [one's] return of having visited the Old World." The tired traveler should "be able to say when somebody mentions an art-gallery or a cathedral or a castle or what-not: 'Oh yes, I've been there.'"[38]

Cobb was often caught between different genres. "On the whole, I think I prefer to write serious stories than humorous ones," he told a publisher in 1929. His last book published by Cosmopolitan in 1931, *Incredible Truth,* was entirely different from *To Be Taken before Sailing,* illustrating this dichotomy. In each of its thirty-four chapters, Cobb used a formula he had not tried before, writing either a first-person account or a later rendition of an important news story from the past. "In compiling the material of this volume, I have endeavored to deal with my subjects as a modern newspaperman would deal with them." Cobb covered events occurring over a period of 500 years—the terrible winter at Valley Forge, witchcraft, Pliny the Younger reporting on the destruction of Pompeii, the St. Bartholomew's Day massacre—but not in chronological order. He employed a method similar to that used by CBS in its *Hear It Now* radio series and in the later television series *See It Now.* Cobb continued to display his versatility, whether writing comedy or drama.[39]

In October 1931 Ray Long left *Cosmopolitan* to fulfill his lifelong ambition of owning a publishing company. The next year, Ray Long and Richard R. Smith Inc. published *Down Yonder with Judge Priest and Irvin S. Cobb,* compiling twelve stories from his magazine repertoire. Most were entirely predictable, with Judge Priest representing the underdog and winning out in the end. Newspaper reviewers were kind but not overly enthusiastic. The *New York Times* pointed out a problem as both Cobb and his favorite character aged: "People who dislike reading dialect will not approve the book, nor will sophisticated tastes find the stories congenial, but for the more easily amused reading public, Judge Priest redivivus should be just the right fare." This was the only Cobb book published by Long, who experienced emotional and financial problems that ended with his suicide in 1935. Cobb stuck with Long through some trying times and considered him a friend, and he attended Long's funeral.[40]

The year 1932 was not a happy one for Cobb. His fiction production seemed to be at a standstill, but he was still making money with "Cobb's Comments," a nearly daily syndicated column that replaced "My Favorite Stories," which he had written in the 1920s. Moreover, his mother, Manie, died on January 27. She had been a widow for three and a half decades. Though Cobb claimed she had no "religious prejudice," like many "southern" women she still held a grudge and distrusted "Yankees." Cobb's spinster sister, Reubie, who had stayed at home to care for her mother, married a local man just three days after Manie's death. "They were engaged for forty years. Forty years!" exclaimed Buff. Unfortunately, both Reubie and her husband died within a year. Buff had a second child, Irvin Cobb Brody, born in 1931, but after her second marriage failed, she and the children moved in with her parents in New York City.[41]

Cobb no longer had a book contract to automatically publish his articles and stories in book form, so in 1933 he published some old *Cosmopolitan* and other pieces in *One Way to Stop a Panic* under the imprimatur of "The Laugh Club, New York," even writing his own prefaces for each piece. The book did not sell well.[42] However, Cobb soon found another legitimate publisher: Bobbs-Merrill of Indianapolis, Indiana. The firm had grown from a bookstore in 1850 to a major publisher of school textbooks, medical and law books, and trade books in the early 1930s. Cobb first shopped a manuscript there in October 1932. Later, while filling out a company questionnaire, Cobb demonstrated his sense of humor. Under "Personal Dislikes," he listed "People who get up fool questionnaires." To "How I happened to write that book," he replied, "I needed the money." He received an advance of $500. Cobb's correspondence with literary editor David Laurance Chambers indicated that his career was back on track. "I must tell you again how proud and happy we are to number you in our family of authors, and how eager we are to start publishing for you," Chambers wrote to Cobb. In a study of Bobbs-Merrill, Chambers is presented as a taskmaster who often quarreled with the authors he handled. In this case, Chambers refused Cobb's proposed title of *Blood Money*, along with eighteen other suggestions. In the end, *Murder Day by Day* was the title chosen by Chambers.[43]

Murder Day by Day followed the device used by Agatha Christie in *The Murder of Roger Ackroyd*, published in 1926, wherein the erudite narrator turns out to be the cold-blooded if well-educated culprit who is presumably doing society a favor by murdering a villain or two. Even today, *Murder Day by Day* is fun to read. It is well plotted and riveting in detail. Cobb leads the reader up several blind alleys and introduces a number of interesting characters. However, the book went almost unnoticed by the press. The *New York Herald-Tribune*'s reviewer called it "a rip-roaring good mystery yarn packed with thrills and told by a prince of story tellers. We won't even tell you to what famous lady novelist Mr. Cobb may or may not owe his main trick—and a very slick one it is, too." In the end, former newspaperman Gilbert Jonathan Redd confesses to his friend, an intrepid police investigator, that he is indeed guilty of murdering a scoundrel, thereby saving a young couple from suspicion. "Being a Southerner-born," Redd downs "a Bourbon toddy" and then takes his own life.[44]

Bobbs-Merrill also picked up another Cobb manuscript, published as *Faith, Hope and Charity,* a compilation of stories that appeared previously in *Cosmopolitan* and other magazines. Cobb preferred the title *To Make a Long Story Short,* but once again, Chambers overruled him. Meanwhile, Cobb's New York literary agent and brother-in-law Hewitt H. Howland suggested the possibility of writing an Old Judge Priest mystery book.[45]

As always, Cobb was good for a news story, such as the time he added extra alcohol to near beer ahead of the complete suspension of Prohibition. "Cobb's eyes bulge" as he enjoys a pint at the "Lion Brewery" in New York City, ran the picture caption. After Prohibition ended, Cobb participated in an alcohol-mixing contest against "Eddie of the Astor, famous bartender," with journalist Heywood Broun as the judge. The event was held in Cobb's Park Avenue apartment, and reporters covered it for a laugh and a story. After tasting several bourbon-laced juleps, Broun declared Cobb the winner and prepared to go home. Cobb, who had sampled a couple of his own concoctions, declared, "Mr. Broun, I thank you on behalf of the people of Kentucky. I think I'll go home too. Oh, I'm already home? Excuse me."[46]

Barely able to hide his glee about the end of Prohibition, Cobb wrote a very short satirical booklet about the "opening of the new-old Waldorf Bar"—a men-only establishment—in New York City in 1934. His over-the-top wording is still worth reading today: "Our generation and succeeding generations surely may go on and on taking joy out of the new Waldorf-Astoria's Gentlemen's Bar, which in spirit and in essence and in the accomplished deed, will be even as the old Waldorf-Astoria Gentlemen's Bar was—a 'Who's Who' of American Gentility and American Genius, a 'Here's How' of typically American good cheer, good fellowship, good companionship—and good things for to eat and for to drink!"[47]

Cobb began to explore more lucrative outlets for his talents. His last real venture in Hollywood had been in 1927, writing the scenario for *Turkish Delight,* a Cecil B. DeMille silent film. Although Bayard Veiller wrote the script for *The Woman Accused,* Cobb and nine other writers contributed to that 1933 movie, which the *New York Times* critic found "rather disappointing." Then a new opportunity came along at just the right time. Friend Will Rogers was about to begin shooting *Judge Priest,* based on Cobb's stories, in early 1934, and he asked the Kentuckian to come to the movie studio and "advise the production." Hal Roach wired Cobb, "If you feel like doing a series of shorts for this shop, why not come on out here at my expense and talk it over." In early April 1934 Cobb informed the Bobbs-Merrill office that he was moving to the West Coast and asked them to forward his mail to the Beverly-Wilshire Hotel in Los Angeles or the Hal Roach Studios in Culver City, California. Buff summed up her father's decision to make the leap to Hollywood: "He said he wanted the trip and the change, and the money. Nonsense! He wanted to act."[48]

11

A New Beginning and the Beginning of the End

Cobb's life to this point had taken several turns—from a small town in Kentucky to New York City, from newspaperman to short story writer, from a struggling young man to a well-to-do and famous fiction writer. But at age fifty-eight, where could he fit into Hollywood? A *Louisville Times* columnist reported that Cobb was "a man who loves cities and peoples and things; a man who has little time for self love." He is "a great big laughing creature who tells you in the first five minutes that he will give Hollywood two years of his time" before returning to his previous life. Was that really Cobb's plan, if he had one? Or was he simply drifting from one role to another in a life that had so far been quite successful?[1]

Cobb's personality always drew an audience. For example, when he sent his definition of "corn whisky" to the Federal Alcohol Control Administration soon after the end of Prohibition, it was a big news story. "There is no solace for the soul, no tonic for the body, like old Bourbon whisky," he intoned, arguing for the reputable variety of alcohol in *Irvin S. Cobb's Own Recipe Book,* published by Frankfort Distilleries in the mid-1930s. Part history and part humor, with a large helping of Old South nostalgia, the book includes a recipe section for the proper use of Kentucky's finest whiskey (usually spelled with an "e" in Kentucky). The recipes are very specific and end with a typical Cobbian tagline. For example, the recipe for the "Georgia Mint Julep" ends with the admonition to drink "and start singing 'Dixie.'" Cobb was always an excellent promoter, whether of himself or of a product (such as the advertisements he wrote for Ford three decades earlier).[2]

Moving to California was exciting for the Cobbs. "We were absolutely delighted with everything," Buff reported upon their arrival in California. "Sunshine, palm trees, . . . people, architecture, the movie business, the Pacific Ocean, Derby hats to eat in and Ye Olde Gasoline Shoppe at which to buy our gas, actors, agents, everything." Hal Roach put on a big welcoming party for them with a prison theme. The guests dressed up in prison uniforms and wore balls and chains; they were even fingerprinted and photographed. Apparently, Louis B. Mayer did not appreciate the humor and "departed in a huff."[3]

As Cobb was working his way into the Roach movie system, he did some advising for the film *Judge Priest*. At the invitation of director John Ford, he viewed the main set and suggested that "Town Hall" be changed to "City Hall" and "Rooming House" to "Boarding House" to fit 1890s Paducah. "'It's the most remarkable motion picture set I've ever seen,'" Cobb told the press.[4]

Cobb enjoyed the companionship of Will Rogers immensely. He sometimes appeared on Rogers's *Good Gulf Show,* broadcast from Los Angeles. Even when he was not a guest on the show, Cobb would sometimes sit in the audience. Rogers, who mostly ad-libbed his lines, once referred to his Kentucky friend as "our greatest humorist and when they remove the mantle at some future time, our historians—from Mr. Mark Twain, they won't have to take it very far—just from the Mississippi River right over to Paducah on the Ohio." On another program, broadcast on May 19, 1935, they engaged in friendly repartee. "Mr. Cobb is the author also of our most popular picture Judge Priest, the best I ever got mixed up in. . . . And now I take great pleasure in introducing my very good friend and one of America's greatest humorists, writers, and all-round human beings, Irvin Cobb. Hello, Irv [applause]." For the next several minutes they joked together like old friends.[5]

Meanwhile, Cobb tried to navigate his way in the highly competitive Hollywood movie business. A promotional page of "Hal Roach's Funnies" intended to highlight "Paducah's first Citizen" included various photographs of Cobb. In his first "two-reeler," Cobb played a steamboat captain, a role he relished because his great-grandfather had been one of the earliest captains on the rivers in and around Paducah. "'Thus it befalls that my title isn't altogether an imaginary one. I will be the fourth direct descent to play the role of Cap'n Cobb.'" Several still photos show him in scenes from the movies *Speaking of Relations, Nosed Out,* and *You Bring the Ducks* and as the character "Cap'n Cobb." Another photo shows Cobb laughing it up on the set with Laurel and Hardy, indicating Cobb's status as a rising star in the Roach studio.[6]

Roach left most of his productions in the hands of capable directors and avoided meddling. He produced not only the unforgettable Laurel and Hardy films but also the successful Harold Lloyd, Charlie Chase, and Our Gang comedies. Roach maintained in 1935 that "the gag's the thing," but it had to be put into a social and personal context. Slapstick worked in silent films, but when talkies came along, there had to be a story line and the audience had to empathize with the characters. Those developed for Laurel and Hardy worked; Cobb's, unfortunately, did not.[7]

Roach and his associates envisioned Cobb playing a homespun character beset by the world's problems. W. C. Fields, who often portrayed a bumbling fat man, may have been Roach's inspiration for Cobb's character, but he used his fat-man image in a more benign fashion. Seven short films were projected for Roach's All-Star series, which had Cobb "wandering through a malevolent world of irritating relatives and escaped convicts, spouting homespun witticisms all the way," according to Roach biographer Richard Lewis Ward. However, "the Cobb series was so unpopular with exhibitors that it was canceled after only four films, one of which was not even released to theaters." A still photo from one of Cobb's movies shows him dressed in female garb between two character actors. I think he was embarrassed by the whole episode. A photograph of Cobb and Roach mulling over a script in Ward's book is captioned: "Irvin S. Cobb wondering why audiences aren't laughing, 1934. Hal Roach seems to know." The "Irvin S. Cobb fiasco" ended the All-Star series.[8]

Nevertheless, Cobb had Laura close up their New York apartment and their house on Long Island and join him in California. Irvin promised they would only rent a place until they had made a firm decision to stay in California. However, after looking at 1717 San Vicente Boulevard in Santa Monica, Irvin surprised his wife with the announcement that he had purchased the home, formerly owned by film star Greta Garbo. The next year Buff and her two children, Pat and Cobbie, joined her parents in California. "Oh, how grateful I was to be able to pack the kids and myself on the train and head for the sunset and my mother's house!" Odd McIntyre, in his "New York Day by Day" column, reported that his friends the Cobbs "will spend six months in California and six months in New York." However, Irvin intended to make California his permanent home.[9]

Neither Cobb in *Exit Laughing* nor Buff in *My Wayward Parent* mentioned his failure to catch on as one of Roach's main attractions. It was as if those movies had never been made. Cobb was not used to failure, and it must have hurt his pride immensely. *Irvin S. Cobb: His Life and Letters,* published in 1938 by Fred G. Neuman of Paducah, mentions the Roach studio episode as only a detour leading to better days. Cobb even quipped about his foray into acting: "'It provides a complete mental rest but it's hard on the feet.'"[10]

Though Cobb was not writing as much as he had earlier in his career, he continued to pen the occasional piece for *Cosmopolitan, Smart Set,* and *Golden Book Magazine.* I think he wrote mostly for pleasure as he aged—not that he couldn't use the money. He wrote mostly mystery stories, with an occasional Judge Priest story and some western pieces. At this late date, there would be no change in either his writing style or the subjects he chose. For example, he wrote a comical piece for *Cosmopolitan* called "Why Are Women Like That?" And he wrote another on food—one of his favorite subjects—entitled, "Thanksgiving . . . with Corn-bread Stuffing." The first banked on Cobb's continuing bewilderment with women, and the latter casually noted, "A black mammy anywhere in the interior South [can] instruct him [a European chef] in the right use of the frying pan."[11]

Once Cobb decided to stay in California, his output tapered off. If he could not make it as a movie star in his own right, there were other roles he could play in Hollywood. He spent considerable time with Will Rogers and other friends such as Leo Carrillo and Gilbert Roland, as he fell into the California lifestyle. Soon after arriving in Hollywood, Irvin and Buff visited the Rogers ranch one day. Along with a group that included Odd McIntyre and Billie Burke, they took a trip up into the hills in a wagon pulled by two mules and driven by Rogers. In his typical boyish style, Rogers described what happened in a posthumously published autobiographical item dated May 6, 1934 (with his typical misspellings and grammatical errors left intact): "Had some fun out here at old Uno

E Dos Mortgages Rancho [First and Second Mortgage Ranch] a couple of Sundays ago. . . . We drove up on a kind of high lookout. Its our local Pikes Peak. Must be at least 400 feet above sea level." As they descended the hill, "Well the brakes dident work." Rogers continued: "Cobb is in the very rear seat, and can't do the coaching that I figured he would be able to aid me with. He is leaning in toward the mountain side at an angle that must a been about horizontal." A mounted ranch hand riding alongside saved the day by leaping on one of the mules and reining it in. When the ladies on board, including Buff, decided to walk down the hill, Cobb "said he dident mind staying in, but he dident like to see the ladies walk down the hill alone as no telling what leading man might attack em."[12]

During the filming of *Judge Priest*, Cobb often hung around the set, making suggestions and gabbing with Rogers when they had time. A still photo from the Will Rogers Museum collection shows Cobb seated between Rogers in his Judge Priest costume and director John Ford. Other photos in this collection demonstrate the same close relationship between the two fast friends.

By the mid-1930s, Rogers had become an established star on radio and in the movies, and his newspaper column was read by millions. He transitioned from silent films into the sound era and became an even bigger attraction. His persona fit the movies of the time, filling a niche that had earlier been occupied by Harry Carey in John Ford's silent films. Rogers was considered a scriptwriter's "worst nightmare" because he would not follow directions. However, "he knew how to play himself superbly," and that is what his audiences loved. His pay grew from $110,000 per movie to $125,000 plus 10 percent of the profits. Though he played "everyman" in his movies and certainly sympathized with the plight of the average person during the Great Depression, he was quite wealthy.[13]

Judge Priest, based on several of Cobb's writings, was filmed in the professional Hollywood style of the day, with a screenplay by veteran writers Dudley Nichols and Lamar Trotti. Director John Ford had a long and distinguished career, despite problems with alcohol and a somewhat tempestuous marriage. Cobb dubbed Mary Ford "the lion tamer." *The Informer* was Ford's "first great success" critically, but three movies starring Rogers filmed between 1933 and 1935 at Fox—*Dr. Bull, Judge Priest,* and *Steamboat 'Round the Bend*—were his "real bread and butter" of the Great Depression era.[14]

Judge Priest is considered one of Rogers's best films. But today it is usually dismissed as an inconsequential and campy period piece full of racism. One website commentator remarked: "If this is the sort of film that appealed to 1930's audiences, then they deserved the Great Depression they were in. *Judge Priest* is one of the most offensive, bitter movies ever made, a low point for all involved. *Judge Priest* is watchable only as a masochistic experiment in how much offensively intolerable material you can stand. If you make it through the entire film without becoming scarlet-red with frustration, you're either a monster or you're Buddha."[15]

A sampling of other Internet comments reveals similar viewpoints. Modern viewers simply abhor the movie. However, as described by Rogers biographer Ben Yagoda, *"Judge Priest* is a misty-eyed depiction of life in the Old South. Thus mint juleps are ubiquitous and the only blacks in evidence are shuffling Stepin Fetchit and the bandana-wearing, spiritual-singing Hattie McDaniel. Yet it is part of the movie's charm that the extremely loose-constructionist jurist played by Will relates to these characters with an affectionate, not unrespectful give-and-take."[16]

Judge Priest opens with the judge, appropriately, reading an issue of the *Louisville Courier-Journal* (although it is a contemporary issue rather than one from the 1890s), slamming down his gavel, and declaring, "Here, Here, Here, court's called to order." Then the opening credits run—"Fox Films Presents Will Rogers in Irvin S. Cobb's Judge Priest"—as a syrupy version of "My Old Kentucky Home" plays in the background against the backdrop of Priest's old mansion. As a sign of its authenticity, a quotation from Cobb is projected on the screen: "The figures of this story are familiar ghosts of my own childhood. The War between the States was over, but its tragedies and comedies haunted every grown man's mind." To Cobb, Priest represented the "tolerance" that pervaded this idyllic scene, where everyone knew his station in life.[17]

The setting is basically a Cobbian version of his Paducah hometown, circa 1890. Priest is a longtime widower and a loner in many ways. The movie includes a love story between Priest's nephew, Rome Cobb (Tom Brown), and a young woman, Ellie May (Anita Louise), whom Rome's mother considers beneath his station (Rome is a lawyer). That is only one source of conflict. Another is the rivalry between Priest and his opponent in an upcoming election, bombastic state senator Maydew. While Priest is a pragmatist and a realist, Maydew follows the letter of the law. Priest is the soul of compromise and reconciliation, and as he did in all Cobb's stories, he will eventually resolve whatever problems there are. Priest is like many of Ford's main characters—played by Harry Carey, Will Rogers, and John Wayne—who are willing to go against the rules of society to do the right thing. To Ford, Priest and these other characters depict the "American Adam," a mythic individual who is always on the side of justice.[18]

All the characters in *Judge Priest* are stereotypical southerners, men and women, black and white. Priest's closest male companions are all Confederate veterans. The African Americans are all hackneyed characterizations. Stepin Fetchit, whose real name was Lincoln Perry (1902–1985), played Jeff Poindexter, who is a defendant in a vagrancy case being prosecuted by the pompous Maydew. Onscreen, Fetchit is a "shuffling, inarticulate, bone-lazy" black underling, just as Cobb described him in all his stories, and just as white audiences envisioned African Americans at the time. As one biographer of Fetchit revealed, to blacks, he was "puttin' on massa" in "a running joke" that blacks understood but escaped whites. "For most blacks, it was ironic farce; for many whites, it was sociological verity," according to Mel Watkins. Hattie McDaniel played Aunt Dilsey, Priest's washerwoman, and she sang solos as well as duets with Rogers. Her "sassiness" contrasted with Fetchit's submissiveness. She is listed in the credits (although her name is misspelled "McDaniels"), testifying to her importance in the movie.[19]

Unlike the website commentator quoted earlier, Ford biographer Tag Gallagher called *Judge Priest* "one of Ford's finest and most convivial works." As the story develops, blacksmith Bob Gillis is arrested for defending the honor of Ellie May against a villainous barber and his cohorts. The centerpiece of the film is Gillis's trial. When challenged by prosecutor Maydew as being biased, Priest steps down as judge. As the case progresses, all the evidence seems to be against Gillis. Young lawyer Rome is out of his element in defending Gillis, but his uncle comes to the rescue, acting as his co-counsel. Priest, of course, has a card up his sleeve, because he has learned the true identity of Gillis, who secretly is the father of Ellie May. Henry B. Walthall, playing Reverend Brand, the local minister, breaks his silence and reveals on the witness stand that Gillis served honorably as a Confederate soldier after being freed from a prison chain gang in the waning months of the war. Walthall, who also appeared in

The Birth of a Nation, steals the scene as he describes the Gillis's heroism, with dramatic footage of a battle playing in the background. The jurors, already sympathetic to any of their Confederate brethren, begin to fall for Priest's plan, as Stepin Fetchit and his fellow blacks outside the courtroom sing a rousing rendition of "Dixie." This is exactly the same ploy Cobb used in one of his first Judge Priest stories, "Words and Music," published in 1911. Ford always inserted elements of comedy in his films, even his most serious ones. Actor Francis Ford, who throughout the trial has been spitting tobacco juice in the direction of the hated Maydew, shouts: "Hooray for Jeff Davis, the Southern Confederacy, and Bob Gillis!" All ends well. Priest is reelected circuit judge, Rome and Ellie May marry, and Gillis, carrying the Stars and Bars, joins a parade of Confederate veterans as happy Negroes sing and cavort on the sidelines. If this ending seems manipulated to modern moviegoers, it is, but this is true of all films. One important segment did not make it into the final film. Ford shot a lynching sequence in which Priest confronts a mob and saves an innocent black man from hanging. However, the studio cut this scene, finding it too controversial for the times.[20]

Judge Priest renewed Cobb's belief in himself and his career. The film received excellent newspaper coverage when it was released in the fall of 1934, owing to the celebrity and success of Will Rogers. All through September and October the film received much press attention, which often included a mention of Cobb as creator of the main character. The *Chicago Tribune* hailed the movie, stating, "You ain't seen 'Judge Priest'? Then you ain't seen nothing yet!" In interviews, Cobb praised the film and explained how he had developed his characterizations. A trade paper, the *Hollywood Reporter,* concluded that the movie was "calculated to bring forth laughter and tears in such rapid succession that you're rather proud of that sentimental streak in you that you've been hiding so long."[21]

While searching for a role in Hollywood, Cobb found work as a "Dixie expert" during the filming of *Mississippi,* starring Bing Crosby, Joan Bennett, and W. C. Fields. In a lighthearted column, Idwal Jones of the *New York Times* described Cobb's impact on the film: "As a judge, Cobb had handed down decisions in the filming of 'Mississippi.' Three concerned hounds, two the right amount of mint in juleps, and one on diction. He made it clear that 'Yo'all' is proper Dixie if addressed to more than one person at a time." However, when Cobb suggested that the word *jute* be substituted for *burlap,* he was overruled by an "indignant Mayor in Texas" who claimed that the name had been used circa 1869, the time frame of the film. Jones described Cobb as looking "solemner than he looks in his photographs," a bit older, and with his ever-present cigar.[22]

By early 1935, Cobb had become enough of a Hollywood insider to be invited to serve as master of ceremonies at the Academy Awards presentations. *It Happened One Night* starring Clark Gable and Claudette Colbert won five awards that year. Cobb played to the audience by shouting over the loudspeaker as he opened the envelope, "It is something that . . . ," and the audience responded, "Happened One Night!" He also had the honor of presenting a special award to child star Shirley Temple, and a photograph of her giving him a kiss appeared in the press. "The whole affair glittered in the best Hollywood tradition and Cobb got a scant two feet away from the platform before lighting his big, black cigar," reported the Louisville newspapers.[23]

Cobb's biggest opportunity in Hollywood came thanks to his friendship with Will Rogers. *Steamboat 'Round the Bend,* based on the novel by Ben Lucien Burman, was another of Ford's attempts to portray an "Edenic timelessness, the river serving as the metaphor for eternal freedom and rebirth." Though this description from Peter Stowell's fine biography of Ford sounds a bit overblown, it perfectly describes the movie's simple yet effective depiction of a post–Civil War Mississippi River community.[24]

Rogers wanted Cobb to play the role of a rival steamboat captain. When "the studio manager told Cobb it was not much of a part," Cobb replied, "'I am not much of an actor.'" Rogers was noted for getting others started in "their motion-picture careers" and letting someone else steal a scene while he stayed in the background. He must have intended to do that for Cobb. Besides, he liked having Cobb around to talk to between scenes.[25]

The story line of *Steamboat* was simple enough, playing to the strengths of Rogers's personality. Though the movie ends with a steamboat race in which Rogers's *Claremore Queen* battles Cobb's *Pride of Paducah,* the subplots include a love story and a miscarriage of justice, as well as humorous scenes interspersed along the way. Filmed on the Sacramento River, Rogers joked on his radio program on May 19, 1935, that they would have filmed on the Los Angeles River, "but they'd have had to haul the water too far." He told listeners, "Cobb is the captain of the *Pride of Paducah,* and I'm the admiral of the *Claremore Queen*. If this news of *Claremore* gets back to Claremore that they had a big steam-wheeler named after 'em, it'll be a surprise to them. . . . Cobb's been on a riverboat before, and he's kind of our technical director, too."[26]

As usual, Rogers played himself. He would typically be given the general idea of the plot and then fill in the details in his own words. Ford did not demand an early work schedule, and this suited Rogers's dilatory ways; he also took time out during filming to type his daily newspaper column. However, once everyone was assembled and Rogers got into character, it usually required only one take to get the scene right. Rogers's acting method has been described as both unorthodox and hilarious. "'I don't think he ever read a script at home,'" Ford later recalled. When Ford asked if he had read the script, Rogers replied, according to Cobb: "'Who, me?' said Will, in pretended surprise. 'When did I ever read one of those fool things? I been too busy roping calves and romancing around.'" According to Cobb, he and Will agreed to make up each other's "speeches." They kept the exasperated Ford and his crew waiting for precious minutes, after which Ford congratulated them on their ad-libbing. One time, however, Ford demanded, "'You'll play this scene and play it right or I'll have you thrown into the river—and I hope neither one of you can swim.'"[27]

As Dr. John Pearly, "a snake-oil hawker and riverboat captain," Rogers shambles along in his usual pattern. Early on, Cobb as Captain Eli challenges Pearly to a race, with the prize being the loser's steamboat. The race becomes a side issue as Pearly's nephew Duke (John McGuire) is falsely accused of murder (he claims self-defense). His girlfriend Fleety Belle (Anne Shirley) stays with Pearly on his riverboat when Duke goes to jail. Meanwhile, Pearly hauls on board a wax museum of historical figures that he renames for his unlettered audiences as he attempts to raise $500 to hire a lawyer for Duke. The cast is small and brilliant. Francis Ford reprises his role in *Judge Priest* as a whiskey-swilling, tobacco-chewing comedian, as does Stepin Fetchit as a stereotypical fawning Negro. Pearly and his motley crew search the river for the "New Moses," hilariously played by white-robed Berton Churchill (who played the pompous Senator Maydew in *Judge Priest*), because he holds the key to exonerating Duke. When Pearly joins the steamboat race, he and Captain Eli engage in repartee as they steam down the river. In one scene, Pearly lassos the back of the *Pride of Paducah* and lets the larger boat tow his throughout the night. When Captain Eli awakes and orders a crew member to cut the rope, Pearly mocks him. Of course, *Steamboat 'Round the Bend* must have a happy ending. Pearly lassos the New Moses from the shore and hauls him aboard, and they proceed toward the finish line, which happens to be located in the town where Duke is scheduled to be executed. Pearly can defeat the *Pride of Paducah* only by throwing his wax figures into maws of his furnaces. As fire belches from the smokestacks of the *Claremore*, Cobb's expression is quite funny as his steamboat falls behind. Duke is saved, and in the final scene Pearly rests on the deck of the *Pride of Paducah*, content that he, like Judge Priest, has saved the day. "This is nostalgia at its best," according to Stowell, though it seems a bit contrived and corny for today's audiences.[28]

At the end of shooting *Steamboat 'Round the Bend*, Rogers invited Cobb to his ranch for some horseback riding, explaining that Cobb on horseback was a most comical sight. Cobb declined, saying he had some writing to do at home. "I waved my hand in farewell and hurried off. I was afraid I would succumb to temptation," Cobb recalled. "'Better change your mind, old-timer,' he called after me. 'I may not be seeing you for quite a spell.'"[29]

An avid supporter of aviation, Rogers left Hollywood for a trip to Alaska in August 1935. Well-known pilot Wiley Post had redesigned a monoplane with a larger engine and pontoons for the arduous journey into the Alaskan wilderness. Soon after takeoff for a flight to Point Barrow, the plane plunged into a river, killing both pilot and passenger instantly. Cobb was visiting New York when he heard the news. "PLEASE COMMAND ME FOR ANY POSSIBLE SERVICE FOR YOU AND YOURS. MRS COBB JOINS ME IN AFFECTIONATE SYMPATHY FOR ALL OF YOU," Cobb wired from the Newark, New Jersey, airport. A photograph of the Cobbs at Rogers's funeral depicted a grief-stricken couple who had lost a dear friend and colleague. A deputy sheriff assigned to crowd control recognized Cobb, Mary Pickford, James A. Farley, Amelia Earhart, Eddie Cantor, and Harry Carey among the "well known people" that passed him on the way to services at the Little Church of the Flowers and internment at Forest Lawn Cemetery in Los Angeles. The deputy reported a solemn and dignified ceremony.[30]

The death of Rogers dealt a heavy blow to Cobb. He had already lost close friends Charley Russell, Ray Long, and Will Hogg, so this loss was devastating. He wrote lovingly of his friendship with Will, whom he often referred to as "Bill" (just as he had Will Hogg). Writing as if Rogers were entering a heaven that looked like a ranch, where his old friends were waiting, Cobb opined that the "Almighty Range Boss" would have said: "So step up, old-timer, and sit down with me by this bunkhouse and let's just talk things over. There's a lot of the boys waiting to meet you!" Cobb went on to lament, "In my heart are a thousand things I'd like to say about Will Rogers—his sweet sanity, his gallantry, his kindliness which was like a well that never went dry—but there's a lump here in my throat that keeps them back." Cobb lost one his best friends in Will Rogers, as well as someone who had championed his career in Hollywood.[31]

The release of *Steamboat 'Round the Bend* a few weeks after the death of Will Rogers only added to his legend. Cobb's role was prominently mentioned in reviews, but he was clearly no actor—neither a natural one like Rogers nor one trained in the art. Though his evocation of Captain Eli was not highly applauded, he had played the part well and understood his limitations as an actor. The *Louisville Times* praised him, noting that "there is in Mr. Cobb a likeableness that no kind of acting, one imagines, can obliterate. Doubtless he will make more friends than enemies in *Steamboat 'Round the Bend.*"[32]

Cobb enjoyed the atmosphere of a film set, claiming that whereas writing was a "lonely, thankless job," there was "a heap of fun connected with the work (of acting). I wish I'd started forty years ago." He was busy from 1936 through 1938 with his movie career; his newspaper columns, variously called "Cobb's Comments" and then "What Irvin S. Cobb Thinks About," syndicated by the North American Newspaper Alliance; and a new radio venture, *Paducah Plantation,* a weekly program on NBC. In the latter he spun tales about his upbringing in Paducah; there were also musical acts, including performances by popular radio star Dorothy Page. Soon he could be seen starring in *Everybody's Old Man,* another Fox film, with Jane Withers, a rising young star. In the final scene, Cobb presents her with a bag containing $5,000 and reportedly devised her line at the last minute. When asked what she is going to do with the money, Withers replies, "Count it!" People in the movie industry appreciated his ability to come up with effective dialogue. To his good friend Alice Hogg (the wife of Mike, Will Hogg's brother), Cobb expressed pride over his reception by members of the press, one of whom claimed he was "Will Rogers with a double chin." In the *Louisville Courier-Journal,* critic Boyd Martin wrote that Cobb "comes through like a veteran of an actor, which he probably has been, at heart, all these years." The Strand Theatre in Louisville billed the movie as "the picture WILL ROGERS would have made." Was Cobb on his way to movie fame? In *Pepper* (1936), with Withers and comic Slim Summerville, Cobb played a minor role as a millionaire. Then he played Captain O'Hare, the commander of a steamship, in *Hawaii Calls*, a 1938 thriller about Japanese spies. The latter movie played all over the United States in and much of the English-speaking world; for example, it was advertised in a local newspaper in Trentham, New Zealand, in July 1938. Cobb's last movie role, a very minor one, was in another 1938 movie, *The Arkansas Traveler*. Although Cobb is credited with writing the story on which *Our Leading Citizen* (1939) is based, the screenplay was written by Jack Moffitt. *New York Times* movie critic Frank S. Nugent disparaged that movie as an unrealistic, Pollyannaish view of how to turn around the American economy. Cobb expected to play a role in *Public Nuisance No. 1*, but he did not get the part; nor did he play an announced role in *The Young in Heart* (1938). All told, his movie career lasted less than five years.[33]

As Cobb aged, health problems compounded by overeating made his life increasingly miserable. Though in public he seemed to be the same unflappable fat man, always good for a quotable quip, his appearance had changed. Even in his earliest pictures his teeth were noticeably mis-aligned, and he had bridgework done during his early days in New York City. He told the Hoggs: "I had a rotten time with my teeth, to begin with—still am having some. There must have been a lot of poison in my system and part of it is still there. Anyhow I lost appetite—think of Ivory [a pet name] without an appetite!" In *My Wayward Parent*, Buff told a humorous story that occurred after her father had all his teeth pulled and he had been fitted with dentures. While attending a movie, he "mislaid his new store teeth. It seems that he had slyly withdrawn them during the performance, and tucked them in his pocket." Somehow, the teeth fell out of his pocket, and according to Buff, "none of us noticed he was as tooth-less as an angleworm, or that his face, sans denture, was folded up like an accordion." The dentures were found the next day by a cleaning woman at the movie theater.[34]

As Cobb's movie career ended and his health declined, so did his wealth. For all his apparent success in Hollywood, the lifestyle took a toll on his pocketbook (as had the stock market crash of 1929). For example, soon after settling in, the Cobbs cut back on throwing lavish parties, owing to the expense. Their finances took another hit when he lost his syndicated column "Cobb's Comments." Buff reported that "the syndicate letter nearly killed him."[35]

Eventually, the Cobbs sold their New York City apartment and their mansion on Long Island. Cobb's life in Hollywood seemed to be going downhill quickly. "Hollywood is the easiest place in the world to drop out of sight," Buff lamented. After the election of Franklin Roosevelt in 1932 and the beginning of the New Deal, Cobb's political and economic views turned more conservative. He moved away from his longtime allegiance to the Democratic Party and toward the Republicans. Owing in part to his southern upbringing, Cobb did not like what was happening in the United States in the 1930s.[36]

Cobb, however, did not have the political stature of a Will Rogers. Perhaps because of his wealth, Rogers was able to chide both political parties without rancor. His humor was direct but not biting or bitter like Cobb's; therefore, Rogers could be on good terms with both President Roosevelt and the Republican leadership of Congress. His most famous political adage—"I am not a member of any organized political party—I'm a Democrat"—endeared him to the public. Rogers's boyish grin and mild demeanor contrasted with Cobb's increasing bitterness. It is obvious that Rogers died at the height of his fame and influence, which may have diminished over time, whereas Cobb had in many ways outlived his time.[37]

Though Cobb had apparently voted for Roosevelt in 1932 and 1936, he was never invited to the White House. He did not approve at all of New Deal legislation or Democratic control of Congress. In his column "Cobb's Comments," Cobb joked in mid-1935, "Congress finally did something that had the approval of everybody. It adjourned." A week later he railed against the unemployed, observing that he had raised himself up by his bootstraps. His articles became sarcastic rather than humorous. In 1934 and 1938 Cobb publicly supported Republican Frank F. Merriam for governor of California.[38]

At last, Cobb and his old nemesis H. L. Mencken agreed on something: they detested Roosevelt and the New Deal. Mencken, who had voted for FDR in 1932, soon soured on the new administration, which he described as a "dreadful burlesque of civilized government." He called the president one of the "obvious demagogues" that populated the Great Depression world. As early as 1934, in a piece for *Cosmopolitan,* Cobb renounced the New Deal and its incessant creation of programs. "As for our President, surely nobody will begrudge him his holiday. But the man won't rest. With twenty-six letters already practically exhausted, he's sure to wear himself to a frazzle trying to think up a lot more new sets of initials for this and that. If this administration ever lands in the soup, it will be alphabet soup!" Cobb and former president Herbert Hoover appeared together when both were guests of honor at a banquet in Los Angeles in 1934, and a few years later he had nothing but praise for Hoover. Cobb noted that the first time he had voted against Hoover in 1928 "it was party gesture," whereas "the second time it was a grievous error which I have since repented in sackcloth and ashes." Having witnessed the actions of the current president and Congress, Cobb preferred the days of the Hoover administration— apparently forgetting that the stock market crash and the beginning of the Great Depression had occurred during his term in office. Addressing Hoover, Cobb said: "Merely let me say to you, sir, that we are grateful because during your occupancy of the White House you never got the idea of burning down the temple of our fathers in order to destroy a few cockroaches in the basement."[39]

Cobb's animadversion of the Roosevelt administration was even more pronounced in his private correspondence. After the death of Will Hogg, Cobb kept up a steady correspondence with Mike and Alice Hogg in Houston, in which he disclosed his deepest feelings about economics and politics. As his financial situation worsened, he blamed it all on Roosevelt and the New Deal: "Well, if Roosevelt takes us to Hell in a hand basket, we'll all go together—if that's any consolation to anybody." To his friend Fred Neuman in Paducah, Cobb railed in mid-1939, "Roosevelt prosperity has ruined me too. If this be recovery, it's undoubtedly the smallest recovery in the history of the world." According to Cobb, the only good thing to come out of the Roosevelt administration was the American Guide series of the Federal Writers' Project. Even though Cobb complained about his finances during the late 1930s, it should be noted that he had a staff of seven at his Santa Monica home overlooking the Rivera Golf Course. This included "a colored couple who know how to cook corn bread and ham and how to fry chicken to the Cobbs' liking," his private secretary, Laura N. Paes, told Neuman. There was also a Swedish nursemaid for the grandchildren, a Japanese gardener, and "Narcissis the colored laundress (direct from Georgia)." Moreover, Paes reported that Cobb's library had grown so large that he found it necessary to give "away three thousand books," indicating both the size of his home and the extent of his reading tastes.[40]

Cobb's writing did not turn off as abruptly as indicated by Buff in *My Wayward Parent*. Although *Faith, Hope and Charity* turned out to be a near disaster, earning him "only about one third of its advance," Cobb later wrote two Judge Priest novellas—his final works starring that character. *Judge Priest Turns Detective* first appeared as a series of syndicated newspaper features in September and October 1936 and was published as a book by Bobbs-Merrill in 1937. The *Louisville Courier-Journal* touted the series with an advertising campaign. Late in his career Cobb turned his talents to writing children's books, perhaps to please his grandchildren; *AZAM: The Story of an Arabian Colt and His Friends* came out in 1937 and *Four Useful Pups* in 1940, both published by Rand-McNally. Neither sold well. I think he was trying to find a direction for his writing.[41]

The two novellas in *Judge Priest Turns Detective*, though interesting to read, are predictable and typical Cobb fare. When Bobbs-Merrill urged Cobb to attend a book signing, he refused. "I appreciate your kindly interest and the courtesy of Robinson's (bookstore) but I've always fought shy of these autography-signing events and I'm too set in my ways to break the rule." Cobb's agent Hewitt Howland told publisher David Chambers, Cobb "isn't in his usual fine spirits, and his usual accommodating mood, and there is nothing for it but to be patient as we can." *Judge Priest Turns Detective* got some decent reviews, but within a few months, sales flattened. Biographer Chatterton concluded, as do I, that this Judge Priest offering "was accepted as the last link in a saga that was ready to end, and did." In early January 1938, after conferring with Cobb, Howland wrote to Chambers: "For the record, Irvin Cobb consents to your dealing with Judge Priest's remains as you see fit." However, Chambers and Howland were already urging Cobb to write his memoirs. When Howland heard no word from Cobb about this project, he wrote to Chambers, "I'll step on his toes."[42]

12

Exit Laughing

Only a few days after the death of Will Rogers, Cobb alluded to his own quest to secure his place in American humor. Once nominated as the heir of Mark Twain, Cobb failed because, of course, there was no successor to Twain. Mocked by Mencken early in his career, Cobb added to his dilemma by becoming more comedian than humorist, and his brief movie career completed that transition. With the death of Rogers, some thought Cobb might step into "the man's beloved cowboy boots," but "they'll probably have to take soundings to find me," Cobb lamented. "But what nobler ambition for any American writing man, even though he fails, than trying to follow in Will's footsteps?"[1]

By early 1938, Cobb's career had apparently hit rock bottom. He continued to blame "Mr. Franklin Delano Roosevelt" for his financial problems, which forced him to borrow money. In personal letters to Alice and Mike Hogg, he poured out his greatest fears and disappointments:

My syndicated column died January 1 [1938] cutting off a source of income which wasn't large but helped mightily in the budget. Radio engagements are nil, seemingly for an indefinite period and good and all. Magazines won't buy my stuff any more at any price. [It] appears I'm old-fashioned or outmoded or something. And nobody at all wants to hire me either to write pictures or act in them. And so on and so forth, with my family obligations piling up on me within shooting distance of my sixtieth birthday. Well, what the hell! I had a good time while the going was good and I've no desire, if I'm to be either sickly or busted or a crabby disappointed dodo, to live to a ripe—or rancid—old age.[2]

Would Cobb fail to secure a lasting place among America's great humorists?

As it turned out, Cobb still had some writing to do. There was one last project. His brother-in-law Hewitt Howland and Bobbs-Merrill publisher David Laurance Chambers were pushing Cobb to write his memoirs. "I am aiming to start the memories within the next few days," he said in early 1938, but "I have been delayed at getting under way by pestiferous matters."[3]

The "pestiferous matters" Cobb referred to were his ongoing health problems. His stomach continued to bother him, and although he tried to lose weight, his love of spicy food and southern-style cooking often won out over his good intentions. He developed diabetes, he joked to the Hoggs, "on a falling sugar market." It seemed that no sooner had his health improved when another siege of illness occurred. "That damnable intestinal trouble has been playing a return date," Cobb said. "It has hung on now for more than two weeks and still bothering me to beat hell." Examination and x-rays showed "no growths, but lingering inflammation in the lower colon." Meanwhile, he found it difficult to work on his memoirs, and his financial condition deteriorated "because most of my investments [are] already pretty well weakened." Cobb suffered a new setback a few weeks later when he came down with pneumonia, necessitating another hospital stay of ten days. Eventually, he told the Hoggs, "I went to Palm Springs to try to bake out."[4]

Cobb's health concerns coincided with Buff's marital problems. As Buff's writing career blossomed, her second marriage began to fail. "Poor kid, she always picks 'em wrong," Cobb wrote to Alice Hogg. After the divorce, Buff reverted to her maiden name and retained custody of the children. "I wish to God she would find a real man," her father lamented. "She hasn't been able to work and goes around with the saddest eyes I ever saw. . . . When I look at her, sometimes, I want to bust out crying myself." Buff did not stay single for long. At age thirty-five she married Robert Cameron "Cam" Rogers (two years her senior) of Santa Barbara, California, in late November 1938 in Las Vegas. Her father told Mike and Alice Hogg that he approved of this marriage and asked whether the newlyweds could visit the Hoggs' estate in Mexico. All this personal turmoil coincided with the release of Cobb's last insignificant roles in motion pictures.[5]

With Buff's marriage, Cobb was relieved of some of his financial obligations. Moreover, once his health had improved somewhat, he began in earnest to write his memoirs. By mid-1939, Cobb's "life story" was well under way, and he had already decided to call it *Exit Laughing*. Howland kept Chambers informed of the status of the manuscript, and the latter replied: "Please tell Mr. Cobb how perfectly delighted I am to hear that he had made such fine progress with his autobiography. The title EXIT LAUGHING, is thoroughly characteristic, the real Cobb touch—but I hope it will be a very long time before he exits." Though Howland found the first two chapters to be excellent, he persuaded Cobb to rewrite the next four, as they were "pretty bad." Cobb reacted positively and made the revisions, believing "he will have enough left over for a follow-up to be called CURTAIN CALL."[6]

However, not long after his sixty-third birthday, Cobb had another serious "gastric disturbance," at first thought to be a heart attack, while at a San Francisco nightclub. Just before his release from the hospital, Cobb joked with the press, "'I couldn't have been stricken in a better place. Most of San Francisco's distinguished physicians and surgeons were there and I got $100,000 worth of free medical advice for nothing. It isn't often that a man can boast he had 15 doctors and lived.'" But to his friend Neuman, Cobb revealed, "I had a pretty close call." He told Alice Hogg, "I had a bad sudden gastric hemorrhage—came very near killing me but my heart saved me." He recovered very slowly into the fall of 1939, limiting his progress on the *Exit Laughing* manuscript. However, he could always find time to write something brief as a diversion, such as the introduction to *Roustabout Songs: A Collection of Ohio River Valley Songs,* published in 1939.[7]

Chambers had initially wanted an early spring 1940 release date for *Exit Laughing,* but Cobb slowed his writing and took an extended vacation to visit the Hoggs in Texas. Cobb continued to work on *Exit Laughing* into 1940, and it would eventually grow to be a 200,000-word manuscript. He insisted that "there are to be no illustrations in his autobiography," and no heavy editing. Chambers was amenable to these demands and even to the possibility of another book. "There is great excitement over your autobiography through our organization," Chambers wrote to

Cobb. "It is most delightful and we offer you our most cordial congratula-
tions. We assure you that EXIT LAUGHING will be featured on our list, and
that we will give it a real sure-nuff, honest-to-God advertising campaign."
Cobb could not have been happier, particularly since his contract provided him with a $1,000 advance and 10 percent of the $5 retail price for
the first 3,000 copies. However, further delays meant that the book would
not be ready for the 1940 Christmas season. Meanwhile, two anthologies
of his work, *Irvin Cobb at His Best* and *Favorite Humorous Stories of Irvin
Cobb,* appeared in 1940, but they were published by minor presses and did
not generate much income.[8]

Cobb also got involved in the presidential election of 1940. Although
he had voted for Roosevelt in 1932 and 1936, he continued to blame his
personal financial problems on the New Deal. Much of Cobb's depleted
energy went into the campaign as he became a leader in the "Democrats for Willkie" faction of the party. "Everywhere I go I find Democrats who either openly or privately are supporting Willkie," Cobb told
Mike Hogg. He hoped other famous Democrats would come out for the
Republican nominee. Rather melodramatically, Cobb privately referred
to Willkie as the "only Democrat running for president this year." Cobb
made public appearances in California and elsewhere in the West and
gave radio speeches in support of Willkie. All the while, *Exit Laughing*
was in production. Howland reported to Chambers: "He's getting some
grand publicity out of his speech for Willkie. Even Roosevelt voters seems
to have enjoyed it." Chambers wrote to Cobb that he had listened to the
humorist's speech from San Francisco and revealed, "I, too, am a Willkie
Democrat." However, when Cobb stated in an Oklahoma City speech
just before Election Day that Hitler and Mussolini had turned into dic-
tators after being elected three times, Henry Ward in the *Paducah Sun-
Democrat* and an editorial in the *Louisville Courier-Journal* corrected his
history. The *Courier-Journal,* owned by the pro-Roosevelt Bingham family, admitted that maybe the Paducah native was "just being funny" but
gently scolded him nevertheless. "Perhaps the moral of this episode is that
a cobbler is always best at his own last. And Mr. Cobb achieved fame as a
humorist—not as a political philosopher." Cobb overconfidently believed
that Willkie still had a chance to win, even on election night. In a letter
to Mike Hogg he wrote, "I think tonight's returns will show him a winner. If he isn't I'm going to start for Canada and stay there [actually, he

wanted to go to Canada on a prolonged hunting trip]." Roosevelt soundly defeated Willkie, carrying a majority of states and winning by a count of 449 to 82 in the Electoral College. Cobb was unhappy about a third term for Roosevelt, and he also opposed the rearming of the United States as World War II began.[9]

Cobb finally realized that his diabetes and his other health problems would severely limit his life. He admitted to "being a semi-invalid and having to take injections and this and that." He complained to Alice Hogg, "I'm puny as hell!" Doctors blamed his current health problems on his exertions during the recent presidential campaign. A trip to San Francisco—a city he dearly loved—revived his spirits some. However, when planning a trip to Paducah, Cobb instructed Neuman that it had to be a low-profile visit, limited to seeing a few old friends. "Since I am forbidden to do much jubilitating and partyfying I prefer to arrive without much publicity," he wrote. Moreover, Cobb had been famous for his after-dinner speeches for more than three decades, but he decided to call it quits in early February 1941 in a speech delivered to the Santa Monica Chamber of Commerce. He said that his doctors and his wife had warned him to cease such activities.[10]

With *Exit Laughing* in press, Howland reported to Chambers that Cobb "has made a real come-back as a result of his campaign speeches. EXIT LAUGHING will be a gainer, I hope." With proofreading and other final issues to be resolved, including the compilation of an extensive index, Cobb told a Bobbs-Merrill official, "It's been a hell of a job for everybody concerned, hasn't it?"[11]

In anticipation of the success of *Exit Laughing*, Bobbs-Merrill issued *Glory, Glory, Hallelujah!* an old-fashioned Paducah tale focused on Cobb's African American characters. The little sixty-one-page book highlights African American efforts in American military history, particularly during World War I. Apparently, it was not successful and is not mentioned in other Cobb biographies.[12]

Chambers kept his word, and Bobbs-Merrill carried out an extensive publicity program before the release of *Exit Laughing*, sending examination copies to bookstores, reviewers, and others. Most reviewers were complimentary, but the owner of a bookstore in Union City, New Jersey, critiqued *Exit Laughing* as "being boresome." Josephus Daniels, the ambassador to Mexico, highly praised the book. In a promotional advertisement, Robert Benchley, himself a famous humorist, claimed: "It's the kind of autobiography every newspaperman promises himself he'll write one day—but can't."[13]

Exit Laughing, at 572 pages, is a long, rambling memoir by one of the premier humorists of the early to mid-twentieth century. In forty-two chapters, Cobb presents what can only be described as a meandering life history, with asides on issues, events, and remembrances of people from his past (many of whom are unknown to modern readers). Cobb analyzes his mission in a long but descriptive sentence: "My purpose is to set down, more or less at random, certain memoirs of events and certain likenesses of individuals that have impressed me as being picturesque or fantastic or glamorous, which means that without too much regard for chronological order I shall range back and forth from the recollections of childhood, which are still so vivid, to happenings of comparatively recent occurrence, which last I'd probably forget altogether did I wait many more years before putting them down."[14]

Unlike Will Rogers, who famously said, "I never met a man I didn't like," Cobb disliked some people and abhorred others. However, he generally spoke favorably of the many individuals he met during his career as a newspaperman, magazine journalist, fiction writer, after-dinner speaker, movie scriptwriter, and "star." Though frank about his opinions of politicians and others, he left out any mention of critics such as H. L. Mencken, who had so bitterly attacked him just as he was trying to break into the very competitive field of humor. Cobb held a grudge against the intelligentsia in America, particularly well-educated easterners. Despite his extensive real-life experience, Cobb never got over his rather humble beginnings and lack of education. He was a prime example of the mythical American "self-made man," fending for himself in a hostile world. His early successes and his ability to make a substantial income appeared effortless, yet he worked very hard at his craft. Even today, a blogger cites this famous quote about the laborious task of writing: "Yes, there I sit, dashing it off at the rate of about an inch and a half an hour, using sweat for punctuation . . . every smooth, graceful line means another furrow in the head of its maker."[15]

Throughout his career, Cobb's critics found his successes galling to some extent. Cobb reacted by touting himself. If anything, he suffered from too much pride. Nevertheless, reviews and opinions of *Exit Laugh-*

ing, Cobb's last major book, were generally positive. In the friendlier ter-
ritory of Kentucky, the Lexington and Louisville papers were effusive, but
even in New York City, the response was positive. "Irvin Cobb's autobiography is journalism at its record best," stated the *Louisville Courier-Journal.* Fellow author and *New York Herald-Tribune* editor Stanley Walker
praised the book: "This is the man the whippersnappers would dismiss as
'overrated.' It cannot be done so easily. When he was going great guns he
was one of the best. . . . The old Cobb gusto, once he gets going cannot
be restrained, which is why his 'Exit Laughing' is, like the man himself,
full-blooded and shot through with what is known in the literary trade
these days as charming human juices. . . . 'Exit Laughing' is a lot of book.
It rambles, and it is unconsciously wordy in spots, but is it friendly and
human—genuine Cobb." Robert van Gelder in the *New York Times* was
not effusive but complimentary, adding that he hoped this was not really
the end of Cobb. Kansan William Allen White, legendary editor of the
Emporia Gazette, took a more long-ranged view of Cobb. In "The Humor
of the Self-Kidder," published in the *Saturday Review of Literature,* White
wrote: "This book is only incidentally the 'life story' of Irvin S. Cobb. It is
an adventure in humorous American humor. Taking it by and large, the
humor of Irvin Cobb's autobiography, which bubbles like eternal Pierian
springs on every page, is the humor of the self-kidder." White could not
restrain his praise. "I know of no book published in recent years which is
so American as 'Exit Laughing.'"[16]

Exit Laughing initially sold well, ranking among the nonfiction best
sellers of 1941, many of which were about the beginning of World War II.
The success gratified Cobb for two reasons. First, he was once again recognized as an important American writer. Second, he made some money
when he badly needed it. "The book is selling well, thank God!" he told
John Wilson Townsend. "I'll need the money." Meanwhile, he was working on a new manuscript with the material left over from *Exit Laughing.*[17]

When his health improved some, Cobb traveled to Kentucky by way
of New York City, where Buff lived, in mid-1942. He made a brief appearance at the Pendennis Club in Louisville and then visited Paducah without fanfare, where he stayed in a special suite kept for him at the Hotel
Irvin Cobb. He took time to publicize his support for the appointment of
a friend, Kentucky's administrator of the Works Progress Administration,
as chief of the Office of Price Administration. However, with his energies

mostly spent, he did not visit the Hoggs in Houston and soon returned to California.[18]

After the attack on Pearl Harbor, Cobb's patriotic spirit returned, reminiscent of his ardor during World War I. To his friend Mike Hogg, Cobb sent a book Bobbs-Merrill published in 1942 entitled *Roll Call.* "Here lately I got to free-versing," Cobb told his Texas friend. While biographer Lawson correctly describes this forty-page book of text and illustrations as "a sentimental mélange of poetry and prose of a Vachel Lindsey flavor," Chatterton, taking a more literary viewpoint, ignores this important insight into Cobb's last years. In seven short chapters, each accompanied by a Warren Chappell illustration, Cobb praises America's heroic past, emphasizing such notables as "Dan'l Boone," "Moll Pitcher," and "Old Hickory," with a patriotic refrain at the end of each free-verse section: "Uncle Sam needn't be ashamed of his seed." Trying to pull together the complete story of America, Cobb praises the immigration of all peoples, but on pages 22–23 he includes an anti-Semitic theme that developed as he aged: "To this simmering brew add a small and canny Jew, a shrewd city trader known as Mister Salomon." On the back of the dust cover is Cobb's plea for Americans to support the war effort. "Buy War Stamps! Buy War Bonds!" Also in 1942, Cobb was still popular enough that *Argosy* republished "Fishhead."[19]

Cobb's health continued to decline in 1943. With many of his old friends gone—Bob Davis died in October 1942—he was lonely. Cobb traveled to the Southwest briefly, then suffered a bout of pneumonia while on a trip to Washington, DC, before returning to California. Buff described these tense days as her mother, whom she always called "Moie," closed up the Santa Monica house and joined her daughter and two grandchildren in the Cobbs' apartment at the Sheraton Hotel in New York. During this time, Cobb had to be hospitalized again for what the doctors described as "nervous exhaustion." As he explained to his friend Fred Neuman, "In other words I've got to play invalid." Urged to join his family in New York, Cobb had difficulty finding railroad connections due to the war. When he finally arrived at the station, Buff was shocked. "We saw him, but for a moment we did not recognize him. This bent old man, this slow-moving, stooped, shambling, thin, old man?" When Buff asked him why he had not ordered a wheelchair, her father replied, "'I thought that Lolly would be here. I thought Lolly would be scared if she saw me in a chair.' We took him home and put him to bed. He never got up again."[20]

"I'm feeling pretty puny," Cobb wrote to Neuman in a letter marked "strictly confidential." "Although the doctor's counterfeit [confident] I'm not fooled. If I lick my ailments nobody will be more surprised than I am. That also is information for your private ear." Along with "dropsy" (an old-fashioned term for edema, or the swelling of tissues because of water accumulation), diabetes, and other ailments, he suffered pain and sleeplessness. In a 1943 address book he wrote, somewhat tongue in cheek, "In case of serious illness notify a doctor and give me a shot of insulin." Cobb tried to write some reminiscence of his Paducah days for Neuman, but his poor health made it difficult.[21]

Cobb also wrote a letter to old friend Kent Cooper, executive director of the Associated Press, which he called an "epistle to the Corinthians and the Paducahans." Cobb had promised Cooper that if "I [Cooper] survived him [Cobb], and he was in his last sickness, he would prove his undying love of humor by writing me an amusing letter." The letter was indeed classic Cobb, handwritten from his bed, according to Cooper. They had known each other since their newspaper days at the turn of the century. Cobb admitted that he was ill, but perhaps not as dangerously ill as hoped for by the "affable undertaker down the block." He told Cooper:

> If, as and when I get ready to depart elsewhere, I promise to keep friendly newspapers fully advised. . . . I take credit for one thing. So far as the available records show, I am the only person who under similar circumstances did not wittily remark—with or without credit to the author—"the reports of my death have been greatly exaggerated." For those who enjoy morbid particulars, I might add that the doctors are still tapping me for impulsive little freshets of dropsy but the results of these aquatic sports and pastimes will, they believe, diminish as time passes. For a while though, they tried too hard to be cheerful, if you get what I mean. And I'm still just a trifle worried about St. Smithin's Day [July 15].

Cobb thanked those who had been concerned about the state of his health. "As of me, I content myself with the refrain: 'Merry symptoms and a tappy new year.'"[22]

If Cobb had stopped there, it would have been best. However, he added a virulent postscript that was published in the nation's newspapers but not in Cooper's memoirs. In his humorous yet scathing way, Cobb called on General Patton to return home and take on management of the Tule Lake Japanese Relocation Center in California, "that nest of scaly, shark-toothed, yellow-bellied concentrates." Then he called for it to be turned into a bloodbath, literally, so the "landscape will look as though somebody had been cleaning fish-gills, gore and guts all over the place." Several commentators considered the last remarks distasteful. In the *Commonweal,* C. G. Paulding went even further, condemning the postscript as "the most revolting [sentences] that have been printed in the English language during this war." With finality he exclaimed, "I wish I had never heard of Irvin S. Cobb."[23]

Pain and sleeplessness fed Cobb's despair. He knew he was dying, and what could only be called rage and bitterness led to even more reactionary writing. He expressed his deepest feelings to Neuman: "Having not much else to do in the long evenings except lie here and cuss out F.D.R. and look up at the ceiling—and when you've seen one you've practically seen 'em all—I think up doggerel verse and the next morning I relieve my spleen by putting it down on paper. I find this has much the same effect as taking a mild laxative." In short, he poured out his anger against FDR, Eleanor Roosevelt, and Senator Alben Barkley of Kentucky. In one of his darker moments, he only halfheartedly praised his fellow Kentuckian's opposition to the president in an unpublished poem: "Can it be, dear Alben Barkley, Lackey, Mouthpiece, caddy, doormat, Has up and left his liege lord Flat—He the New Deal's prize malarkey?" As Cobb's health declined, so did his tolerance. When asked by a reporter for ten words "expressing my dearest hope for 1944," Cobb replied, "Freedom from Eleanor Roosevelt, Freedom from Eleanor, Freedom from Eleanor, Amen!" He railed against miscegenation, the Democratic Party, Jews, and anyone else he had developed a disliking for. His anti-Semitism was tied to his contempt for the Roosevelt family and the New Deal. In the end, he longed for a return of "the old Democratic Party," the one he had grown up with in Paducah, which had been dominated by his white southern mores.[24]

Cobb suffered in his last days. In December 1943 he wrote to his good friends Fred Neuman and Edwin J. Paxton Sr., of the *Paducah Sun-Democrat,* about his impending death and his last wishes. A fair amount of Cobbian humor came through in his "To Whom It May Concern" letter to Neuman and Paxton: "In death I desire that no one shall look upon my face and once more I charge my family, as already and repeatedly I have done, that they shall put on none of the habiliments of so-called mourning. Folds of black crepe never administered to the memory of the departed; they only made the wearers unhappy and self-conscious." He asked that his body be cremated. "If anybody tries to insert me into one of those dismal numbers run up by the undertaker's dressmaking department, I'll come back and ha'nt 'em." He asked that his ashes be buried without fanfare in Paducah, with a short epitaph carved on native stone—something simple like "I Have Come Back Home." "And, thank you, no flowers. . . . Above all I want no long faces and no show of grief at the burying ground. Kindly observe the final wishes of the undersigned and avoid reading the so-called Christian burial service which, in view of the language employed in it, I regard as one of the most cruel and paganish things inherited by our forbears from our remote pagan ancestors." A reading of the Twenty-Third Psalm and a few words would suffice. In the rest of this document, he expounded on the good and the bad of various religious sects. With his characteristic impiety, he described Jesus Christ as only "the first true gentleman of recorded history and the greatest gentleman that ever lived." He added parenthetically: "(One advantage of dying is that it affords a fellow opportunity to say a lot of things that have been curdling in his system all these years. Frankly, I'm enjoying myself.)"[25]

Laura wired Neuman on March 10, 1944: "IRVIN PASSED AWAY THIS MORNING AT ELEVEN O'CLOCK." Cobb, who was sixty-seven, died in the family apartment at the Sheraton Hotel. In Cobb's last letter to George H. Goodman, he said, "I'm sick of being tired and tired of being sick." Newspapers large and small carried obituaries. The *Mt. Vernon (NY) Daily Argus* declared, "We need a good laugh now and then, even in the midst of tragedy. And that is why we shall miss Irvin S. Cobb and men like him." The *New York Times* editorialized the day after his death, "Not yet 68, Irvin Cobb died too early." Rejecting the idea that Cobb wrote too much, the editor characterized this as "a rather highbrow and crabbed view." "For more than a generation Irvin Cobb worked for the pleasure of his countrymen. He became in time almost like a character in a novel himself. There was a sort of legendary Cobb beside the real one. His irony and his humor have amused, refreshed and rested multitudes." The *Saturday Review of Literature,* edited by Norman Cousins, called Cobb a fine writer "who almost became a legend in his own lifetime," but his short time in Hollywood "surprised and diverted him." "A selection of Cobb's work would make a book of characteristically American humor, to last for a long time. He stands somewhere between Mark Twain and Joel Chandler Harris in the American pantheon," which was high praise indeed.[26]

Cobb's request for a simple funeral went awry. He was cremated, and a service was conducted in New York a few days after his death. Held in a small chapel at the funeral home, it probably would have displeased Cobb. His friend, sportswriter Grantland Rice, wrote a piece headlined "New York Pays Last Tribute to Cobb at the Simplest Possible Service" for the North American Newspaper Alliance. A Presbyterian minister "was selected to conduct the simplest possible service and give Irv Godspeed on his way back home, to find the dreamless peace he had wanted for so many months through the broken world of today," Rice wrote. As Cobb requested, the minister read the Twenty-Third Psalm and Robert Louis Stevenson's *Requiem.*[27]

Rice, who had known Cobb for thirty-four years, had visited him often during his last few months of life and witnessed his suffering. He eulogized his old friend in print: "A fine writer—one of our best—a fine orator and after-dinner speaker, a master of the anecdote and snap-shot repartee, he loved the majority of his fellow human beings and the majority of his fellow humans loved Irv." However, "there were exceptions when he could be violent in his sarcasm. For his beliefs in what he thought was right and proper were fixed and firm. And he had no gods to serve beyond his own Kentucky conscience." Finally, Rice finished by attesting to Cobb's great love of life.[28]

Cobb's interment in Paducah was delayed by the extended illness of his widow. Finally, on October 7, nearly seven months after his death, Laura, Buff, granddaughter Pat (who had recently married Gregson Bautzer), and Cobb's sister Manie joined a large crowd at Paducah's Oak Grove Cemetery for Irvin S. Cobb's final services. George H. Goodman carried a marble box containing Cobb's ashes, which was buried in front of a dogwood tree. As requested by Cobb, Mattie Copeland, a former servant in the Cobb household in Paducah, led an African American choir in two spirituals: "Swing Low, Sweet Chariot" and "Deep River." A local

Presbyterian minister read the Twenty-Third Psalm, and a few friends made remarks.[29]

Though Cobb had fretted about his finances, his estate amounted to $478,592, five-sixths of which went to his wife, Laura. Despite heavy losses in the stock market crash and the subsequent downturn in the economy as well as his career, this was a substantial legacy. Laura continued to live in New York City until her death in 1967 and is buried beside her husband in Paducah. Their daughter Buff, who died in 1956, is also buried there.[30]

Irvin S. Cobb was not soon forgotten. Bobbs-Merrill published Elisabeth "Buff" Cobb's *My Wayward Parent,* a loving yet realistic and insightful biography of her father, in 1945. A *Chicago Sunday Tribune* reviewer found the book to be a charming family portrait. Buff described him as "bumbling and awkward and lovable, like a gangling boy or half grown puppy. That was Irvin S. Cobb, and that was why he had a legion of friends." Since the publication of *Cobb's Cavalcade* in 1945, reprints of his work have been few. Cobb's name did not disappear from public view, however. On October 7, 1951, WLW-T in Cincinnati, as part of its weekly *Our America* series, presented a profile of Cobb in a dramatized script written by Rod Serling. From time to time, an article about Cobb would appear in one of the Louisville, Lexington, Paducah, or even big-city newspapers into the 1970s, but he soon faded from memory as his style of writing and humor lost popularity in the postwar years.[31]

The greatest legacy of Cobb's long career turned out to be a movie made nearly ten years after his death and nearly two decades after the film *Judge Priest.* John Ford revisited the Judge Priest character in 1953 with *The Sun Shines Bright,* an adaptation of three Cobb stories: "The Sun Shines Bright," "The Mob from Massac," and "The Lord Provides." Screenwriter Laurence Stallings blended the three stories into a script. Ford's new evocation of the saintly Kentucky judge starred Charles Winninger as Priest, Arlene Whelen as Lucy Lee Lake, and John Russell as Ashby Corwin. Stepin Fetchit reprised his role as Jeff Poindexter, as did Francis Ford as a moonshine-swilling backwoodsman for comic effect. Whereas Will Rogers had played Priest as an extension of his own personality, Winninger played him as an actor would. Distributed by Republic Pictures, the ninety-two-minute film has some of the "southern" impediments of *Judge Priest* but focuses more on reconciliation of North and

South in the early twentieth century. Again, there is a love story, small-town racial and class prejudice, and a verbal and electoral duel between Priest and Senator Maydew. However, this time, the lynching story from "The Mob from Massac" is not cut and is a crucial part of the movie. It is a plea for African American civil rights, and it sends as strong a message for freedom and justice as the studio would allow at the time (the film was released a year before the Supreme Court's decision in *Brown v. Board of Education*). And Ford, who could be something of a crusader, based it all on Cobb's writings from previous decades. *The Sun Shines Bright* can be watched today by a modern audience without flinching, whereas *Judge Priest* is too laden with racism. In two decades, Hollywood had indeed changed. *The Sun Shines Bright* is a much better version but a "period piece" just the same.[32]

I have had the advantage of reading not only Buff's biography of her father and the uncritical biography by Fred Neuman but also the two fine biographies by Anita Lawson and Wayne Chatterton that appeared in the mid-1980s. Lawson's book is a chronologically organized view of Cobb's entire career; it exposes his racism while giving him credit for his accomplishments. Chatterton, who interviewed Cobb's last surviving friends in Paducah and carefully studied his literary efforts, particularly *Exit Laughing*, places him in the context of American humor and humorists. Throughout her book, Lawson critiques Cobb's literary output and concludes with the words of Tom Waller, a longtime Paducah friend: "He had the touch, and he used it." Though Chatterton admits that Cobb's style of short story writing and his brand of humor were outdated in 1986, he agrees with Norman W. Yates that Cobb aptly used "three type figures" in his writing—"the cracker-box sage, the solid citizen, and the Little Man"—at various stages of his career. Chatterton praises Cobb's evocation of the "Great American Funny Man" and ends with a suggestion that Cobb's words in the last paragraph of his autobiography were prescient: "Who knows what the end of anything is? Who knows when a thing begins or when it may end? By your leave then, we will put down here that line that sometimes is to be found in the stage business of a play to cue a character who is leaving the stage, and may or may not be back again: EXIT LAUGHING."[33]

What are we to make of Irvin S. Cobb in the second decade of the twenty-first century? In his lifetime, Cobb won fame and fortune for his many accomplishments as a newspaperman, short story writer, after-dinner speaker, and columnist. Though less successful as a playwright and during his short-lived movie career, Cobb had the grit to venture into genres that frightened many others in his day. He wrote extensively to make a living and to take care of his family. He no doubt thought of himself as an example of the American dream, as someone who, though not well educated, could succeed in the larger world despite his parochial western Kentucky upbringing. If Cobb is virtually unknown today, so are most of his contemporaries. Even Will Rogers is largely forgotten, except for some of his most famous witticisms. Latter-day humorists and comedians such as Steve Allen, Erma Bombeck, Art Buchwald, Sam Levinson, and the redoubtable Johnny Carson are fading from memory. How long before late-night television stars David Letterman and Jay Leno disappear from view as new humorists and comedians take the stage? As Shakespeare famously wrote: "All the world's a stage. And all the men and women merely players; They have their exits and entrances." Cobb exited laughing, or did he?

For all the candor in his autobiography, Cobb was embittered that the world had passed him by. In his last years, travel was nearly impossible. He was tortured by his ailments, spending his last months in agony as a bedridden invalid. Most of his close male friends had died, and he missed the camaraderie of the campfire, the duck blind, and the fishing stream. His political, economic, and social conservatism became more pronounced as he aged.

Late in life, Cobb became a cliché for a barely reconstructed southerner. Though he retained his benevolent form of racism to the end, it should be remembered that he stood up against the resurgence of the Ku Klux Klan in the early 1920s. If his short stories were considered too long for "modern" tastes in the late 1930s, his earlier stories, particularly the "grim" tales, held audiences spellbound. His record as a journalist of the early twentieth century, particularly his coverage of the early months of World War I, exemplified the era of the "great reporter." Cobb's record as a multitalented writer and performer is unmatched in his time.

If Cobb eventually became a caricature of his earlier self, that is the fate of most of those we call celebrities, if they live long enough. Irvin Shrewsbury Cobb knew the hazards of his trade and the pitfalls of celebrity, but he lived a valuable life. He made people laugh, and for most of his life, he was able to laugh at himself.

Acknowledgments

This book is the result of reading and studying humor for nearly a lifetime, and more than six years' worth of labor. Irvin S. Cobb wrote millions of words in his newspaper articles, commentary, short stories, memoirs, autobiographies, books, and novels. I cannot claim to have read everything he wrote and published, but I have read, digested, and thought carefully about most of it.

I thank the readers and editors of the University Press of Kentucky for their painstaking efforts to bring this book to publication. Copyeditor Linda Lotz and Ila McEntire, senior editing supervisor, deserve special thanks for helping this old-fashioned historian. Archivists at all of the repositories listed have been of great help, often searching out bits and pieces that have not seen the light of day for many years.

Special thanks to the interlibrary loan staff at Eastern Kentucky University for helping an old researcher find sometimes arcane sources of Cobbian material, much of it more than one hundred years old.

I also thank Irvin S. Cobb, who often frustrated me with his line of thought and humor. However, he was always interesting to read. It is difficult to understand the energy he put into his many efforts. He was indefatigable.

Notes

Introduction

1. Dayton Duncan, *The National Parks: America's Best Idea* (New York: Alfred A. Knopf, 2009), 183; Irvin S. Cobb, "Roughing It De Luxe: Canonized Pilgrims," *Saturday Evening Post,* June 7, 1913, 5.

2. Duncan, *National Parks,* 183, 185; Cobb, "Roughing It De Luxe," 5, 44.

1. The Making of an American Humorist

1. Constance Rourke, *American Humor: A Study of the National Character* (New York: Harcourt, Brace, 1931); Wade Hall, *The Smiling Phoenix: Southern Humor from 1865 to 1914* (Gainesville: University of Florida Press, 1965); Irvin S. Cobb, *Exit Laughing* (Indianapolis: Bobbs-Merrill, 1941), 330.

2. John E. Kleber, ed., *The Kentucky Encyclopedia* (Lexington: University Press of Kentucky, 1992), 211–12; Berry Craig, *Kentucky Confederates: Secession, Civil War, and the Jackson Purchase* (Lexington: University Press of Kentucky, 2014), 1–10, 88, 281–94, 312n; Cobb, *Exit Laughing*, 66, 102, 440; Cobb to John Wilson Townsend, September 21, 1921, John Wilson Townsend Collection, Eastern Kentucky University Special Collections and Archives; Marion B. Lucas, *A History of Blacks in Kentucky: From Slavery to Segregation, 1760–1891* (Frankfort: Kentucky Historical Society, 1992), 1–3, 188–89, 199–200, 202, 204, 261; George C. Wright, *A History of Blacks in Kentucky,* vol. 2, *In Pursuit of Equality, 1890–1980* (Frankfort: Kentucky Historical Society, 1992), 39, 53, 78, 80, 84–86, 92–94, 110.

3. Kleber, *Kentucky Encyclopedia,* 211–12; Irvin S. Cobb, *The Glory of the Coming: What Mine Eyes Have Seen of Americans in Action in the Year of Grace and Allied Endeavor* (New York: George H. Doran, 1918), 453; Cobb to Townsend, September 20, 1921, Townsend Collection; Anita Lawson, *Irvin S. Cobb* (Bowling Green, OH: Bowling Green State University Popular Press, 1984), 1–10, 20; Cobb, *Exit Laughing,* 342.

4. Cobb to Townsend, September 27, 1921, Townsend Collection; Irvin S. Cobb, *The Works of Irvin S. Cobb: Stickfuls (Myself to Date)* (New York: George H. Doran, 1923), 18.

5. Cobb, *Exit Laughing*, chaps. 4–8; Fred G. Neuman, *The Story of Paducah* (Paducah, KY: Young Printing, 1927), 97,115; Lawson, *Cobb*, 1, 15; Wayne Chatterton, *Irvin S. Cobb* (Boston: Twayne, 1986), 5; Cobb, *Works: Stickfuls*, 36.

6. Chatterton, *Cobb*, 4–10; Robert H. Davis, "Introducing Mr. Cobb," *Golden Book Magazine*, January 1934, 15; Norris W. Yates, *The American Humorist: Conscience of the Twentieth Century* (Ames: Iowa State University Press, 1964), 128–29.

7. Elisabeth Cobb, *My Wayward Parent* (Indianapolis: Bobbs-Merrill, 1945), 23–24, 243; Cobb, *Exit Laughing*, 333; LeRoy Ashby, *With Amusement for All: A History of American Popular Culture since 1830* (Lexington: University Press of Kentucky, 2011), chaps. 1–3.

8. Cobb, *Exit Laughing*, 48–60, 330–32. For an up-to-date interpretation of Kentucky's post–Civil War southern and Confederate identity, see Jacob F. Lee, "Unionism, Emancipation, and the Origins of Kentucky's Confederate Identity," *Register of the Kentucky Historical Society* 111 (Spring 2013): 199–233.

9. Cobb, *Exit Laughing*, 49–52, 89–90, 247, 425, 551–53; Cobb, *My Wayward Parent*, 98, 135. One of Cobb's most successful books, *Fibble, D.D.* (New York: George H. Doran, 1916), concerned the life of an "incredibly naïve clergyman, the Reverend Roscoe Titmarsh Fibble," demonstrating Cobb's displeasure with formal, particularly conservative or mainline Christianity. Lawson, *Cobb*, 143.

10. Fred G. Neuman, *Irvin S. Cobb: His Life and Letters* (Emmaus, PA: Rodale Press, 1938), 50–55; Cobb, *Works: Stickfuls*, 15–43; William E. Ellis, "Dream Big," *Kentucky Monthly*, August 2011, 56; Lawson, *Cobb*, 20; Cobb, *Exit Laughing*, 96.

11. Cobb, *Works: Stickfuls*, 31–88; Ellis, "Dream Big," 56; Lawson, *Cobb*, 21–27; Chatterton, *Cobb*, preface; Cobb, *My Wayward Parent*, 56–59.

12. *Chicago Tribune*, December 1, 1897; Cobb, *Exit Laughing*, 97–101.

13. *Chicago Tribune*, December 16, 17, 1897; Cobb, *Exit Laughing*, 103–10.

14. Cobb, *Works: Stickfuls*, 31–38; Lawson, *Cobb*, 25–27; *Chicago Tribune*, December 1, 16, 17, 20, 1897, April 23, 1898; Cobb, *Exit Laughing*, 97–112.

15. John E. Kleber, ed., *The Encyclopedia of Louisville* (Lexington: University Press of Kentucky, 2001), 655–66.

16. Kleber, *Kentucky Encyclopedia*, 377–78. See also James C. Klotter, *William Goebel: The Politics of Wrath* (Lexington: University Press of Kentucky, 1977).

17. *Louisville Evening Post*, January 30–February 8, 1900; Kleber, *Encyclopedia of Louisville*, 655–56; Kleber, *Kentucky Encyclopedia*, 377–78; Steven H. Gale, ed., *Encyclopedia of American Humorists* (New York: Garland, 1988), 91–93; Lawson, *Cobb*, 28–39; Cobb, *Works: Stickfuls*, 89–97; Neuman, *Cobb*, 56–61, Cobb, *Exit Laughing*, 198–211.

18. Robert H. Davis, *Irvin S. Cobb: Storyteller* (New York: George H. Doran, 1924), 6–16, 17–26. "Miss Pennyroyal's Scar," written by Cobb while in Paducah, was apparently sent out to publishers during this period and may have been one of his first stories. Boxes 1–14 of the Irvin S. Cobb Papers in the Pogue Library at Murray State University contain many handwritten stories that went through numerous versions before being typed for submission to publishers.

19. Neuman, *Cobb*, 56–58; Lawson, *Cobb*, 45; *Louisville Evening Post*, May 25, 27, 28, 30, 31, June 1, 12, July 4, 1901; Cobb to Cyril Clemens, January 23, 1937, Irvin S. Cobb Papers, Filson Historical Society; Chatterton, *Cobb*, 27–29.

20. Kleber, *Encyclopedia of Louisville*, 722–73, 925–26; George D. Prentice, *Prenticeana: Or Wit and Humor in Paragraphs* (New York: Derby and Jackson, 1860); Daniel S. Margolies, *Henry Watterson and the New South* (Lexington: University Press of Kentucky, 2006).

21. Lawson, *Cobb*, 38–39; Opie Read, *I Remember New York* (New York: Richard H. Smith, 1930), 49; Willard Rouse Jillson, *Irvin S. Cobb at Frankfort, Kentucky* (Carrollton, KY: News Democrat Press, 1944), 6; Kent Cooper, *Kent Cooper and the Associated Press: An Autobiography* (New York: Random House, 1959), 15; Joyce Milton, *The Yellow Kids: Foreign Correspondents in the Heyday of Yellow Journalism* (New York: HarperCollins, 1989), xiii–xiv, 58.

22. Cobb, *My Wayward Parent*, 21–61; Lawson, *Cobb*, 40–48.

23. Lawson, *Cobb*, 44–45; Cobb, *Exit Laughing*, 223–25; Jillson, *Cobb at Frankfort*, 6.

24. Lawson, *Cobb*, 45–50; Cobb, *Exit Laughing*, 70, 94, 550.

25. Cobb, *My Wayward Parent*, 48–51; Orville Vernon Burton, "The South as 'Other,' the Southerner as 'Stranger,'" *Journal of Southern History* 79 (February 2013): 7–50.

26. Cobb, *Works: Stickfuls*, 97–103; Lawson, *Cobb*, 47–48.

27. *Paducah News-Democrat*, September 29, October 6, 13, 23, 24, November 6, 11, December 28, 1901.

28. Cobb, *My Wayward Parent*, 54–56, *Paducah News-Democrat*, October 6, 1901.

29. *Paducah News-Democrat*, July 22, 1904; Lawson, *Cobb*, 49–50; Cobb, *My Wayward Parent*, 60–61; Cobb, *Works: Stickfuls*, 100–103.

30. Lawson, *Cobb*, 51–53; Neuman, *Cobb*, 68–87; Cobb, *Exit Laughing*, 111–12; Cobb, *Works: Stickfuls*, 97–151.

31. Cobb, *Works: Stickfuls*, 101–51.

2. Big-City Newspaperman

1. James C. Klotter, *Kentucky: Portrait in Paradox, 1900–1950* (Frankfort: Kentucky Historical Society, 1996), 169–73, 318–19.

2. John Tebbel, *The Compact History of the American Newspaper* (New York: Hawthorn Books, 1963), 209, 211, 219–20; Lawson, *Cobb*, 54–58; Neuman, *Cobb*, 68–73.

3. Lawson, *Cobb*, 61–62; Cobb, *My Wayward Parent*, 61–84; Neuman, *Cobb*, 74–76.

4. *New York Sun*, July 11, 1905; Eugene P. Trani, *The Treaty of Portsmouth: An Adventure in American Diplomacy* (Lexington: University of Kentucky Press, 1969), 79–122.

5. Trani, *Treaty of Portsmouth,* 123–28; *New York Sun,* August 6, 12, 1905.

6. *New York Sun,* August 8, 10, 12, 14, 15, 17–23, 26, 1905.

7. *New York Sun,* August 28–31, September 2, 5, 1905; Trani, *Treaty of Portsmouth,* 156–70; Lawson, *Cobb,* 55–62; Cobb, *My Wayward Parent,* 62–89; Neuman, *Cobb,* 68–77.

8. Lawson, *Cobb,* 62–64; Neuman, *Cobb,* 76–79; George Juergens, *Joseph Pulitzer and the* New York World (Princeton, NJ: Princeton University Press, 1966), 27, 331–65; Meyer Berger, *The Story of the* New York Times (New York: Simon and Schuster, 1951), 100, 115; John D. Stevens, *Sensationalism and the New York Press* (New York: Columbia University Press, 1991), 67–80; Justin Fox, "Start the Presses! *Atlantic,* May 2014, 26.

9. Michael Emery, Edwin Emery, and Nancy L. Roberts, *The Press in America: An Interpretative History of the Mass Media* (Boston: Allyn and Bacon, 2000), 213–15; Lawson, *Cobb,* 62–67; Neuman, *Cobb,* 76–94; James Wyman Barrett, *Joseph Pulitzer and His World* (New York: Vanguard Press, 1941), 275–79; W. A. Swanberg, *Pulitzer* (New York: Scribner, 1971), 301; Charles E. Chapin, *Charles Chapin's Story: Written in Sing Sing Prison* (New York: Putnam's, 1920), 190, 284–334; Cobb, *Exit Laughing,* 119; Tebbel, *Compact History,* 216–18. In a strange twist of fate, after sensationalizing many murder cases, Chapin killed his invalid wife after they both became despondent over outstanding debts. Lacking the nerve to kill himself, he spent the remainder of his life in prison. Until Chapin's death in 1930, Cobb sent him a monthly check that the ex-editor used for his garden and other sundry items.

10. Gerald Langford, *The Murder of Stanford White* (New York: Notable Trials Library, 1996); *New York Evening World,* June 26, 29, July 19, 1906; Paula Uruburu, *American Eve: Evelyn Nesbit, Stanford White, the Birth of the "It" Girl, and the Crime of the Century* (New York: Riverhead, 2008); *New York Times,* June 1, 2008.

11. Cobb, *My Wayward Parent,* 91; *New York Evening World,* January 2, 4, 18–26, 30, 31, February 7, 14, 19, 20, 22, 27, 28, March 4–7, 18, 26, May 24, 1907.

12. Robert Mason, "The Supreme Court and Press Fashions," *William and Mary Law Review* 22 (1980): 261, commenting on Louis L. Snyder and Richard B. Morris, *A Treasury of Great Reporting* (New York: Simon and Schuster, 1949), 283–91; *Washington Post,* January 4, 1999.

13. *New York Evening World,* January 3, 1907; Chapin, *Chapin's Story,* 189–90.

14. *New York Evening World,* April 23, 1906, January 1, 3, 5, 15, 22, 29, 31, February 21, March 5, April 11, 1907, January 1, 7, 1908; Lawson, *Cobb,* 79–80; Cobb, *Exit Laughing,* 359–60; "Grinnan Barrett" columns, box 7, Cobb Papers, Murray State University Special Collections and Archives.

15. *New York Evening World,* January 7, 1908; Cobb, *Exit Laughing,* 359–60; Lawson, *Cobb,* 79–80; Neuman, *Cobb,* 180; program for "Funabashi, a Musical Comedy by Irvin Cobb and Stafford Waters," Cobb Papers, Murray State University Special Collections and Archives.

16. *New York Evening World,* January 6, 9–11, 13–31, February 1, 2, 1908; Langford, *Murder of Stanford White,* 93, 102–4, 234–62.

17. Cobb, *Exit Laughing*, 246–47. A "creek crane" is a western Kentucky nickname for a great blue heron.

18. Lawson, *Cobb*, 75–80; W. A. Swanberg, *Theodore Dreiser* (New York: Charles Scribner's Sons, 1935), 207; Corey Ford, *The Time of Laughter* (Boston: Little, Brown, 1967), 13; Chatterton, *Cobb*, 139.

19. Lawson, *Cobb*, 66–67; Neuman, *Cobb*, 79.

20. Emery, Emery, and Roberts, *Press in America*, 213–15; Cobb, *Exit Laughing*, 150–57; Lawson, *Cobb*, 83–85.

21. Cobb, *Exit Laughing*, 156–62.

3. From Newspaperman to Short Story Writer

1. Lawson, *Cobb*, 68–74; David E. E. Sloane, "Samuel Langhorne Clemens," in *Encyclopedia of American Humorists*, ed. Steven H. Gale (New York: Garland, 1988), 83–90; Cobb, *My Wayward Parent*, 75; Cobb, *Exit Laughing*, 260–61.

2. Lawson, *Cobb*, 69–70; Cobb, *My Wayward Parent*, 97–98; Irvin S. Cobb, *Irvin Cobb at His Best* (Garden City, NY: Sun Dial Press, 1940), 202.

3. Lawson, *Cobb*, 68–74; Yates, *American Humorist*, 129–33; Cobb, *Exit Laughing*, 260–61; *New York Tribune*, November 21, 1921.

4. Cobb, *Exit Laughing*, 260–61; Thomas L. Masson, *Our American Humorists* (New York: Moffat, Yard, 1922), 102–3; Gordon McLauchlan, *A History of New Zealand Humour* (Auckland, New Zealand: Penguin Books, 1989), 18.

5. *New York Evening World*, August 2, 1906.

6. *Evening World*, April 13, 1908.

7. *Evening World*, August 8, 1908, March 26, 29, 30, April 1, 3, 8, July 3, 1909.

8. *Evening World*, April 25, 1909, July 8, 16, 1910. Johnson finally lost the heavyweight championship to the "Great White Hope" Jess Willard on April 5, 1915, in Havana, Cuba. Randy Roberts, *Papa Jack: Jack Johnson and the Era of White Hopes* (New York: Free Press, 1983), 90–91, 106–111; A-Tony Gilmore, *Bad Nigger! The National Impact of Jack Johnson* (Port Washington, NY: Associated Faculty Press, 1975), 9, 36–37, 46–47, 110–11, 149–50; Denzil Batchelor, *Jack Johnson and His Times* (London: Phoenix Sports Books, 1956), 80–87.

9. *Evening World*, June 5, July 9, 10, 1909, October 14, 16, 17, 1911.

10. *Evening World*, January 29, February 2, 5, March 2, 16, 30, April 2, 6, 9, 13, 16, 27, May 18, 21, 24, 25, June 16, July 30, August 9, 20, October 5, 13, 22, November 10, 1910, March 4, 11, 18, May 27, 1911.

11. *Evening World*, August 21, 24, December 28, 1908, February 3, June 16, 20, 1909, June 21, 1911, August 13, 1912, May 6, 13, 20, 27, 1913.

12. *Sunday World*, August 9, 1908; Neuman, *Cobb*, 79–82; Lawson, *Cobb*, 68–73.

13. *Sunday World*, December 5, 1909; Lawson, *Cobb*, 68–71; Neuman, *Cobb*, 77–87.

14. *Sunday World*, January 17, July 5, 12, 19, August 9, September 27, 1908, November 14, 1909.

15. Lawson, *Cobb,* 86–87; Cobb, *Exit Laughing,* 468–70; Cobb to H. H. Mc-Clure, undated letters (circa 1908) and checks to Cobb, August 24, October 15, November 18, December 2, 1908, McClure Publishing Company Archives, University of Delaware Library, Special Collections.

16. Cobb, *My Wayward Parent,* 100–107; Cobb, *Exit Laughing,* 296–97; Lawson, *Cobb,* 82–83, 92–93; George H. Doran, *Chronicles of Barabbas, 1884–1934* (New York: Rinehart, 1935), 244; Chatterton, *Cobb,* 148–51.

17. Cobb, *My Wayward Parent,* 100–106; *Sunday World,* August 15, 1909; Chatterton, *Cobb,* 54, 148; Lawson, *Cobb,* 76, 145–54.

18. *Sunday World,* February 7, May 28, July 11, November 7, 1909; *Evening World,* February 16, 23, 1908.

19. *Sunday World,* February 13, 20, 27, March 6, 1910; Chatterton, *Cobb,* 49–50.

20. Chatterton, *Cobb,* 49–50; *Sunday World,* April 17, May 1, 1910.

21. Cobb, *My Wayward Parent,* 174–76; Cobb, *Exit Laughing,* 260; Neuman, *Cobb,* 79.

22. Ashby, *With Amusement for All,* 64–175.

23. Lawson, *Cobb,* 68–73; Neuman, *Cobb,* 79; Cobb, *Exit Laughing,* 127.

24. Cobb, *My Wayward Parent,* 110–11.

25. Cobb, *Exit Laughing,* 322–32, 468–70; Cobb, *My Wayward Parent,* 110–14; Lawson, *Cobb,* 87–90.

26. Lawson, *Cobb,* 87–91; Neuman, *Cobb,* 86–87; Cobb, *Exit Laughing,* 323–25; Cobb, *My Wayward Parent,* 110–11; Chatterton, *Cobb,* 93–107.

27. Lawson, *Cobb,* 88–89; Cobb, *Exit Laughing,* 322–33; Chatterton, *Cobb,* 90.

28. Jan Cohn, *Creating America: George Horace Lorimer and the* Saturday Evening Post (Pittsburgh: University of Pittsburgh Press, 1989), introduction; Irvin S. Cobb, "The Escape of Mr. Trimm," *Saturday Evening Post,* November 27, 1909, 12–13. "The Escape of Mr. Trimm" is also included in Cobb, *Cobb's Cavalcade* (Cleveland, OH: World Publishing, 1945), 135–59.

29. Cobb, "Escape of Mr. Trimm," 12–13.

30. Ibid., 14–15; Chatterton, *Cobb,* 108–111.

31. Cobb, "Escape of Mr. Trimm," 25–27.

32. One of Lorimer's biographers mistakenly dates Cobb's entry into the *Post's* inner circle of writers as occurring in 1908. Cohn, *Creating America,* 7–8; Doran, *Chronicles of Barabbas,* 245; Irvin S. Cobb, "Tale of the Hard Luck Guy," *Popular Magazine,* October 1909, 57–60.

4. Crossroads Again

1. Scott Stossel, "My Anxious, Twitchy, Phobic (Somehow Successful) Life," *Atlantic,* January–February 2014, 74–92; Cobb, *My Wayward Parent,* 49–51, 112–13; Donald Elder, *Ring Lardner* (Garden City, NY: Doubleday, 1956), 129.

2. Chatterton, *Cobb,* 84–85.

3. Robert H. Davis, "Who's Cobb and Why?" *New York Sun,* October 19, 1912, reprinted in Davis, *Cobb,* 8; Lawson, *Cobb,* 96.

4. Davis, *Cobb,* 10, 12, 13.

5. Ibid., 14–15.

6. Ibid., 15.

7. Ibid., 15–16.

8. Lawson, *Cobb,* 88–89. See chapter 3 for an explanation of the "Cos Cob" items, which continued into mid-1913.

9. Cobb, *My Wayward Parent,* 113; Doran, *Chronicles of Barabbas,* 245–46.

10. Lawson, *Cobb,* 90; Chatterton, *Cobb,* 108, 114; Irvin S. Cobb, "The Exit of Anse Dugmore," in *Cobb's Cavalcade,* 209–20. One assumes "Anse" is short for Anderson, borrowed from "Devil Anse" Hatfield of the famous Hatfield-McCoy feud.

11. John Tebbel and Mary Ellen Zuckerman, *George Horace Lorimer and the* Saturday Evening Post (Garden City, NY: Doubleday, 1948), 1–40, 63; Cohn, *Creating America,* 3–59; Cobb, *Exit Laughing,* 113–16, 121.

12. Cohn, *Creating America,* 7, 81, 83–85, 166, 243, 280–82.

13. Cobb, *Exit Laughing,* 127–29; Lawson, *Cobb,* 90–91. There was a slight Kentucky connection between Lorimer and Cobb. Lorimer's father, a Baptist minister, had moved from Paducah to Louisville just before Lorimer's birth.

14. Irvin S. Cobb, "An Occurrence up a Side Street," *Saturday Evening Post,* January 21, 1911, 6–7, 32.

15. Cobb, "An Occurrence up a Side Street," in *Cobb's Cavalcade,* 199–207.

16. Irvin S. Cobb, "The Trail of the Lonesome Laugh," *Everybody's Magazine,* April 1911, 467–75; Cobb, "The Perquisites of Public Life," *Munsey's,* October 11, 1911, 68–74; Cobb, "Who's Who at the Zoo," *Hampton-Columbian Magazine,* October 1911, 421–30.

17. Irvin S. Cobb, "An Open Season for Ancestors," *Saturday Evening Post,* October 7, 1911, 8–9, 57–58; Cobb, "In the Haunt of the Deadly a La," *Saturday Evening Post,* October 14, 1911, 8, 53–54.

18. Cohn, *Creating America,* 83–84; Chatterton, *Cobb,* 86–87; Yates, *American Humorist,* 129; Cobb, *Exit Laughing,* 333; Jeanette Tandy, *Crackerbox Philosophers in American Humor and Satire* (Port Washington, NY: Kennikat Press, 1925), 167. There is some disagreement among Cobb's biographers over the number of Judge Priest stories, but Chatterton's number is most accurate. The title "Judge Priest—Murder Witness" was changed to "Words and Music" in Irvin S. Cobb, *Back Home: Being the Narrative of Judge Priest and His People* (New York: George H. Doran, 1912).

19. Cobb, *Exit Laughing,* 333–47; Lawson, *Cobb,* 90; Chatterton, *Cobb,* 86–107; Neuman, *Cobb,* 88–99; Yates, *American Humorist,* 128–31; Alben W. Barkley, *That Reminds Me—* (New York: Doubleday, 1954), 64.

20. Irvin S. Cobb, "Words and Music," *Saturday Evening Post,* October 28, 1911, 9–11; J. K. Van Dover and John F. Jebb, *Isn't Justice Always Unfair? The Detective in Southern Literature* (Bowling Green, OH: Bowling Green State University Popular Press, 1996), 83–84.

21. Chatterton, *Cobb*, 86–88; Sloane Gordon, "The Story of Irvin S. Cobb," *Pearson's Magazine* 33 (March 1915): 278–84; Neuman, *Cobb*, 93.

22. Van Dover and Jebb, *Isn't Justice Always Unfair*, 84–85; Charles Sellers, Henry May, and Neil R. McMillen, *A Synopsis of American History* (Chicago: Ivan R. Dee, 1992), 214; Mark Steadman, "Humor," in *Encyclopedia of Southern Culture*, ed. Charles Reagan Wilson and William Ferris (Chapel Hill: University of North Carolina Press, 1989), 855–56; Amy Louise Wood, *Lynching and Spectacle: Witnessing Racial Violence in America, 1890–1980* (Chapel Hill: University of North Carolina Press, 2009); Yates, *American Humorist*, 130–31; William Allen White, "The Humor of the Self-Kidder," *Saturday Review of Literature*, March 22, 1941, 5.

23. Yates, *American Humorist*, 130–31; Karen L. Cox, *Dreaming of Dixie: How the South Was Created in American Popular Culture* (Chapel Hill: University of North Carolina Press, 2011); Gordon, "Story of Irvin S. Cobb," 278–84; James C. Cobb, *Away down South: A History of Southern Identity* (New York: Oxford University Press, 2005), 67–184, 283; David W. Blight, *Race and Reunion: The Civil War in American Memory* (Cambridge, MA: Belknap Press, 2001), 1–5, 236–39, 350–55, 378, 394–97.

24. *St. Louis Post-Dispatch*, December 10, 17, 24, 1911 (copies in Cobb Papers, Murray State University Special Collections and Archives).

25. Lawson, *Cobb*, 92–96; Reginald Pound, *Arnold Bennett* (New York: William Heinemann, 1953), 226–29, 234–35; Tebbel and Zuckerman, *Lorimer*, 144.

26. Arnold Bennett, *Your United States* (New York: George H. Doran, 1912), 147–48; Arnold Bennett, *The Journal of Arnold Bennett* (Garden City, NY: Literary Guild, 1933), 422–25, 438–39, 444–45, 448–49; Irvin S. Cobb, "Arnold Bennett," *American Magazine*, November 1912, 36, 38; Cobb, *Exit Laughing*, 353–56; Lawson, *Cobb*, 94–95.

27. *Saturday Evening Post*, February 10, March 2, April 6, 27, May 11, June 1, 15, 22, July 6, 13, August 3, 10, 17, 31, September 7, 14, 28, October 5, 19, December 7, 21, 28, 1912.

28. Irvin S. Cobb, "The Mob from Massac," *Saturday Evening Post*, February 10, 1912, 5–7, 32–33; Lawson, *Cobb*, 98–100.

29. Irvin S. Cobb, *Cobb's Anatomy* (New York: George H. Doran, 1912); Chatterton, *Cobb*, 50–53; Lawson, *Cobb*, 97.

30. Cobb, *Cobb's Anatomy*, 11, 61; Lawson, *Cobb*, 97.

31. *Saturday Evening Post* cover, December 28, 1912.

32. Lawson, *Cobb*, 97–101; Cobb, *Back Home*, vii–xi; review of *Back Home* in *Bookman*, January 1913, 237, clipping in Louisville Free Public Library (LFPL).

33. Irvin S. Cobb, "Black and White," *Saturday Evening Post*, September 7, 1912, 18–20, 40–41.

34. Cobb, *Exit Laughing*, 469; Irvin S. Cobb, "The Belled Buzzard," *Saturday Evening Post*, September 28, 1912, 3–5, 37, reprinted in *Fiction Parade and Golden Book*, October 1935, 762–63.

35. Cobb, "Belled Buzzard," in *Fiction Parade*, 766–67.

36. Chatterton, *Cobb*, 108–9, 116; Masson, *Our American Humorists*, 101.

37. Chatterton, *Cobb,* 52; Lawson, *Cobb,* 103, 138; Irvin S. Cobb, *Cobb's Bill of Fare* (New York: George H. Doran, 1913), 1–148; *Fielding Star* (New Zealand), September 6, 1915.

38. Neuman, *Cobb,* 103: Irvin S. Cobb, "Fishhead: The Rejected Story," *Cavalier,* January 11, 1913, 321–23; Cobb to Townsend, January 4, 1913, Townsend Collection.

39. Cobb, "Fishhead," in *Cobb's Cavalcade,* 125–32.

40. Ibid.

41. Chatterton, *Cobb,* 122–23; Grant Overton, "Irvin S. Cobb: Ask Him Another," *Bookman,* August 1927, 673–77, clipping in LFPL.

42. H. L. Mencken, "The Burden of Humor," *Smart Set,* February 1913, 153, 155.

43. Guy J. Forgue et al., eds., *Letters of H. L. Mencken* (Boston: Northeastern, 1981), 36; Masson, *Our American Humorists,* 93.

44. Cobb to Townsend, April 19, 1913, March 20, 1914, Townsend Collection.

45. *Saturday Evening Post,* June 7, 28, July 19, August 2, 16, 1913; Lawson, *Cobb,* 105–7.

46. Irvin S. Cobb, *Roughing It De Luxe* (New York: George H. Doran, 1914), 15–17, 40–51.

47. Ibid., 56–94.

48. Ibid., 97–132.

49. Ibid., 135–72.

50. Ibid., 175–219.

51. *Saturday Evening Post,* September 13, November 1, 15, December 6, 27, 1913, January 10, 24, 1914.

52. Lawson, *Cobb,* 106–11; Neuman, *Cobb,* 129–30; Chatterton, *Cobb,* 55–56; Irvin S. Cobb, *Europe Revised* (New York: George H. Doran, 1914), 19–20.

53. Cobb, *Europe Revised,* 138–60.

54. Ibid., 176–256.

55. Ibid., 282.

56. Ibid., 343–465.

57. Ibid., 467.

58. Kipling to Cobb, October 13, 1913, Cobb Papers, Murray State University Special Collections and Archives; Lawson, *Cobb,* 107–11; Chatterton, *Cobb,* 55–57; *New York Evening Post,* December 13, 1913; Irvin S. Cobb, "Kipling at Home," *Book News Monthly,* February 1914, 274–75, clipping in LFPL.

59. Cobb, *My Wayward Parent,* 113–18; Cobb, *Works: Stickfuls,* 320–27; Lawson, *Cobb,* 110.

60. Lawson, *Cobb,* 111; Margaret (Case) Harriman, *The Vicious Circle: The Story of the Algonquin Round Table* (New York: Rinehart, 1951), 4.

5. World War I

1. Cobb to Townsend, June 10, 1914, Townsend Collection.

2. Jeanne Boydson et al., *Making a Nation* (Upper Saddle River, NJ: Prentice-

Hall, 2002), 627–33; John Keegan, *The First World War* (New York: Vintage, 1999), 3–23.

3. Emmet Crozier, *American Reporters on the Western Front, 1914–1918* (New York: Oxford University Press, 1959), 17–18; Cohn, *Creating America,* 105, 296n; Lawson, *Cobb,* 113; John Tebbel and Mary Ellen Zuckerman, *The Magazine in America, 1741–1990* (New York: Oxford University Press, 1991), 80; Barbara W. Tuchman, *The Guns of August* (New York: Ballantine, 1962), 227.

4. Crozier, *American Reporters,* 42; Lawson, *Cobb,* 113–14; Neuman, *Cobb,* 154–55; Cohn, *Creating America,* 105.

5. Keegan, *First World War,* 24–47; Irvin S. Cobb, "A Little Town Called Montignies St. Christophe," *Saturday Evening Post,* October 10, 1914, 3–5; Cobb, *Paths of Glory: Impressions of War Written at and Near the Front* (New York: George H. Doran, 1915), 1–10. All pages cited are from an electronically produced version of *Paths of Glory;* the original 414-page book sold for $1.50.

6. Cobb, *Paths of Glory,* 4.

7. Ibid., 3–10.

8. Ibid., 12–21.

9. Ibid., 21–22. Western painter Frederic Remington became a close friend of Cobb, who admired and collected his work. Cobb, *Exit Laughing,* 402.

10. Cobb, *Paths of Glory,* 28–82, 93; Cobb, "Punitives versus Primitives," *Saturday Evening Post,* November 14, 1914, 14–15; Cobb, "Being a Guest of the German Kaiser," *Saturday Evening Post,* October 24, 1914, 14 (the cover advertised "Cobb's Story of the War"); Tuchman, *Guns of August,* 315; *Louisville Herald,* September 9, 1914, clipping in LFPL.

11. Lawson, *Cobb,* 118–19; Irvin S. Cobb, "The Funniest Thing that Ever Happened to Me," in *"Here Comes the Bride—" and so Forth* (New York: George H. Doran, 1925), 104–9.

12. Lawson, *Cobb,* 120–22; *New York Times,* September 7, 1914; Cobb, *Paths of Glory,* 83–100, 115–28; Cobb, *Exit Laughing,* 520–28; Crozier, *American Reporters,* 41–42; Joseph J. Mathews, *Reporting the Wars* (Westport, CT: Greenwood Press, 1972), 163, 280; message in German via the American consul in Aachen, Germany, from Chancellor Bethmann-Hollweg to Cobb, September 14, 1914, Cobb Papers, Murray State University Special Collections and Archives, translation by Juergen Rudolph and Charles Rohrer.

13. Irvin S. Cobb, "Being a Guest of the German Kaiser," *Saturday Evening Post,* October 24, 1914, 6–9, 65–68; Cobb, *Paths of Glory,* 37, 150; Lawson, *Cobb,* 121–29.

14. Irvin S. Cobb, "Europe's Rag Doll," *Saturday Evening Post,* January 9, 1915, 11–13, 26, 29–30; Cobb, *Paths of Glory,* 38, 212.

15. Cobb, *Paths of Glory,* 116, 130–31; Lawson, *Cobb,* 122–23.

16. Lawson, *Cobb,* 125; *New York Times,* October 14, 17, 1914. In one of the most recently published histories of World War I, *Catastrophe 1914: Europe Goes to War* (New York: Alfred A. Knopf, 2013), Max Hastings disputes Cobb's claim that

the German army committed no atrocities in the early part of the war. Hastings argues that the Germans did not expect civilians to put up a defense, and their retaliatory acts qualified as atrocities (192–94).

17. J. Lee Thompson, *Politicians, the Press, and Propaganda: Lord Northcliffe & the Great War, 1914–1919* (Kent, OH: Kent State University Press, 1999), 35, 118–19; Irvin S. Cobb, "An Interview with Lord Kitchener," *Saturday Evening Post*, December 5, 1914, 3–4, 34–38; Cobb, *Paths of Glory*, 102–15; Lawson, *Cobb*, 125–26; Cobb, *Works: Stickfuls*, 204–16; Doran, *Chronicles of Barabbas*, 246.

18. Neuman, *Cobb*, 159–60; Cobb, *Works: Stickfuls*, 204–14; Cobb, "Interview with Lord Kitchener," 38; Cobb, *Exit Laughing*, 192–97.

19. Lord Northcliffe to Cobb, December 21, 1914, Cobb Papers, Murray State University Special Collections and Archives; Lawson, *Cobb*, 126; Phillip Knightley, *The First Casualty: From Crimea to Vietnam; the War Correspondent as Hero, Propagandist, and Myth Maker* (New York: Harcourt, Brace, Jovanovich, 1975), 117–19; *Saturday Evening Post*, August 22, 1914, cover; Thompson, *Politicians, the Press, and Propaganda*, 238–44.

20. Lawson, *Cobb*, 127–28; Cobb, "Europe's Rag Doll"; Tebbel and Zuckerman, *Lorimer*, 117; *Manchester Guardian*, March 27, 28, 1915, and *London Daily Telegraph*, March 26, 1915, clippings in LFPL; *New Republic*, clipping used for promotion, Townsend Collection.

21. Lawson, *Cobb*, 123; Cobb, *Exit Laughing*, 303–4; Cobb, *My Wayward Parent*, 153–56; *New York Times*, December 2, 1914.

22. Cobb, *My Wayward Parent*, 155; Neuman, *Cobb*, 160–61; Cobb, *Paths of Glory*, 100; Cobb, *Exit Laughing*, 380–87.

23. Irvin S. Cobb, "Unaccustomed as I Am—," in *Prose and Cons* (New York: George H. Doran, 1926), 263, 268; Lawson, *Cobb*, 128–29.

24. Cobb, "Unaccustomed as I Am—," *Saturday Evening Post*, March 25, 1916, 3–5, 77; Lawson, *Cobb*, 131.

25. Cobb, "Unaccustomed as I Am—," in *Prose and Cons*, 264–68; Chatterton, *Cobb*, 69–70.

26. Cobb, *My Wayward Parent*, 155–56.

27. Cobb, "Unaccustomed as I Am—," in *Prose and Cons*, 277; *Louisville Herald*, February 17, 1915; *Louisville Post*, February 13, 1915; *Louisville Times*, February 13, 1915; *Louisville Courier-Journal*, February 18, 1915; *Paducah Evening Sun*, April 16, 1915, clippings in LFPL; Lawson, *Cobb*, 129–31; program for "Illustrated Talk by Irvin S. Cobb, Macauley's Theatre, February 17, 1915," Townsend Collection.

28. *Dinner Tendered to Irvin S. Cobb* (New York, 1915), 1–2 (copies exist in several locations, including the Kentucky Digital Library); Lawson, *Cobb*, 131; *New York Times*, April 26, 1915.

29. Lawson, *Cobb*, 131; *New York Times*, April 26, 1915; *Louisville Post*, April 28, 1915, clippings in LFPL.

30. *Dinner Tendered to Cobb*, 3–4, 6, 12–13.

31. Irvin S. Cobb Papers, McCracken County Public Library, Paducah, KY;

Dinner Tendered to Cobb, 49. Doran also published a version of the celebration with several illustrations entitled *Irvin Cobb: His Book: Friendly Tributes upon the Occasion of a Dinner Tendered to Irvin Shrewsbury Cobb at the Waldorf-Astoria Hotel* (New York: George H. Doran, 1915).

32. *Dinner Tendered to Cobb,* 50–56.

6. Midlife

1. *Louisville Post,* May 5, 1915; *New York Times,* May 14, 1915, clippings in LFPL.

2. Cobb, *My Wayward Parent,* 156–57; Cobb, *Exit Laughing,* 516; *Lexington Herald,* May 19, 1915, clipping in LFPL.

3. Mary Roberts Rinehart, *My Story: Mary Roberts Rinehart* (Chicago: E. M. Hale, 1931), 204; Lawson, *Cobb,* 136; *Louisville Courier-Journal,* June 27, 1915.

4. Cobb's articles appeared in the *Saturday Evening Post* on August 7, August 28, October 16, and November 6, 1915.

5. Yates, *American Humorist,* 131; Irvin S. Cobb, *Speaking of Operations* (New York: George H. Doran, 1915), 38; Lawson, *Cobb,* 136–38; "Book Reviews," *American Journal of Nursing,* May 1916, 781; *Louisville Times,* March 22, 1916, clippings in LFPL.

6. Doran, *Chronicles of Barabbas,* 246; James Montgomery Flagg, "Portraits in Mud," *Metropolitan,* February 1915, 23, Townsend Collection. This clay figure was cast in bronze, and one of the statues is in the archives at Eastern Kentucky University.

7. Gary Engle, "Irvin Shrewsbury Cobb," in Gale, *Encyclopedia of American Humorists,* 92; Cobb, *Cobb's Cavalcade,* 16; Lawson, *Cobb,* 136–38.

8. Doran, *Chronicles of Barabbas,* 249; Chatterton, *Cobb,* 88–89; J. L. Woodbridge to Cobb, October 27, 1917, Cobb Papers, Murray State University Special Collections and Archives; *New York Times,* November 1, 1914, clipping in LFPL.

9. Kleber, *Kentucky Encyclopedia,* 972; *Louisville Post,* April 16, May 18, 1916; *Louisville Courier-Journal,* May 19, 1916, clippings in LFPL; Charles Reagan Wilson, *Baptized in Blood: The Religion of the Lost Cause, 1885–1920* (Athens: University of Georgia Press, 2004), 30–32, 116, 181–82. In *Blood and Irony: Southern White Women's Narratives of the Civil War, 1861–1937* (Chapel Hill: University of North Carolina Press, 2004), 213–19, Sarah E. Gardner explains the role of the United Daughters of the Confederacy in the development of the Lost Cause and the blending of their views, like those of the United Confederate Veterans, into the militancy of the World War I era. In its often hilarious comments section, *American Magazine* noted that a Birmingham reporter had spotted Cobb wearing a wristwatch, a habit he must have picked up in Europe. The writer commented, "Mark Twain once visited New York in a white duck suit in midwinter, but even he never appeared in Alabama wearing a wrist-watch." "A Humorist and His Wrist-Watch," *American Magazine,* August 12, 1916, 318–19, clipping in LFPL.

10. Irvin S. Cobb, "My Country, 't Is of Thee," *Smart Set,* May 1913, 70; H. L. Mencken, "Critics of More or Less Badness," *Smart Set,* November 14, 1914, 156, Townsend Collection; *Smart Set,* May and June 1913, covers, Townsend Collection.

11. Irvin S. Cobb, "A Card to the Public from Rev. Roscoe T. Fibble," *Saturday Evening Post,* October 24, 1914; Cobb, "Fibble, D.D., Takes Pen in Hand," *Saturday Evening Post,* December 23, 1915, 6; Cobb, *Fibble, D.D.;* review, *New York Times,* circa late 1917, Townsend Collection.

12. Irvin S. Cobb, "The Undoing of Stonewall Jackson Bugg," *McClure's,* September 1915, 38–39; Cobb, "Big Moments of Big Trials," *McClure's,* November 1915, 90–94; Tebbel and Zuckerman, *Lorimer,* 26, 139, 237; Cobb, "The Gold Brick Twins," *Red Book,* December 1915, 226–38. Unlike *McClure's,* which folded in 1929, *Red Book* is still published by the Hearst Corporation and is one of the most important women's magazines in America.

13. Cobb's articles appeared in the *Saturday Evening Post* on January 15, March 11, 25, April 8, 15, 29, May 13, July 1, 22, August 12, September 9, 23, October 7, 14, and November 4, 1916. "Scandalous Doolan, C.S.A.," which appeared in *Red Book* in July 1916, was another southern story.

14. Lawson, *Cobb,* 143; Chatterton, *Cobb,* 93–107; Irvin S. Cobb, *Old Judge Priest* (New York: George H. Doran, 1916); Cobb, "The Glory of the States: Kentucky," *American Magazine,* May 1916, 18–20.

15. Cobb, *Old Judge Priest,* 141–97.

16. "Current Fiction," review of *Old Judge Priest, Nation,* June 1, 1916, 595; "Irvin S. Cobb Proves that Humorists Are Able to Buy Food," *Literary Digest,* July 19, 1919, 58–60, clippings in LFPL.

17. Irvin S. Cobb, *Local Color* (New York: George H. Doran, 1916), 11–17, 19–20.

18. Ibid., 35–46.

19. Ibid., 408–60. Grosset and Dunlap, a larger publisher than Doran, published *Local Color* in an edition that deleted "Smooth Crossing." Grosset and Dunlap also published books by other popular novelists of the day, including Zane Grey, Kathleen Norris, Booth Tarkington, Jack London, and Kentuckian John Fox Jr.

20. *Louisville Times,* August 24, 28, 1916, clipping in LFPL; Cobb, *Exit Laughing,* 287, 295–99; Wilson to Cobb, June 23, 1916, Cobb Papers, Murray State University Special Collections and Archives.

21. *New York Times,* July 5, 1914; "Cobb Acts for the 'Movies,'" *Motion Pictures,* September 1914, 257–58, clippings in LFPL.

22. Lawson, *Cobb,* 140; Gabe Essoe and Raymond Lee, *DeMille: The Man and His Pictures* (New York: Castle Books, 1970), 313; Cecil B. DeMille, *The Autobiography of Cecil B. DeMille,* ed. Donald Hayne (Englewood, NJ: Prentice Hall, 1959), 136–37.

23. *Boston Transcript,* October 9, 1915; *Louisville Courier-Journal,* October 9, 1915; *Louisville Times,* October 9, 1915, clippings in LFPL; Cobb to Townsend, January 7, 1922, Townsend Collection.

24. *New York Times,* November 16, 1915, clipping in LFPL.

25. *Chicago Tribune,* November 28, 1915, clipping in LFPL; *New York Dramatic Mirror,* November 1915, clipping in Townsend Collection; *Louisville Times,* November 22, 1915; *Louisville Courier-Journal,* November 24, 1915, clippings in LFPL.

26. *New York Times,* November 23, 1915, clipping in LFPL; Cobb to Townsend, November 23, 1915, Townsend Collection; Cobb, *Exit Laughing,* 359.

27. Lawson, *Cobb,* 139; *New York Times,* October 4, 1916, clipping in LFPL; Cobb, *Exit Laughing,* 363–65; Cobb to Townsend, August 30, 1921, Townsend Collection.

28. Lawson, *Cobb,* 140–41; *Louisville Courier-Journal,* November 19, 1916; *Chicago Tribune,* August 28, 1916, clippings in LFPL.

29. Irvin S. Cobb, "I Am Strangely Moved by the Movies," *Woman's Home Companion,* July 1917, 15.

30. *Louisville Post,* July 22, 1916; *Louisville Times,* March 21, 1916, clippings in LFPL; "Paul Plaschke," *Lambick Comiclopedia* website (Plaschke later moved on to Hearst's *Chicago Herald-Examiner*); Kleber, *Encyclopedia of Louisville,* 708; program for Authors' League of America, Third Annual Dinner, April 11, 1916, Filson Historical Society; Cobb to Townsend, September 19, 1916 (?), Townsend Collection.

31. Irvin S. Cobb, "Looking Both Ways from Forty," *American Magazine,* May 1917, 11–14, 118–20.

32. Robert H. Davis, "Irvin S. Cobb, a Paducah, Kentucky, Gentleman," *American Magazine,* May 1917, 14.

33. Cohn, *Creating America,* 100–21.

34. Irvin S. Cobb, "The Garb of Men," *Saturday Evening Post,* January 20, 1917; other Cobb articles appeared in the *Saturday Evening Post* on March 24, 31, April 7, 14, 1917.

35. Irvin S. Cobb, "Thrice Is He Armed," *Saturday Evening Post,* April 21, 1917, 7, 133–34, 137–38; Cobb, "The Prussian Paranoia," *Saturday Evening Post,* May 5, 1917, 3–4, 49, 51; Cobb, "Ex-Fightin' Billy: A Timely 'Judge Priest' Story," *Pictorial Review,* June 1917, 8–9, 29–32, 48, 70; George Lorimer, "Peace Terms," *Saturday Evening Post,* June 30, 1917, 22; Cohn, *Creating America,* 120–21.

36. Irvin S. Cobb, *Speaking of Prussians*— (New York: George H. Doran, 1918), 11–80; *Louisville Post,* June 2, 1917; *Chicago Tribune,* June 2, 1917, clippings in LFPL.

37. Cobb, *Exit Laughing,* 552; *Louisville Times,* October 2–4, 15, 1917; *Louisville Post,* April 21, 1917, clippings in LFPL; "Town Gossip," undated newspaper clipping quoting Sunday, Townsend Collection.

38. Irvin S. Cobb, *Those Times and These* (New York: George H. Doran, 1917); review of *Those Times and These, Louisville Baptist World,* November 29, 1917, clipping in LFPL.

39. Irvin S. Cobb, "'Twixt the Bluff and the Sound," *Saturday Evening Post,* May 19, July 7, 28, August 11, September 1, 1917; Cobb, "The Luck Piece," *Saturday Evening Post,* February 2, 1918; Cobb, "Boys Will Be Boys," *Saturday Evening Post,* October 17, 1917, 5–7, 34, 37–39, 41–42, 44–46; Cobb, *Exit Laughing,* 362–63;

Boston Transcript, November 19, 1919; *Louisville Courier-Journal,* October 11, 24, 1919; *New York Times,* October 14, 1919, clippings in LFPL.

40. Irvin S. Cobb, "The Thunders of Silence," *Saturday Evening Post,* February 9, 1918, 3–5, 38, 41–42. Doran rushed to publish this story as a booklet, also titled *The Thunders of Silence,* in early 1918, not long after it appeared in the *Post.*

41. John Tebbel, *Between Covers: The Rise and Transformation of Book Publishing in America* (New York: Oxford University Press, 1987), 195.

42. Irvin S. Cobb, "The Gallowsmith," *All-Story Weekly,* February 9, 1918, 529–43.

7. Momentum

1. Cobb, *My Wayward Parent,* 110–11, 129–82; Lawson, *Cobb,* 46–48, 64.

2. Cobb, *My Wayward Parent,* 100–28; Doran, *Chronicles of Barabbas,* 244–45.

3. Irvin S. Cobb, "Life among the Abandoned Farmers," *Saturday Evening Post,* September 13, 1913. This article was also published as the final chapter in *Those Times and These,* 343–74, and was expanded into a book, *The Abandoned Farmers* (New York: George H. Doran, 1920), detailing the development of Cobb's land into a homesite; Chatterton, *Cobb,* 54–55.

4. Lawson, *Cobb,* 145–50; Irvin S. Cobb, "Back to the Land," *Saturday Evening Post,* November 3, 1917, 3–4, 59; Cobb, "Back to the Land—Leading the Abandoned Life," *Saturday Evening Post,* December 1, 1917, 18–19, 73–77; Cobb, *My Wayward Parent,* 173.

5. "They Spin Yarns to Please You," *Collier's,* November 18, 1916, 3; Neuman, *Cobb,* 212; Cobb, *My Wayward Parent,* 141–42; Cobb to James B. Pond, May 12, 1921, Cobb Papers, Filson Historical Society.

6. Cobb, *Exit Laughing,* 464–66; Ed Weiner, *The Damon Runyon Story* (New York: Longmans, Green, 1948), 99; Edwin P. Hoyt, *A Gentleman of Broadway* (Boston: Little, Brown, 1964), 112, 136, 163, 231; Tom Clark, *The World of Damon Runyon* (New York: Harper and Row, 1978), 39; John Mosedale, *The Men Who Invented Broadway: Damon Runyon, Walter Winchell & Their World* (New York: R. Marek, 1981), 117; Raphael James Cristy, *Charles M. Russell: The Storyteller's Art* (Albuquerque: University of New Mexico Press, 2004), 34; Irvin S. Cobb, "Battling with Bogey," *American Golfer,* April 3, 1920, 4–6, clipping in Murray State University Special Collections and Archives; Cobb, *My Wayward Parent,* 176–77.

7. Cobb, *My Wayward Parent,* 152–53.

8. Cobb, *Exit Laughing,* 295–314. Irvin and Laura hobnobbed with President Wilson soon after his second marriage in 1915 at a dinner in the residence of Secretary of the Navy Josephus Daniels. Cobb, *Exit Laughing,* 467.

9. Boydson et al., *Making a Nation,* 645–50; John Toland, *No Man's Land: 1918—The Last Year of the Great War* (Garden City, NY: Doubleday, 1980), 405–510.

10. *Louisville Courier-Journal,* December 25, 1917, clipping in LFPL; Kleber, *Encyclopedia of Louisville,* 158–59.

11. *Louisville Courier-Journal,* February 10, 1918.

12. The *Saturday Evening Post* articles published in *The Glory of the Coming* were those in the March 9, April 27, May 18, 25, June 1, 15, 22, 29, July 20, August 24, 31, September 7, and November 23, 1918, issues. In her biography of Cobb, Anita Lawson maintains that "many" of the chapters in *The Glory of the Coming* "were written after he returned" from Europe. I suspect that, given Cobb's ability to write off the cuff, he already had these well in hand when he returned in June 1918. Lawson, *Cobb,* 161; Cobb, *Glory of the Coming,* ix, xvi.

13. Cobb, *Glory of the Coming,* 21–24; *Louisville Courier-Journal,* February 10, 1918, clipping in LFPL.

14. Cobb, *Glory of the Coming,* 27–30.

15. Ibid., 27–34.

16. Cobb, *Exit Laughing,* 428–34.

17. Knightley, *First Casualty,* 127.

18. "Bozeman Bulger," in *Encyclopedia of Alabama Online;* Cobb, *Exit Laughing,* 306; George Creel, *Rebel at Large: Recollections of Fifty Crowded Years* (New York: G. P. Putnam's Sons, 1947), 153, 158–59, 221, 286.

19. Cobb, *Glory of the Coming,* 40–41.

20. Ibid., 67, 195–234, 435.

21. Ibid., 170.

22. Ibid., 172, 186–87, 279–307, 368, 424–35, 452–53. The *Louisville Courier-Journal* editorialized on August 29, 1918 (clipping in LFPL), that "no man writing for the press to-day qualified better than Cobb" to write about African American soldiers because of his knowledge of both southern and northern blacks.

23. Lawson, *Cobb,* 164–66: Cobb, *Glory of the Coming,* 296–97; Cobb, *Exit Laughing,* 435–36; *Louisville Courier-Journal,* August 28, 29, 1918; *New York Times,* November 3, 1918, clippings in LFPL.

24. Cobb, *Glory of the Coming,* 352–33.

25. Ibid., 359; Cobb, *My Wayward Parent,* 174.

26. Cobb, *My Wayward Parent,* 174; *Louisville Courier-Journal,* June 27, 1918; Keegan, *First World War,* 372–414.

27. *Louisville Herald,* December 15, 18, 1918, clippings in LFPL; Cobb, *Exit Laughing,* 435–45; Lawson, *Cobb,* 164–66.

28. *New York Times,* January 12, 1919, clipping in LFPL. Cobb's book retailed for $1.75.

29. *Boston Transcript,* January 9, 1919; *Chicago Tribune,* January 7, 11, 1919; *New Orleans Picayune,* January 19, 1919; *Louisville Courier-Journal,* January 7, 19, June 26, 1919; *Louisville Herald,* June 26, 1919, clippings in LFPL; Lawson, *Cobb,* 167. For an example of the buildup of American propaganda, see Craig W. Campbell, *Reel America and World War I: A Comprehensive Filmography and History of Motion Pictures in the United States, 1914–1920* (Jefferson, NC: McFarland, 1985).

30. Cobb, *Exit Laughing,* 307.

31. Ibid., 307–12. In contrast, Cobb had high praise for Theodore Roosevelt's ability to fit into any type of political crowd and situation.

32. H. L. Mencken, "The Burden of Humor," *Smart Set,* February 1913, 155; Mencken, "A Review of Reviewers," *Smart Set,* October 1914, 158; Mencken, "A Massacre in a Mausoleum," *Smart Set,* February 1916, 151; Mencken, "The Great American Art," *Smart Set,* March 1916, 309; Lawson, *Cobb,* 167–68.

33. Edward J. O'Brien, "The Best Sixty-Three American Short Stories of 1917," *Bookman,* February 1918, 698–99.

34. Carl Bode, ed., *The New Mencken Letters* (New York: Dial Press, 1977), 85.

35. H. L. Mencken, *Prejudices: First Series* (New York: Alfred A. Knopf, 1919), 97–104; Edgar Kemler, *The Irreverent Mr. Mencken* (Boston: Little, Brown, 1950), 114.

36. H. L. Mencken, *Prejudices: Second Series* (New York Alfred A. Knopf, 1920), 32; Mencken, *Prejudices: First, Second, and Third Series* (New York: Library of America, 2010), 496.

37. Gerald W. Johnson, foreword to Fred C. Hobson Jr., *Serpent in Eden: H. L. Mencken and the South* (Chapel Hill: University of North Carolina Press, 1974), ix–xi.

38. Kemler, *Irreverent Mr. Mencken,* 90; Forgue et al., *Letters of H. L. Mencken,* 186–87; Lawson, *Cobb,* 168.

39. Irvin S. Cobb, "I Admit I Am a Good Reporter," *American Magazine,* August 1919, 60–61, 75–76, 79–80, 83.

40. Townsend to Cobb, January 13, [no year], August 23, 1924; Mencken to Townsend, circa early 1920s (two letters); Townsend to "The Smart Set," March 22, 1922, Townsend Collection.

41. "Mint Condition: The History of the Julep," April 22, 2012, http://www.thelouisvillepaper.com/mint-condition-the-history-of-the-julep/; "Drink This Tonight: Mint Juleps," April 9, 2013, http://www.charlestoncitypaper.com/charleston/drink-this-tonight-mint-juleps/Content?oid=3323830.

42. Harriman, *Vicious Circle,* 4, 32, 201–2; Samuel Hopkins Adams, *A. Woollcott: His Life and His World* (New York: Reynal and Hitchcock, 1945), 121; Lawson, *Cobb,* 76.

43. Neuman, *Cobb,* 183–99; Lawson, *Cobb,* 170–72; Chatterton, *Cobb,* 61–62.

44. Cobb's work appeared in the *Saturday Evening Post* on January 25, May 10, 24, July 19, August 9, 20, 23, October 11, 25, November 1, and December 6, 1919.

45. "Life of the Party" appeared in the *Saturday Evening Post* on January 25, 1919, and was reprinted in several of Cobb's books, including *Irvin Cobb at His Best,* 95–159. Doran initially published *The Life of the Party,* a sixty-six-page booklet, in 1919.

46. *Boston Transcript,* September 20, 1919, clipping in LFPL; Cobb to Mr. Kane, November 10, 1919, Cobb Papers, Filson Historical Society; Irvin S. Cobb, "When August the Second Was April the First," *Saturday Evening Post,* November 1, 1919, 10–11, 101, 104.

47. Cobb, "Life among the Abandoned Farmers," 3–5, 65–66; Cobb, "Back to the Land—Leading the Abandoned Life," 3–4, 59; Lawson, *Cobb*, 76, 145–49, 161, 186–87, 202; Cobb, *My Wayward Parent*, 171.

48. Irvin S. Cobb, "Some Things H. Hoover Overlooked," *Saturday Evening Post*, May 24, 1919, 10–11, 130; Cobb, "In Which We Build a House," *Saturday Evening Post*, September 20, 1919, 10–11, 133–35; Cobb, "And Sold To—Irvin S. Cobb," *Saturday Evening Post*, October 11, 1919, 3–4, 165–66, 169–70; Cobb, "Life among Us Landed Proprietors," *Saturday Evening Post*, October 25, 1919, 6–7, 153.

49. Cobb, *Abandoned Farmers*, 11–14.

50. Ibid., 17–247.

51. Margaret McElroy, "Irvin Cobb Builds Himself a House," *House and Garden*, February 1922, 26–27; Clarence Fowler, "The Gardens at 'Rebel Ridge,'" *Garden Magazine*, December 1921, 202–3; "Irvin S. Cobb and Peter B. Kyne Telling Each Other Stories," *Hearst's International*, August 1923; Cobb to Townsend, circa 1922, Townsend Collection. Cobb preferred a female African American cook, owing to his enjoyment of southern food. As he was moving to Rebel Ridge, he told a friend, "We hope . . . to land a nigger." Cobb to Claire Lingley, circa early 1920s, Cobb Papers, Murray State University Special Collections and Archives.

52. Mary Stewart Cutting Jr., "What He Thinks about Himself: America's Beloved Humorist," circa early 1920s, Townsend Collection.

53. Irvin S. Cobb, "The Advantages of Being Homely," *American Magazine*, July 1918, 43–45, 87.

8. Accommodation

1. Tebbel and Zuckerman, *Magazine in America, 1741–1990*, 83, 157; Emery, Emery, and Roberts, *Press and America*, 403, 569; Pendennis, "'My Types'—Irvin S. Cobb," *Forum*, October 1917, 471–80; Patricia Ward D'Itri, *Damon Runyon* (Boston: Twayne, 1982), 137–51.

2. Hoyt, *Gentleman of Broadway*, 93–95, 112, 130, 136, 163–64, 231.

3. Charles B. Driscoll, *The Life of O. O. McIntyre* (New York: Greystone Press, 1938), 72–81, 232–33, 322–33; Cobb to Bill Hogg, October 26, 1921, William Clifford Hogg Papers, University of Texas at Austin (Cobb usually referred to Hogg as Bill, though others called him Will); "William Clifford Hogg," *The Handbook of Texas Online;* Jonathan Yardly, *Ring: A Biography of Ring Lardner* (New York: Random House, 1977), 327; Elder, *Ring Lardner*, 129, 198–99, 216–17, 316; Cobb, *Exit Laughing*, 115–16; Irvin S. Cobb, "Speaking of Corporations," *National Pictorial Brain Power Monthly*, November 1921, 16, clipping in LFPL.

4. E. V. Lucas, "From an American Note-Book," *Outlook*, September 15, 1920, 100; Cobb, *Exit Laughing*, 391–93.

5. Irvin S. Cobb, *Eating in Two or Three Languages* (New York: George H. Doran, 1919), 47, 58; *New York Times*, February 16, 1919; *Louisville Post*, February 22, 1919, clippings in LFPL; Chatterton, *Cobb*, 58–59.

6. *Louisville Courier-Journal,* December 20, 1919. The full text of "The American's Creed" is as follows: "I believe in the United States of America, as a government of the people, by the people, for the people; whose just powers are derived from the consent of the governed; a democracy in a republic; a sovereign nation of many sovereign States; a perfect union; one and inseparable; established upon these principles of freedom, equality, justice and humanity for which American patriots sacrificed their lives and their fortunes. I therefore believe it is my duty to my country to love it, to support its Constitution, to obey its laws, to respect its flag, and to defend it against all enemies." "The American's Creed," USHistory.org; *Houston Post,* February 4, 1920, clipping in LFPL; Tebbel, *Between Covers,* 195–96.

7. Jan Cohn, *Improbable Fiction: The Life of Mary Roberts Rinehart* (Pittsburgh: University of Pittsburgh Press, 1980), 78–79, 108; Mary Roberts Rinehart, "Roughing It with the Men," *American Magazine,* December 1922, 18–21, 125–28.

8. Irvin S. Cobb, "Oh, Well, You Know How Women Are!" and Mary Roberts Rinehart, "Isn't that Just Like a Man!" *American Magazine,* October 1919, 10–13, 183–87; *Chicago Tribune,* March 13, 1920, clipping in LFPL; Chatterton, *Cobb,* 64–66.

9. Irvin S. Cobb, "'Miste-er Chairma-an!'" *Saturday Evening Post,* June 5, 1920, 3–4, 50, 53–54, 57; *Louisville Courier-Journal,* April 3, 1921, clipping in LFPL.

10. *Louisville Post,* June 5, 9, 11, 14, 23, 28, 30, July 1–3, 1920, clippings in LFPL; "Politics on the Cobb, *Nation,* July 17, 1920, 62–63; *New York Times,* July 6, 1926. Harding won in a landslide in 1920, with only the "Solid South," minus Tennessee, supporting Cox. This began a decade of domination by the Republican Party.

11. Irvin S. Cobb, *From Place to Place* (New York: George H. Doran, 1920), 11–407; Chatterton, *Cobb,* 78; *Louisville Courier-Journal,* April 4, 1920; *New York Times,* February 1, 1920.

12. *Louisville Courier-Journal,* March 26, April 2, 3, 21, 1921; *Louisville Herald,* April 2, 9, 21, 1921, clippings in LFPL.

13. *New York Times,* October 11, 12, 16, 17, 1917; *Louisville Post,* October 13, 1921, clippings in LFPL.

14. *Louisville Post,* June 30, July 1, 2, 1921, clippings in LFPL.

15. Jack Dempsey with Barbara Piattelli Dempsey, *Dempsey* (New York: W. H. Allen, 1977), 145–49; Randy Roberts, *Jack Dempsey: The Manassa Mauler* (Baton Rouge: Louisiana State University Press, 1979), 120–21; *New York Times,* July 3, 1921; *Louisville Evening Post,* July 5, 1921.

16. George Kimball and John Schulian, eds., *At the Fights: American Writers on Boxing* (New York: Library of America, 2011), 10–19; *New York Times,* July 3, 1921, clipping in LFPL.

17. Irvin S. Cobb, "Cobb Fights It over Again," in Kimball and Schulian, *At the Fights,* 15.

18. Ibid., 17–19; Roberts, *Jack Dempsey,* 126.

19. Irvin S. Cobb, "A Plea for Old Cap Collier," *Saturday Evening Post,* July 3, 1920, 1, 3–4, 49–50, 52; Cobb, *A Plea for Old Cap Collier* (New York: George H.

Doran, 1921). The latter, a forty-five-page booklet, fit Doran's formula for a light comical publication with instant appeal to Cobb's fans and a sure moneymaker.

20. John Lomax to Hogg, December 21, 1921, and Arthur LeFevre Jr. to Hogg, December 7, 1921, William Hogg Papers.

21. Chatterton, *Cobb*, 52–53; Irvin S. Cobb, "The Great Reduction," *Saturday Evening Post*, July 16, 1921, 3–4, 67, 70; Cobb, "One Third Off," *Saturday Evening Post*, July 23, 1921, 6–7, 74, 77–79, 82; Cobb, *One Third Off* (New York: George H. Doran, 1921); *Louisville Herald*, November 18, 1923; *Times Literary Supplement*, May 18, 1922, clippings in LFPL.

22. Cobb to Townsend, September 13, 1921, Townsend Collection; *Louisville Courier-Journal*, April 21, 1918; *Louisville Herald*, July 3, 1921; *Louisville Post*, April 1, 1921, clippings in LFPL.

23. Neuman, *Cobb*, 240–41; Irvin S. Cobb, "The Nearest I Ever Came to Death," *American Magazine*, December 1922, 5–7, 123–25.

24. Cobb, "Nearest I Ever Came to Death," 5; Cobb, *Exit Laughing*, 516–19.

25. Cobb, "Nearest I Ever Came to Death," 5–7, 123–25.

26. Cobb to Will Hogg, March 4, 24, 1922, William Hogg Papers; Townsend to Cobb, April 13, 1922, Townsend Collection.

27. Kleber, *Kentucky Encyclopedia*, 218, 237–38, 347–49; Lucas, *History of Blacks in Kentucky*, 192–96, 199–200, 244, 293, 321; Wright, *History of Blacks in Kentucky*, 2:84–86, 92, 94, 101–3.

28. Wright, *History of Blacks in Kentucky*, 2:79–84; Wood, *Lynching and Spectacle*, 113–18; *Louisville Courier-Journal*, April 21, 1911, clipping in LFPL.

29. Kenneth T. Jackson, *The Ku Klux Klan in the City, 1915–1930* (New York: Oxford University Press, 1967), 236–38; M. William Lutholtz, *Grand Dragon: D. C. Stephenson and the Ku Klux Klan in Indiana* (West Lafayette, IN: Purdue University Press, 1991); Jim Ruiz, *The Black Hood of the Ku Klux Klan* (Lanham, MD: Austin and Winfield, 1998), 30.

30. David M. Chalmers, *Hooded Americanism: The History of the Ku Klux Klan* (Durham, NC: Duke University Press, 1987), 154–56; Lawson, *Cobb*, 174–77.

31. *Paducah News-Democrat*, December 28–31, 1922; *Louisville Herald*, December 29, 1922, clippings in LFPL; Chalmers, *Hooded Americanism*, 156.

32. Brian Ward, "Music, Musical Theatre, and the Imagined South in Interwar Britain," *Journal of Southern History* 80 (February 2014): 39–72. Though not a close friend of D. W. Griffith, Cobb knew the famous filmmaker and certainly agreed with his rendering of the immediate post–Civil War Ku Klux Klan in *Birth of a Nation*. They also appeared together in a silent film clip about the making of one of Griffith's early films in New Jersey. Robert M. Henderson, *D. W. Griffith: His Life and Work* (New York: Oxford University Press, 1972), 145, 229.

33. Irvin S. Cobb, *J. Poindexter, Colored* (New York: George H. Doran, 1922); Chatterton, *Cobb*, 124.

34. Chatterton, *Cobb*, 103; Lawson, *Cobb*, 178–79; Benjamin Brawley, "The Negro in American Literature," *Bookman* (1923), online.

35. Cobb, *Poindexter,* 11–40.

36. Ibid., 41–139.

37. Ibid., 140–270.

38. *Louisville Courier-Journal,* August 13, 1922; *New York Times,* July 30, 1922; *Literary Review,* September 1922, clippings in LFPL and in other scrapbooks.

39. Lawson, *Cobb,* 179; Walter F. White, *The Fire in the Flint* (New York: Alfred A. Knopf, 1924).

40. Charles Scruggs, *The Sage in Harlem: H. L. Mencken and the Black Writers of the 1920s* (Baltimore: Johns Hopkins University Press, 1984), 10–11, 24, 119; Edward E. Waldron, *Walter White and the Harlem Renaissance* (Port Washington, NY: Associated Faculty Press, 1978), 47–50, 57–58, 69–71; Walter F. White, *A Man Called White: The Autobiography of Walter White* (New York: Viking Press, 1948), 67.

41. Lawson, *Cobb,* 186; Neuman, *Cobb,* 177; Cobb to Townsend, September 13, 1921, August 14, 1922, Townsend Collection; *Louisville Courier-Journal,* February 4, 1923 (photo of Cobb and Buff). I have never found anything directly addressing Laura Cobb's health at this time. Another humorist, S. J. Perelman, had a similar experience after moving from Manhattan and trying farm life in Bucks County, Pennsylvania. As related in *Acres and Pains,* published in 1947, he and his wife moved again after becoming frustrated with country living. Perelman's "rueful tale" became the basis for the 1960s television sitcom *Green Acres.* Franz Lidz, "Welcome to Farmtopia," *Smithsonian,* May 1915, 76.

42. Irvin S. Cobb, *The Works of Irvin S. Cobb: Sundry Accounts* (New York: George H. Doran, 1922); Neuman, *Cobb,* 107–8.

43. Lawson, *Cobb,* 182–83; *New York Times,* May 14, 1922, clipping in Cobb Papers, Murray State University Special Collections and Archives; Neuman, *Cobb,* 107–8; Irvin S. Cobb, "Darkness," in *The Best Short Stories of 1921,* ed. Edward J. O'Brien (Boston: Small, Maynard, 1921), 52–81; *New York Evening Post,* June 10, 1922, clipping in LFPL.

44. The *Louisville Evening Post* published this brief column for one year until it was taken over by the *Louisville Courier-Journal,* which ran it for several years into the late 1920s. See clippings in LFPL and Cobb Papers, Murray State University Special Collections and Archives.

9. From the "Boss" to the "Chief"

1. Irvin S. Cobb, "George Horace Lorimer, Original Easy Boss," *Bookman,* December 1918, 389–94, clipping in LFPL.

2. Tebbel and Zuckerman, *Magazine in America, 1741–1990,* 178, 180.

3. Cobb to Townsend, August 14, 1922, Townsend Collection. During the 1920s, Townsend attempted to publish a biography of Cobb with Doran. Doran did not accept the manuscript, and Cobb finally suggested that Townsend send it to another publisher. The book was never published. Cobb may have torpedoed the project himself. He admitted to Townsend that he had told Doran, "I doubted whether

the biography in book form would sell well while I was living but that should I die or live to be an old man perhaps it might have a real market." Cobb to Townsend, January 7, October 1, 1922, August 15, 1924, April 24, 1928; Townsend to Cobb, April 13, 25, 1922, Townsend Collection.

4. W. A. Swanberg, *Citizen Hearst* (New York: BBS, 1961), 230, 266, 366; David Nasaw, *The Chief: The Life of William Randolph Hearst* (Boston: Houghton Mifflin Harcourt, 2000), 190–92, 209.

5. Tebbel and Zuckerman, *Magazine in America, 1741–1990,* 153; John Tebbel and Mary Ellen Zuckerman, *The Magazine in America: A Compact History* (New York: Oxford University Press, 1969), 172–73, 189; Cohn, *Creating America,* 66–69, 178–79.

6. A. L. Lazarus, ed., *The Best of George Ade* (Bloomington: Indiana University Press, 1985), ix; Lee Coyle, *George Ade* (New York: College and University Press, 1964), 136–41; Terence Tobin, ed., *Letters of George Ade* (West Lafayette, IN: Purdue University Press, 1973), 180.

7. *New York Times,* March 24, 1923; *Louisville Courier-Journal,* April 1, 1923, clippings in LFPL; Lawson, *Cobb,* 183.

8. Chatterton, *Cobb,* 108, 116–17; Irvin S. Cobb, "Snake Doctor," *Cosmopolitan,* November 1922, 14–22, 100, 102.

9. Irvin S. Cobb, *Snake Doctor and Other Stories* (New York: George H. Doran, 1923). "The Second Coming of a First Husband" was also published under a different title, "Her First Husband's Second Coming," in several newspapers, including the *Louisville Courier-Journal,* January 14, 1923, clipping in LFPL.

10. *Louisville Courier-Journal,* March 24, 25, April 1, 1923; *New York Evening Post,* May 19, 1923; *New York Times Book Review,* July 22, 1923; *Boston Evening Transcript,* July 28, 1923, clippings in LFPL.

11. Masson, *Our American Humorists,* 91–96; Tandy, *Crackerbox Philosophers,* 167; Townsend to Cobb, September 1, 1925, Townsend Collection.

12. O'Brien, *Best Short Stories of 1916,* 85–114; *1917,* 86–127; *1921,* 52–81; *1923,* 144–169; *1928,* 94–112.

13. Cobb, *Works: Stickfuls; New York Evening Post,* June 16, 1923; *Boston Evening Transcript,* May 12, 1923, clipping in LFPL; Cobb to Townsend, December 27, 1923, Townsend Collection.

14. *Louisville Courier-Journal,* March 9, 1923, January 3, December 30, 1924, July 2, October 11, 1925; *Louisville Times,* January 1, December 30, 1924, clippings in LFPL.

15. Cobb to Townsend, January 19, 1923, Townsend Collection; Cobb's secretary to Townsend, September 17, 1924, Townsend Papers; Cobb quoted in *Literary Digest,* June 23, 1923, 28–29; *Louisville Times,* November 28, 1923; *New York Times,* July 30, 1924; *Louisville Courier-Journal,* April 10, November 28, 29, 1923, January 1, 1925; *Louisville Post,* November 28, 1923; Irvin S. Cobb, "How to Begin at the Top and Work Down," *American Mercury,* August 1925, 34–35, clippings in LFPL.

16. Ray Long, ed., *My Story I Like Best* (New York: International Magazine, 1924), 7–10, 53–110.

17. Cobb to Will Hogg, circa 1922, William Hogg Papers.

18. Lawson, *Cobb*, 186–88; *New York Times*, January 28, 1923, clipping in LFPL.

19. Wedding notice in the Townsend Collection; *Louisville Post*, June 7, 1923, clipping in LFPL; Lawson, *Cobb*, 186–88; *Louisville Courier-Journal*, June 18, 1923; Neuman, *Cobb*, 178–79; Cobb to Will Hogg, July 8, 1926, and Hogg to Cobb, November 19, 1926, William Hogg Papers.

20. Cobb to Townsend, January 7, 1922, Townsend Collection; Cobb to John M. Saunders, March 2, 1925, Irvin S. Cobb Collection, University of Kentucky Special Collections; *Louisville Herald*, July 1, 1925; Elisabeth Cobb Chapman, "What His Family Thinks of Irvin S. Cobb," *Liberty Magazine*, May 30, 1925, 11–12; O. J. Cadwallader to Hogg, November 27, 1925, and Cobb to Hogg, June 17, 1925, William Hogg Papers.

21. Cobb, *Exit Laughing*, 374–84; Cobb, *A Laugh a Day Keeps the Doctor Away: His Favorite Stories as Told by Irvin S. Cobb* (New York: George H. Doran, 1923), vii–xii; Cobb, *Many Laughs for Many Days: Another Year's Supply (365) of His Favorite Stories* (New York: George H. Doran, 1925); *New York Times*, November 22, 1925, clipping in LFPL.

22. Chatterton, *Cobb*, 14–17, 69, 148; *Louisville Courier-Journal*, October 12, 1924; Irvin S. Cobb, *Goin' on Fourteen: Being Cross-Sections out of a Year in the Life of an Average Boy* (New York: George H. Doran, 1924). Lawson's biography of Cobb does not mention this book.

23. Irvin S. Cobb, "Little Lord Pantsleroy," *Cosmopolitan*, July 1924, 80–83, 134, 136–38; Chatterton, *Cobb*, 15; Cobb, *Goin' on Fourteen*.

24. Chatterton, *Cobb*, 14–17, 69; Cobb, *Goin' on Fourteen*.

25. *New York Times*, October 26, 1924; *New York Evening Post*, November 8, 1924; *Louisville Herald*, September 28, 1924, clippings in LFPL.

26. Irvin S. Cobb, "Standing Room Only," *Cosmopolitan*, October 1924, 16–21, 102, 104, 106, 108.

27. *Louisville Herald*, November 18, 1923; *Louisville Post*, March 29, 1924; *The Great White Way* website; *New York Times*, January 4, 1924, clippings in LFPL; Lawson, *Cobb*, 181.

28. Chatterton, *Cobb*, 130.

29. Lawson, *Cobb*, 181–82; *Everready Hour* website; Cobb, *Exit Laughing*, 368–69; George H. Douglas, *The Early Days of Radio Broadcasting* (Jefferson, NC: McFarland, 1987), 34–37, 137, 219; *Louisville Times*, March 8, 1927, clipping in LFPL.

30. Irvin S. Cobb, *Cobb's American Guyed Books: Kentucky, the Proud State* (New York: George H. Doran, 1924).

31. Ibid.; *Boston Transcript*, April 30, 1924; *New York Times Book Reviews*, April 20, 1924, clippings in LFPL. *Irvin Cobb at His Best* contained six of Cobb's best-known stories.

32. Irvin S. Cobb, *Alias Ben Alibi* (New York: George H. Doran, 1925). On several occasions Cobb dealt with the issue of suicide. For example, in "A Letter to

a Relative," *Good Housekeeping* (another Hearst magazine), November 1923, 10–13, 117–18, Cobb explored the life of an elderly man who commits suicide after he has a stroke and his wife suddenly dies. The story ends with the man writing a letter to his son explaining his actions.

33. *Saturday Review of Literature,* February 21, 1925; *New York Evening Post,* March 14, 1925; *Boston Transcript,* March 18, 1925; *New York Times,* March 1, 1925, clippings in LFPL; Chatterton, *Cobb,* 124.

34. Cobb, *"Here Comes the Bride—"; "*Chatterton, *Cobb,* 66–68.

35. *Boston Transcript,* June 13, 1925; *New York Post,* August 22, 1925; *Saturday Review of Literature,* September 16, 1925, clippings in LFPL.

36. Cobb, *Prose and Cons;* Chatterton, *Cobb,* 69–70; Lawson, *Cobb,* 111, 195, 203.

37. Cobb, *Prose and Cons,* 279–93.

38. Chatterton, *Cobb,* 69; *New York Times,* July 25, 1926; *Boston Transcript,* August 11, 1926, clippings in LFPL.

39. *New York Herald Tribune,* September 12, 1926, clipping in LFPL; Cobb to Townsend, March 11, 1927, Townsend Collection; *New York Post,* October 2, 1926, clipping in LFPL.

40. *Paducah News-Democrat,* May 5, 1926, February 20, 1927; *Louisville Herald,* April 30, 1926, clippings in LFPL.

41. Lawson, *Cobb,* 181–82; Cobb, *Exit Laughing,* 473–90.

42. Cobb, *Exit Laughing,* 475–81.

43. Ibid., 481–90; Lawson, *Cobb,* 199–200; *Louisville Times,* November 1, 1926, clipping in LFPL; Cobb's secretary to Townsend, August 16, 1926, Townsend Collection.

44. *Louisville Courier-Journal,* April 19, 1926; Cobb, *My Wayward Parent,* 161–62; Cobb, *Exit Laughing,* 199; Lawson, *Cobb,* 199–200; *New York Times,* August 19, November 9, 1926.

45. *Louisville Herald,* March 26, 1926; *Louisville Times,* March 30, 1926, clippings in LFPL; Lawson, *Cobb,* 195–96.

46. *Louisville Herald-Post,* March 21, 1926, clipping in LFPL.

47. Lawson, *Cobb,* 195–96; *Louisville Herald,* March 26, 1926; *Louisville Times,* March 26, 1926, clippings in LFPL; Charles Fisher, *The Columnists* (New York: Soskin, 1944), 111.

48. Irvin S. Cobb, "The Convict Who Made a Garden on the Road to Hell," *Hearst's International and Cosmopolitan,* March 1925, 40–41, 180–84.

49. Irvin S. Cobb, "The Principle of the Thing," in *On an Island that Cost $24.00* (New York: George H. Doran, 1926), 178–214.

50. Irvin S. Cobb, "The Unbroken Chain," ibid., 49–82.

51. Ibid., 67–82.

52. *Saturday Review of Literature,* August 21, 1926. The March 7, 1926, edition of the *New York Times* was not much kinder to Cobb (clippings in LFPL).

53. Lawson, *Cobb,* 202.

10. From Prosperity to Depression

1. Irvin S. Cobb, "Do I Like Being Famous?" *Smart Set,* April 1928, 18–19; *Paducah News-Democrat,* April 1, 1928; *Louisville Courier-Journal,* February 5, 1928, clippings in LFPL; Lawson, *Cobb,* 215.

2. Cobb to Townsend, August 21, 1928, Townsend Collection.

3. Irvin S. Cobb, *Ladies and Gentlemen* (New York: Cosmopolitan, 1927), 38–39, 73–116, 145–161 (I am citing an electronically produced version of this book); Lawson, *Cobb,* 94.

4. *New York Times,* February 27, 1927; *Saturday Review of Literature,* April 23, 1927, clippings in LFPL.

5. Lawson, *Cobb,* 203; Chatterton, *Cobb,* 124. See *Cosmopolitan,* January–December 1929, for the variety of contributors mentioned.

6. Irvin S. Cobb, *Chivalry Peak* (New York: Cosmopolitan, 1927); *New York Times,* September 25, 1927; *Louisville Courier-Journal,* October 7, 1927, clippings in LFPL.

7. Irvin S. Cobb, *All Aboard: Saga of the Romantic River* (New York: Cosmopolitan, 1928), 1–3; *Louisville Courier-Journal,* August 26, 1928; *New York Times,* August 12, 1928.

8. *Louisville Herald-Post,* October 17, 1928, clipping in LFPL; Cobb, *Exit Laughing,* 41, 548–49; press release, July 29, 1929, Cobb Papers, McCracken County Public Library.

9. Irvin S. Cobb, *Red Likker* (New York: Cosmopolitan, 1929); *Louisville Courier-Journal,* February 5, 1928; Cobb to Townsend, January 5, 1928, Townsend Collection; Cobb to Otto Rothert, January 5, 27, June 16, 1928, and Rothert to Cobb, January 11, 1928, Otto Rothert Collection, Filson Historical Society; Jillson, *Cobb at Frankfort,* 7.

10. Arthur Bartlett Maurice, "The History of Their Books, VII. Irvin S. Cobb," *Bookman,* July 1929, 511–14, clipping in LFPL; Ray Long, "Red Likker," *Cosmopolitan,* February 1929, 74.

11. Chatterton, *Cobb,* 124–25; Lawson, *Cobb,* 205–9. See also reviews dismissing *Red Likker* in *New York Times,* August 15, 1929.

12. *Louisville Herald-Post,* April 29, November 23, 27, 1928, clippings in LFPL; *Louisville Courier-Journal,* June 10, 1928.

13. Irvin S. Cobb, *This Man's World* (New York: Cosmopolitan, 1929); Chatterton, *Cobb,* 12.

14. Cobb, *This Man's World,* 1–28.

15. Lawson, *Cobb,* 212–13; Chatterton, *Cobb,* 82–83.

16. *Saturday Review of Literature,* April 6, 1929; *Louisville Herald-Post,* April 28, 1929; *Louisville Times,* April 29, 1929; *New York Times,* March 24, 1929, clippings in LFPL.

17. Lawson, *Cobb,* 213; *New York Times,* April 8, 1928, July 30, 1929; *Louisville Courier-Journal,* April 30, 1929; *Louisville Herald-Post,* April 26, 1929, clippings in

LFPL; dedication program for the Hotel Irvin Cobb, April 29, 1929, box 11, Cobb Papers, Murray State University Special Collections and Archives. The bridge is still in use, but the Hotel Irvin Cobb has been turned into apartments for seniors, although the ballroom is available for events.

18. Grantland Rice, "A Swordfishing Story by Grantland Rice, Fin Ahead!" *Collier's*, September 24, 1927, 30; telegram from Cobb to Laura Cobb, December 17, 1929, William Hogg Papers.

19. Cobb, *Exit Laughing*, 408–12; John Wilson Townsend, Irvin S. Cobb, and Will Rogers, *Piano Jim and the Impotent Pumpkin Vine or "Charley Russell's Best Story—To My Way of Thinking"* (Lexington, KY: Blue Grass Book Shop, 1947), 9–23.

20. Irvin S. Cobb, "Pure Reason, I Call It," *Smart Set*, March 1928, 18, 102; *New York Times*, October 28, 1928; *Louisville Courier-Journal*, November 3, 1928; *Louisville Herald-Post*, November 4, 1928, clippings in LFPL.

21. Cobb, *My Wayward Parent*, 17; Donald B. Smith, *Long Lance: The True Story of an Impostor* (Lincoln: University of Nebraska Press, 1982), 149–54; Chief Long Lance, "My Trail Upward," *Cosmopolitan*, June 1926, 72–73, 138. Cobb contributed the foreword to *Long Lance*, published in late 1928 by Cosmopolitan Book Company.

22. Eva Marie Garroutte, *Real Indians: Identity and the Survival of Native America* (Berkeley: University of California Press, 2003), 1–4, 140–41; Smith, *Long Lance*, 196, 226–29.

23. Irvin S. Cobb, *Both Sides of the Street* (New York: Cosmopolitan, 1930), 54–55; *La Cronica* (Lima, Peru), January 4, 1929; *Houston Press*, March 5, 1929. Moving in wealthy circles, Cobb dedicated *Both Sides of the Street* to "Thomas J. Watson, Esq.," chairman and CEO of International Business Machines.

24. Irvin S. Cobb, "These Folks Know How to Play: Brazil," *Cosmopolitan*, March 1930, 170 (in the book, the title was changed to "'B' Stands for Brazil and Beauty"); Cobb, *Both Sides of the Street*, 158.

25. Cobb, *Both Sides of the Street*, 161–239, 243–317.

26. Press release, January 1929; Charles Cason to Hogg, April 15, 1929; Cobb to Hogg, May 11, 1929, all in William Hogg Papers; Lawson, *Cobb*, 209–13.

27. Robert H. Davis, "The Literati under the Lens," *Bookman*, August 1929, 639, clipping in LFPL; Cobb to Townsend, December 30, 1929, Townsend to Cobb and return by Cobb with handwritten replies, no date, Townsend Collection; *Louisville Times*, February 13, 1928; *New York Times*, January 5, 20, 1928, clippings in LFPL.

28. Cobb, *Exit Laughing*, 421.

29. Cobb, *My Wayward Parent*, 180–81; Lawson, *Cobb*, 215.

30. *New York Times*, January 24, 1928, July 28, 1929; *Louisville Times*, June 15, 1929; *London Times Literary Review*, March 27, 1930; *New York World-Telegram*, January 29, 1934, clippings in LFPL.

31. *Louisville Courier-Journal*, March 19, 1930; *New York Times*, March 11, 1930, clippings in LFPL; Cobb to "Colonel Shinbolts" [Will Hogg], August 29, 1930, and Buff to "Now Uncle Bill," September 9, 1930, William Hogg Papers.

32. "William Clifford Hogg," in *The New Handbook of Texas*, vol. 3 (Austin: University of Texas Press, 1996), 654–55; John A. Lomax, *Will Hogg, Texan* (Austin: University of Texas Press 1956), vii–51; Neuman, *Cobb*, ix–xi; Cobb, *Exit Laughing*, 135, 554–57. Will and Mike Hogg developed the exclusive River Oaks housing development in Houston, which I suspect Cobb invested in. See Cheryl Caldwell Ferguson, *Highland Park and River Oaks: The Origins of Garden Suburban Community Planning in Texas* (Austin: University of Texas Press, 2014).

33. D. J. Dooley, *The Art of Sinclair Lewis* (Lincoln: University of Nebraska Press, 1967), 35–36; Sheldon Norman Grebstein, *Sinclair Lewis* (New York: Twayne, 1962), 72; James Lundquist, *Theodore Dreiser* (New York: Frederick Ungar, 1978), 120–21; Lundquist, *Sinclair Lewis* (New York: Frederick Ungar, 1972), 89.

34. Mark Schorer, *Sinclair Lewis: An American Life* (New York: McGraw-Hill, 1961), 230, 561–64; Swanberg, *Theodore Dreiser*, 372–73; Lawson, *Cobb*, 216–17.

35. Irvin S. Cobb, *To Be Taken before Sailing* (New York: Cosmopolitan, 1930), 13; *Louisville Courier-Journal*, October 1, 1930. Roosevelt said, famously: "The only thing we have to fear is fear itself."

36. *Louisville Herald-Post*, March 23, 1923, clipping in LFPL.

37. *Louisville Times*, October 8, 1930; *Louisville Herald-Post*, December 5, 1930, clippings in LFPL; Neuman, *Cobb*, 151, 228–29; handwritten question-and-answer script by Cobb for a radio program, January 2, 1931, Cobb Papers, McCracken County Public Library; *Publisher's Weekly*, January 16, 1932; *Louisville Courier-Journal*, February 5, April 1, 15, 1932; *Louisville Herald-Post*, February 6, March 23, 1932, clippings in LFPL.

38. Cobb, *To Be Taken before Sailing*, 1–45.

39. Cobb to Josephine Piercy, April 8, 1929, Bobbs-Merrill Manuscripts, Lilly Library, Indiana University; Irvin S. Cobb, *Incredible Truth* (New York: Cosmopolitan, 1931), x, 1–362; *New York Times*, March 8, 1931.

40. Irvin S. Cobb, *Down Yonder with Judge Priest and Irvin S. Cobb* (New York: Ray Long and Richard R. Smith, 1932); Chatterton, *Cobb*, 91–92; *Louisville Courier-Journal*, April 7, 1932; *Christian Science Monitor*, May 28, 1932; *New York Times*, April 3, 1932, clippings in LFPL; Lawson, *Cobb*, 216–17.

41. *Louisville Courier-Journal*, January 29, 1932; Cobb, *Exit Laughing*, 547–49; Lawson, *Cobb*, 219–21; Cobb, *My Wayward Parent*, 34–35. Irvin Cobb Brody changed his name to Thomas Cobb Brody. Patrizia, known as Pat, used her mother's nickname, Buff, when she entered the acting profession. Lawson, *Cobb*, 220.

42. Irvin S. Cobb, *One Way to Stop a Panic* (New York: R. M. McBride, 1933).

43. Jack O'Bar, *The Origins and History of the Bobbs-Merrill Company* (Champaign-Urbana: University of Illinois Press, 1985), 25–27; check receipt, October 18, 1932; Chambers to Cobb, February 9, 1933; Cobb to Chambers, June 17, August 4, 1933, Bobbs-Merrill Manuscripts. As noted earlier, Cobb often wrote his replies on correspondence and mailed the letter back to the sender.

44. Lawson, *Cobb*, 217–18; *New York Herald-Tribune Books*, clippings in LFPL; Irvin S. Cobb, *Murder Day by Day* (Indianapolis: Bobbs-Merrill, 1933), 302–3.

238 Notes to Pages 176–182

45. Chambers to Cobb, March 13, 15, 1934, with Cobb's handwritten responses, Bobbs-Merrill Manuscripts; Irvin S. Cobb, *Faith, Hope and Charity* (Indianapolis: Bobbs-Merrill, 1934); Hewitt H. Howland to Cobb, May 26, 1934, Bobbs-Merrill Manuscripts.

46. *New York Journal-American,* April 7, 1933; *Louisville Courier-Journal,* April 30, May 3, 1933, clippings in LFPL.

47. Irvin S. Cobb, *"Who's Who" Plus "Here's How!"* (New York: Hotel Waldorf-Astoria, 1934), 4–10.

48. *Louisville Courier-Journal,* December 1, 1927; *New York Times,* March 13, 1933; Irvin S. Cobb, "Hal Roach: The Cosmopolitan of the Month," *Cosmopolitan,* April 1940, 11; Cobb to Bobbs-Merrill office, April 13, 1934, Bobbs-Merrill Manuscripts; Cobb, *My Wayward Parent,* 181–82; Lawson, *Cobb,* 222–23.

11. A New Beginning and the Beginning of the End

1. David Shipman, *The Great Movie Stars: The Golden Years* (New York: Crown, 1970), 476; *Louisville Times,* September 29, 1934, clipping in LFPL.

2. *New York Times,* December 4, 1934; *Boston Transcript,* November 21, 1934, clippings in LFPL; Irvin S. Cobb, *Irvin S. Cobb's Own Recipe Book* (Frankfort, KY: Frankfort Distillers, 1936), foreword, 1–51.

3. Cobb, *My Wayward Parent,* 183; *Louisville Courier-Journal,* May 17, 1934; Lawson, *Cobb,* 222.

4. *Louisville Courier-Journal,* July 1, 1934.

5. Will Rogers Memorial Commission and Oklahoma State University, *Radio Broadcasts of Will Rogers* (Will Rogers Heritage Trust, n.d.), 71–72, 148–55; Richard D. White Jr., *Will Rogers: A Political Life* (Lubbock: Texas Tech University Press, 2011), 167.

6. *Chicago Tribune,* May 27, 1934, clipping in LFPL; "Hal Roach's Funnies," no date, Mike and Alice Hogg Papers, Archives of the Museum of Fine Arts, Houston, TX.

7. Richard Koszarski, *Hollywood Directors: 1914–1940* (New York: Oxford University Press, 1976), 283–83; William K. Everson, *The Films of Hal Roach* (New York: Museum of Modern Art, 1971), 34–35, 62.

8. Richard Lewis Ward, *A History of the Hal Roach Studios* (Carbondale: Southern Illinois University Press, 2005), 78–79, 94, 158; "Hal Roach's Funnies."

9. Cobb, *My Wayward Parent,* 185–87; *Louisville Courier-Journal,* August 20, 1934.

10. Neuman, *Cobb,* 200–206.

11. Irvin S. Cobb, "Why Are Women Like That?" *Cosmopolitan,* April 1933, 56–57, 124–27; Cobb, "Thanksgiving . . . with Corn-bread Stuffing," *Cosmopolitan,* December 1933, 44–45, 105–6.

12. Will Rogers, *The Autobiography of Will Rogers,* ed. Donald Day (Boston: Peoples Book Club, 1949), 342–44; William R. Brown, *Will Rogers and the American Dream* (Columbia: University of Missouri Press, 1970), 252.

13. Shipman, *Great Movie Stars*, 475–78.

14. Joseph Mcbride, *Searching for John Ford* (New York: St. Martin's Press, 2001), 35, 126, 207; Dan Ford, *Pappy: The Life of John Ford* (Englewood Cliffs, NJ: Prentice-Hall, 1979), 71, 92; Peter Stowell, *John Ford* (Boston: Twayne, 1986), 3–6.

15. Amos Dane, Yahoo! Contributor Network, April 23, 2012.

16. Ben Yagoda, *Will Rogers: A Biography* (New York: Alfred A. Knopf, 1993), 312.

17. *Louisville Courier-Journal*, October 6, 1934.

18. Stowell, *John Ford*, 1–13.

19. Richard Schickel, "Serving up Subversion," a review of Mel Watkins, *The Life and Times of Lincoln Perry, Wilson Quarterly*, Autumn 2005, 114–16; Carlton Jackson, *Hattie: The Life of Hattie McDaniel* (Lanham, MD: Madison Books, 1990), 22–23. Hattie McDaniel's career was ascending as Fetchit's was descending. She would later win an Academy Award for best supporting actress in *Gone with the Wind*. Offstage, Fetchit's behavior was abrasive and somewhat erratic, and eventually the NAACP turned against him because of his portrayal of subservient African Americans.

20. Tag Gallagher, *John Ford: The Man and His Films* (Berkeley: University of California Press, 1986), 100–107.

21. *Louisville Courier-Journal*, September 16, 23, 24, 30, October 4, 1934; *Chicago Tribune*, September 10, 1934; "Fox Has Smash Hit with Rogers in 'Judge Priest,'" *Hollywood Reporter*, August 4, 1934, clippings in LFPL; Chatterton, *Cobb*, 106–7.

22. *New York Times*, February 10, 1935; Lawson, *Cobb*, 224–25.

23. Lawson, *Cobb*, 226–27; *Louisville Courier-Journal*, February 28, 1935; *Louisville Times*, March 16, 1935, clippings in LFPL.

24. Stowell, *John Ford*, 10–13.

25. Richard M. Ketchum, *Will Rogers: His Life and Times* (New York: American Heritage, 1973), 259; Rogers, *Autobiography*, 336–37; *Steamboat 'Round the Bend*, online review, *New York Times*, April 11, 2013.

26. *Radio Broadcasts of Will Rogers*, 152, 156.

27. Mcbride, *Searching for John Ford*, 209; Cobb, *Exit Laughing*, 404–5; Ketchum, *Will Rogers*, 259–62.

28. Stowell, *John Ford*, 10–13; Gallagher, *John Ford*, 125–30, 524.

29. Cobb, *Exit Laughing*, 405–6.

30. *Louisville Courier-Journal*, August 11, 16, 17, 22, 1935; telegram from Cobb to Mrs. Will Rogers, August 18, 1935, Will Rogers Museum Collections; Steven K. Gragert and M. Jane Johansson, eds., *The Papers of Will Rogers: The Final Years*, vol. 5, *August 1928–August 1935* (Norman: University of Oklahoma Press, 2006), 613–15. Cobb wrote an introduction to Joe De Yong's *"Friend Will"* (Santa Barbara, CA, circa 1936).

31. Irvin S. Cobb document, November 2, 1935, Cobb Papers, Filson Historical Society. Cobb wrote several tributes to Rogers for the North American Newspaper Alliance; see *New York Times*, August 22, 1935, and *Louisville Herald-Post*, August 23,

1935, clippings in LFPL. Cobb is pictured in the November 24, 1935, edition of the *New York Times* standing beside Shirley Temple unveiling a bronze plaque dedicated to Rogers on a sound stage at Twentieth Century–Fox Studios in Hollywood. Others in the picture include film moguls Louis B. Mayer and Darryl Zanuck. Cobb also contributed to the founding of the Will Rogers Memorial.

32. *Louisville Courier-Journal,* August 25, 27, 29, September 1, 1935; *Louisville Times,* September 26, 1935, clippings in LFPL.

33. *Louisville Courier-Journal,* March 11, 23, October 11, 1936, September 11, 1938; *Louisville Times,* April 8, October 1, 24, 1936, October 18, 1938; *Louisville Herald-Post,* May 9, 1936, clippings in LFPL; Neuman, *Cobb,* 204–6; Lawson, *Cobb,* 228–34; Cobb to Alice Hogg, May 7, September 13, 1938, Mike and Alice Hogg Papers; *Upper Hutt Weekly Review* (Trentham, New Zealand), July 15, 1938; *New York Times,* August 24, 1939.

34. Cobb to "Dearest You-all," April 23, 1935, Mike and Alice Hogg Papers; Cobb, *My Wayward Parent,* 207–8.

35. Cobb, *My Wayward Parent,* 200–205. Apparently, the last of "Cobb's Comments" was published in the *Louisville Courier-Journal* on September 21, 1936, although it stopped appearing in other papers some time before that.

36. Odd McIntyre noted the pending sale of these properties in his syndicated "New York Day by Day" column, *Louisville Courier-Journal,* September 22, 1936; Lawson, *Cobb,* 231–32; Cobb, *My Wayward Parent,* 200–207.

37. Bryan B. Sterling, *The Best of Will Rogers* (New York: Crown, 1979), 55. Also see Sterling's sections on political parties, bankers, and lawyers for some of Rogers's best humor. The most complete study of Rogers's political influence is White, *Will Rogers.*

38. *New York Times,* September 16, 1934; *Louisville Courier-Journal,* August 29, September 4, 7, 1935.

39. William Manchester, *Disturber of the Peace: The Life of H. L. Mencken* (Amherst: University of Massachusetts Press, 1986), 270, 282; S. T. Joshi, ed., *Mencken on Mencken: A New Collection of Autobiographical Writings* (Baton Rouge: Louisiana State University Press, 2010), 5, 164–65; Forgue et al., *Letters of H. L. Mencken,* 403; Irvin S. Cobb, "Here Again—Good Old Silly Season!" *Cosmopolitan,* August 1934, 44–45, 173; Bode, *New Mencken Letters,* 204–5; "To Herbert Hoover at WOOF," July 22, 1938, manuscript in Cobb Papers, Murray State University Special Collections and Archives.

40. Cobb to "Dearest You-all," February 6, 1938, and Cobb letters to the Hoggs, various dates, 1933–1943, Mike and Alice Hogg Papers; *Lexington Herald,* January 29, 1936; Cobb to Fred Neuman, July 4, 1939, and Laura N. Paes to Neuman, December 19, 1937, January 15, 1938, Cobb Papers, McCracken County Public Library.

41. D. L. Chambers to Hewitt Howland, November 30, 1937, Bobbs-Merrill memo to Cobb, August 25, 1936, and "MK" to Cobb, December 3, 1936, all in Bobbs-Merrill Manuscripts; *Louisville Courier-Journal,* September 26–28, 30, Oc-

tober 1–3, 7–11, 28, 1936; *Louisville Times,* September 25, 1936; Irvin S. Cobb, *AZAM: The Story of an Arabian Colt and His Friends* (Chicago: Rand-McNally, 1937); Cobb, *Four Useful Pups* (Chicago: Rand-McNally, 1940).

42. Chambers to Howland, January 27, November 30, 1937; Cobb to Philip M. Anderson, February 4, 1937; Chambers to Cobb, February 9, 1937; Howland to Chambers, February 17, December 21, 1937, January 5, February 9, 1938, all in Bobbs-Merrill Manuscripts; Chatterton, *Cobb,* 100–101, 124.

12. Exit Laughing

1. *Louisville Courier-Journal,* August 26, 1935.

2. Cobb to Alice Hogg, March 28, 1938, Mike and Alice Hogg Papers. Cobb added at the end of his letter that he would write "again when I'm more cheerful."

3. O'Bar, *Origins and History of Bobbs-Merrill,* 32; Howland relaying a message from Cobb to Chambers, February 24, 1938, and Chambers to Howland, February 28, 1938, Bobbs-Merrill Manuscripts.

4. Cobb to "You-all," April [no day] 1937; Cobb to "Dear Chilluns," October 24, 1937, March 24, 28, 1938; Cobb to "Alice Honey," May 7, 1938, Mike and Alice Hogg Papers.

5. *Louisville Courier-Journal,* March 9, May 24, November 23, 27, 1938; Cobb to "Alice Honey," May 7, 1938, and Cobb to "Dearest You-all," November 3, 1938, Mike and Alice Hogg Papers.

6. Howland to Chambers, June 7, 12, 22, 1939, and Chambers to Howland, June 9, 1939, Bobbs-Merrill Manuscripts.

7. Telegram from Howland to Chambers, August 1, October 11, 17, 1939; Chambers to Howland, October 19, 1939; Chambers to Cobb, October 19, 1939, all in Bobbs-Merrill Manuscripts; telegram from Cobb to Mike Hogg, August 7, 1939, and Cobb to "You-all," August 14, 1939, Mike and Alice Hogg Papers; Cobb to Neuman, August 15, 1939, Cobb Papers, McCracken County Public Library; *New York Times,* August 1, 1939; *Louisville Times,* August 1, 11, 1939; *Louisville Courier-Journal,* August 11, 1939; Cobb, introduction to *Roustabout Songs: A Collection of Ohio River Valley Songs* (1939).

8. Cobb to "You-all," October 28, 1939, Mike and Alice Hogg Papers; Laura N. Paes to Chambers, November 17, 1939; Howland to Chambers, May 29, August 14, 23, September 5, 1940; Chambers to Howland, August 21, 1940; Chambers to Cobb, August 20, 1940; copy of contract, August 3, 1940, all in Bobbs-Merrill Manuscripts. *Irvin Cobb at His Best* included six of his most famous pieces, opening with "Speaking of Operations"; *Favorite Humorous Stories of Irvin Cobb* (New York: Triangle Books, 1940) included "Speaking of Operations," "Judge Priest Comes Back," and old newspaper columns.

9. Cobb to "Dear Majah" [Mike Hogg], August 6, 1940; telegram from Cobb to Mike Hogg, September 19, 1940; Cobb to Mike Hogg, November 5, 1940, Mike and Alice Hogg Papers; *Louisville Courier-Journal,* July 20, November 3, 1940, Au-

gust 6, 1941; *Paducah Sun-Democrat,* reprint in *Louisville Courier-Journal,* November 3, 1940.

10. Cobb to Neuman, January 27, 1940, Cobb Papers, McCracken County Public Library; Cobb to "Alice Honey," January 19, February 10, May 1, 1941, Mike and Alice Hogg Papers; *New York Times,* February 2, 1941; *Louisville Times,* January 28, 1941, clippings in LFPL.

11. Cobb to Chambers, November 15, 16, 18, 1940; Howland to Chambers, November 18, 1940; Cobb to Mr. McAdam, December 27, 1940, Bobbs-Merrill Manuscripts.

12. Irvin S. Cobb, *Glory, Glory, Hallelujah!* (Indianapolis: Bobbs-Merrill, 1941).

13. Raymond Simon to Bobbs-Merrill, March 1, 1941; Josephus Daniels to Cobb, March 7, 1941; promotional material dated March 8, 1941, Bobbs-Merrill Manuscripts; *New York Times,* March 18, 1941.

14. Cobb, *Exit Laughing,* 17.

15. "Chris Crowley's Writing Blog," August 27, 2012.

16. *Louisville Courier-Journal,* March 16, 1941; *Lexington Herald,* March 30, 1941; *New York Herald-Tribune,* March 16, 1941; *Saturday Review of Literature,* March 22, 1941, 5, clippings in LFPL.

17. Note added to letter from Townsend to Cobb, April 5, 1941, Cobb Collection, University of Kentucky Special Collections; Cobb to Neuman, August 22, 1942, Cobb Papers, McCracken County Public Library; Cobb to "Alice Honey," September 2, 1941, Mike and Alice Hogg Papers.

18. *Louisville Courier-Journal,* May 22, 29, 1942; *Louisville Times,* June 5, 1942, clippings in LFPL; Lawson, *Cobb,* 239; Cobb to "Alice Honey," June 4, 1942, Mike and Alice Hogg Papers.

19. Irvin S. Cobb, *Roll Call* (Indianapolis: Bobbs-Merrill, 1942); Cobb to "Alice Honey," June 4, 1942, and Cobb to "Dear Majah," September 29, 1942, Mike and Alice Hogg Papers; Lawson, *Cobb,* 240; H. F. Alexander to Cobb, July 20, 1943, Cobb Papers, McCracken County Public Library; Cobb, "Fishhead," *Argosy,* October 1942, 13–17. To some extent, Cobb's patriotism was rewarded. A liberty ship, built at the Jacksonville, Florida, shipyard, was named for him and commissioned in 1944.

20. *New York Times,* October 12, 1942; Cobb to Neuman, May 17, 1943, Cobb Papers, McCracken County Public Library; Rufus Rockwell Wilson, *New York in Literature: The Story Told in the Landmarks of Town and Country* (Elmira, NY: Primavera Press, 1947), 143; Cobb, *My Wayward Parent,* 246–47.

21. Cobb to Neuman, November 9, December 6, 1943, Cobb Papers, McCracken County Public Library; written statement in 1943 address book, Cobb Papers, Murray State University Special Collections and Archives.

22. Cooper, *Kent Cooper,* 285–86.

23. *Louisville Courier-Journal,* December 9, 1943; *New York Times,* December 10, 1943; C. G. Paulding, "On All Fours," *Commonweal,* December 24, 1943, clippings in LFPL.

24. Cobb to "Alice Honey," September 2, 1941, March 10, 1943, Mike and

Alice Hogg Papers; Cobb to Neuman, undated (late 1943 or early 1944), January [12], February 11, 1944, Cobb Papers, McCracken County Public Library; Cobb comments in file of unpublished poems, box 8, Cobb Papers, Murray State University Special Collections and Archives. Not long after Cobb's death, one of his Santa Monica friends wrote to Neuman about a conversation they had had about making a movie on the life of Luther Burbank. "Yes, honey," Cobb said. "I agree with you perfectly. Burbank was a wonderful man; pity he died too soon—he was just on the point of inventing a seedless JEW." Blanche B. Flournoy to Neuman, May 18, 1944, Cobb Papers, McCracken County Public Library.

25. Collection #23, Cobb Papers, McCracken County Public Library.

26. Telegram from Laura Cobb to Neuman, March 10, 1944, Cobb Papers, McCracken County Public Library; *Louisville Times,* March 10, 1944; *Louisville Courier-Journal,* March 11, 1944; *Mt. Vernon (NY) Daily Argus,* March 11, 1944; *New York Times,* March 11, 12, 1944; *Christian Science Monitor,* May 13, 1944; *Saturday Review of Literature,* March 25, 1944, clippings in LFPL. Box 15 of the Cobb Papers at Murray State University contains a rather ghoulish "death mask" plaster cast with a hole in the left side of the mouth for a cigar.

27. *Louisville Courier-Journal,* March 14, 1944.

28. Ibid.

29. *Lexington Herald,* March 13, 1944; *Louisville Courier-Journal,* September 28, October 6, 8, 1944.

30. *Louisville Times,* September 22, 1945, November 4, 1967; *Paducah Sun-Democrat,* April 19, 1983, clippings in LFPL.

31. *Chicago Sunday Times,* November 4, 1945; *Louisville Courier-Journal,* June 28, 1953, August 29, 1973, September 13, 1976; *Paducah Sun-Democrat,* March 12, 1969, clippings in LFPL. *Cobb's Cavalcade,* published in 1945 by the World Publishing Company of Cleveland and New York, with an introduction by B. D. Zevin, led off with "Speaking of Operations" and included "gay," "grim," and Judge Priest stories. Script for *Our America,* October 7, 1951, WLW-T, Cobb Papers, McCracken County Public Library.

32. McBride, *Searching for John Ford,* 521–25; *Louisville Courier-Journal,* June 28, July 2, 3, 1953.

33. Lawson, *Cobb,* 244; *Paducah Sun-Democrat,* March 14, 1944, clipping in LFPL; Chatterton, *Cobb,* 124–32; Yates, *American Humorist,* 127–33; Cobb, *Exit Laughing,* 558.

Bibliography

Archives

Bobbs-Merrill Manuscripts. Lilly Library, Indiana University, Bloomington, Indiana.
Brody Collection. Murray State University Special Collections and Archives, Murray, Kentucky.
Cobb, Irvin S., Collection. Eastern Kentucky University Special Collections and Archives, Richmond.
Cobb, Irvin S., Collection. University of Kentucky Special Collections, Lexington.
Cobb, Irvin S., Papers. Filson Historical Society, Louisville, Kentucky.
Cobb, Irvin S., Papers. McCracken County Public Library, Paducah, Kentucky.
Cobb, Irvin S., Papers. Murray State University Special Collections and Archives, Murray, Kentucky.
Hogg, Mike and Alice, Papers. Archives of the Museum of Fine Arts, Houston, Texas.
Hogg, William Clifford, Papers. University of Texas at Austin.
McClure Publishing Company Archives. University of Delaware Library, Special Collections, Newark.
Rogers, Will, Museum Collections. Claremore, Oklahoma.
Rothert, Otto, Collection. Filson Historical Society, Louisville, Kentucky.
Townsend, John Wilson, Collection. Eastern Kentucky University Special Collections and Archives, Richmond.

Books by Irvin S. Cobb

The Abandoned Farmers. New York: George H. Doran, 1920.
Alias Ben Alibi. New York: George H. Doran, 1925.
All Aboard: Saga of the Romantic River. New York: Cosmopolitan, 1928.
AZAM: The Story of an Arabian Colt and His Friends. Chicago: Rand McNally, 1937.
Back Home: Being the Narrative of Judge Priest and His People. New York: George H. Doran, 1912.
Both Sides of the Street. New York: Cosmopolitan, 1930.
Chivalry Peak. New York: Cosmopolitan, 1927.
Cobb's America Guyed Books: Kentucky, the Proud State. New York: George H. Doran,

1924. Other books in this series included New York, Kansas, Indiana, Maine, and North Carolina, all published in 1924.

Cobb's Anatomy. New York: George H. Doran, 1912.

Cobb's Bill of Fare. New York: George H. Doran, 1913.

Cobb's Cavalcade. Cleveland, OH: World Publishing, 1945.

Down Yonder with Judge Priest and Irvin S. Cobb. New York: Ray Long and Richard R. Smith, 1932.

Eating in Two or Three Languages. New York: George H. Doran, 1919.

The Escape of Mr. Trimm: His Plight and Other Plights. New York: George H. Doran, 1913.

Europe Revised. New York: George H. Doran, 1914.

Exit Laughing. Indianapolis: Bobbs-Merrill, 1941.

Faith, Hope and Charity. Indianapolis: Bobbs-Merrill, 1934.

Favorite Humorous Stories of Irvin Cobb. New York: Triangle Books, 1940.

Fibble, D.D. New York: George H. Doran, 1916.

Four Useful Pups. Chicago: Rand-McNally, 1940.

From Place to Place. New York: George H. Doran, 1920.

Glory, Glory, Hallelujah! Indianapolis: Bobbs-Merrill, 1941.

The Glory of the Coming: What Mine Eyes Have Seen of Americans in Action in the Year of Grace and Allied Endeavor. New York: George H. Doran, 1918.

Goin' on Fourteen: Being Cross-Sections out of a Year in the Life of an Average Boy. New York: George H. Doran, 1924.

"Here Comes the Bride—" and so Forth. New York: George H. Doran, 1925.

Incredible Truth. New York: Cosmopolitan, 1931.

Irvin Cobb at His Best. Garden City, NY: Doubleday, Doran, 1929. Reprint, Garden City, NY: Sun Dial Press, 1940.

Irvin S. Cobb's Own Recipe Book. Frankfort, KY: Frankfort Distillers, 1936.

J. Poindexter, Colored. New York: George H. Doran, 1922.

Judge Priest Turns Detective. Indianapolis: Bobbs-Merrill, 1937.

Ladies and Gentlemen. New York: Cosmopolitan, 1927.

A Laugh a Day Keeps the Doctor Away: His Favorite Stories as Told by Irvin S. Cobb. New York: George H. Doran, 1923.

The Life of the Party. New York: George H. Doran, 1919.

Local Color. New York: George H. Doran, 1916.

Many Laughs for Many Days: Another Year's Supply (365) of His Favorite Stories. New York: George H. Doran, 1925.

Murder Day by Day. Indianapolis: Bobbs-Merrill, 1933.

"Oh, Well, You Know How Women Are!" and "Isn't that Just Like a Man!" New York: George H. Doran, 1920 (with Mary Roberts Rinehart).

Old Judge Priest. New York: George H. Doran, 1916.

On an Island that Cost $24.00. New York: George H. Doran, 1926.

One Third Off. New York: George H. Doran, 1921.

One Way to Stop a Panic. New York: R. M. McBride, 1933.

Paths of Glory: Impressions of War Written at and Near the Front. New York: George H. Doran, 1915.
Piano Jim and the Impotent Pumpkin Vine or "Charley Russell's Best Story—To My Way of Thinking." Lexington, KY: Blue Grass Book Shop, 1947 (with John Wilson Townsend and Will Rogers).
A Plea for Old Cap Collier. New York: George H. Doran, 1921.
Prose and Cons. New York: George H. Doran, 1926.
Red Likker. New York: Cosmopolitan, 1929.
Roll Call. Indianapolis: Bobbs-Merrill, 1942.
Roughing It De Luxe. New York: George H. Doran, 1914.
Snake Doctor and Other Stories. New York: George H. Doran, 1923.
Speaking of Operations. New York: George H. Doran, 1915.
Speaking of Prussians—. New York: George H. Doran, 1918.
This Man's World. New York: Cosmopolitan, 1929.
Those Times and These. New York: George H. Doran, 1917.
The Thunders of Silence. New York: George H. Doran, 1918.
To Be Taken before Sailing. New York: Cosmopolitan, 1930.
"Who's Who" Plus "Here's How!" New York: Hotel Waldorf-Astoria, 1934.
The Works of Irvin S. Cobb: Stickfuls (Myself to Date). New York: George H. Doran, 1923.
The Works of Irvin S. Cobb: Sundry Accounts. New York: George H. Doran, 1922.

Books and Articles

Adams, Samuel Hopkins. *A. Woollcott: His Life and His World.* New York: Reynal and Hitchcock, 1945.
Ashby, LeRoy. *With Amusement for All: A History of American Popular Culture since 1830.* Lexington: University Press of Kentucky, 2011.
Barkley, Alben W. *That Reminds Me—.* New York: Doubleday, 1954.
Barrett, James Wyman. *Joseph Pulitzer and His World.* New York: Vanguard Press, 1941.
Batchelor, Denzil. *Jack Johnson and His Times.* London: Phoenix Sports Books, 1956.
Bennett, Arnold. *The Journal of Arnold Bennett.* Garden City, NY: Literary Guild, 1933.
———. *Your United States.* New York: George H. Doran, 1912.
Berger, Meyer. *The Story of the* New York Times. New York: Simon and Schuster, 1951.
Blight, David W. *Race and Reunion: The Civil War in American Memory.* Cambridge, MA: Belknap Press, 2001.
Bode, Carl, ed. *The New Mencken Letters.* New York: Dial Press, 1977.
Boydson, Jeanne, et al. *Making a Nation.* Upper Saddle River, NJ: Prentice-Hall, 2002.
Brown, William R. *Will Rogers and the American Dream.* Columbia: University of Missouri Press, 1970.

Burton, Orville Vernon. "The South as 'Other,' the Southerner as 'Stranger.'" *Journal of Southern History* 79 (February 2013): 7–50.

Campbell, Craig W. *Reel America and World War I: A Comprehensive Filmography and History of Motion Pictures in the United States, 1914–1920.* Jefferson, NC: McFarland, 1985.

Chalmers, David M. *Hooded Americanism: The History of the Ku Klux Klan.* Durham, NC: Duke University Press, 1987.

Chapin, Charles E. *Charles Chapin's Story: Written in Sing Sing Prison.* New York: Putnam's, 1920.

Chatterton, Wayne. *Irvin S. Cobb.* Boston: Twayne, 1986.

Clark, Tom. *The World of Damon Runyon.* New York: Harper and Row, 1978.

Cobb, Elisabeth. *My Wayward Parent.* Indianapolis: Bobbs-Merrill, 1945.

Cobb, James C. *Away down South: A History of Southern Identity.* New York: Oxford University Press, 2005.

Cohn, Jan. *Creating America: George Horace Lorimer and the* Saturday Evening Post. Pittsburgh: University of Pittsburgh Press, 1989.

———. *Improbable Fiction: The Life of Mary Roberts Rinehart.* Pittsburgh: University of Pittsburgh Press, 1980.

Cooper, Kent. *Kent Cooper and the Associated Press: An Autobiography.* New York: Random House, 1959.

Cox, Karen L. *Dreaming of Dixie: How the South Was Created in American Popular Culture.* Chapel Hill: University of North Carolina Press, 2011.

Coyle, Lee. *George Ade.* New York: College and University Press, 1964.

Craig, Berry. *Kentucky Confederates: Secession, Civil War, and the Jackson Purchase.* Lexington: University Press of Kentucky, 2014.

Creel, George. *Rebel at Large: Recollections of Fifty Crowded Years.* New York: G. P. Putnam's Sons, 1947.

Cristy, Raphael James. *Charles M. Russell: The Storyteller's Art.* Albuquerque: University of New Mexico Press, 2004.

Crozier, Emmet. *American Reporters on the Western Front, 1914–1918.* New York: Oxford University Press, 1959.

Davis, Robert H. "Introducing Mr. Cobb." *Golden Book Magazine,* January 1934, 15.

———. "Irvin S. Cobb, a Paducah, Kentucky, Gentleman." *American Magazine,* May 1917, 14.

———. *Irvin S. Cobb: Storyteller.* New York: George H. Doran, 1924.

DeMille, Cecil B. *The Autobiography of Cecil B. DeMille.* Edited by Donald Hayne. Englewood, NJ: Prentice Hall, 1959.

Dempsey, Jack, and Barbara Piattelli Dempsey. *Dempsey.* New York: W. H. Allen, 1977.

Dinner Tendered to Irvin S. Cobb. New York, 1915.

D'Itri, Patricia Ward. *Damon Runyon,* Boston: Twayne, 1982.

Dooley, D. J. *The Art of Sinclair Lewis.* Lincoln: University of Nebraska Press, 1967.

Doran, George H. *Chronicles of Barabbas, 1884–1934.* New York: Rinehart, 1935.

Douglas, George H. *The Early Days of Radio Broadcasting.* Jefferson, NC: McFarland, 1987.

Driscoll, Charles B. *The Life of O. O. McIntyre.* New York: Greystone Press, 1938.

Duncan, Dayton. *The National Parks: America's Best Idea.* New York: Alfred A. Knopf, 2009.

Elder, Donald. *Ring Lardner.* Garden City, NY: Doubleday, 1956.

Ellis, William E. "Dream Big." *Kentucky Monthly,* August 2011, 56.

Emery, Michael, Edwin Emery, and Nancy L. Roberts. *The Press and America: An Interpretative History of the Mass Media.* Boston: Allyn and Bacon, 2000.

Essoe, Gabe, and Raymond Lee. *DeMille: The Man and His Pictures.* New York: Castle Books, 1970.

Everson, William K. *The Films of Hal Roach.* New York: Museum of Modern Art, 1971.

Ferguson, Cheryl Caldwell. *Highland Park and River Oaks: The Origins of Garden Suburban Community Planning in Texas.* Austin: University of Texas Press, 2014.

Fisher, Charles. *The Columnists.* New York: Soskin, 1944.

Ford, Corey. *The Time of Laughter.* Boston: Little, Brown, 1967.

Ford, Dan. *Pappy: The Life of John Ford.* Englewood Cliffs, NJ: Prentice-Hall, 1979.

Forgue, Guy J., et al., eds. *Letters of H. L. Mencken.* Boston: Northeastern, 1981.

Fox, Justin. "Start the Presses! *Atlantic,* May 2014, 26.

Gale, Steven H., ed. *Encyclopedia of American Humorists.* New York: Garland, 1988.

Gallagher, Tag. *John Ford: The Man and His Films.* Berkeley: University of California Press, 1986.

Gardner, Sarah E. *Blood and Irony: Southern White Women's Narratives of the Civil War, 1861–1937.* Chapel Hill: University of North Carolina Press, 2004.

Garroutte, Eva Marie. *Real Indians: Identity and the Survival of Native America.* Berkeley: University of California Press, 2003.

Gilmore, A-Tony. *Bad Nigger! The National Impact of Jack Johnson.* Port Washington, NY: Associated Faculty Press, 1975.

Gordon, Sloane. "The Story of Irvin S. Cobb." *Pearson's Magazine* 33 (March 1915): 278–84.

Gragert, Steven K., and M. Jane Johansson, eds. *The Papers of Will Rogers: The Final Years.* Vol. 5, *August 1928–August 1935.* Norman: University of Oklahoma Press, 2006.

Grebstein, Sheldon Norman. *Sinclair Lewis.* New York: Twayne, 1962.

Hall, Wade. *The Smiling Phoenix: Southern Humor from 1865 to 1914.* Gainesville: University of Florida Press, 1965.

Harriman, Margaret (Case). *The Vicious Circle: The Story of the Algonquin Round Table.* New York: Rinehart, 1951.

Hastings, Max. *Catastrophe 1914: Europe Goes to War.* New York: Alfred A. Knopf, 2013.

Henderson, Robert M. *D. W. Griffith: His Life and Work.* New York: Oxford University Press, 1972.

Hobson, Fred C., Jr. *Serpent in Eden: H. L. Mencken and the South.* Chapel Hill: University of North Carolina Press, 1974.

Hoyt, Edwin P. *A Gentleman of Broadway.* Boston: Little, Brown, 1964.

Irvin S. Cobb: His Book: Friendly Tributes upon the Occasion of a Dinner Tendered to Irvin Shrewsbury Cobb at the Waldorf-Astoria Hotel. New York: George H. Doran, 1915.

Jackson, Carlton. *Hattie: The Life of Hattie McDaniel.* Lanham, MD: Madison Books, 1990.

Jackson, Kenneth T. *The Ku Klux Klan in the City, 1915–1930.* New York: Oxford University Press, 1967.

Jillson, Willard Rouse. *Irvin S. Cobb at Frankfort, Kentucky.* Carrollton, KY: News Democrat Press, 1944.

Joshi, S. T., ed. *Mencken on Mencken: A New Collection of Autobiographical Writings.* Baton Rouge: Louisiana State University Press, 2010.

Juergens, George. *Joseph Pulitzer and the* New York World. Princeton, NJ: Princeton University Press, 1966.

Keegan, John. *The First World War.* New York: Vintage, 1999.

Kemler, Edgar. *The Irreverent Mr. Mencken.* Boston: Little, Brown, 1950.

Ketcham, Richard M. *Will Rogers: His Life and Times.* New York: American Heritage, 1973.

Kimball, George, and John Schulian. *At the Fights: American Writers on Boxing.* New York: Library of America, 2011.

Kleber, John E., ed. *The Encyclopedia of Louisville.* Lexington: University Press of Kentucky, 2001.

———. *The Kentucky Encyclopedia.* Lexington: University Press of Kentucky, 1992.

Klotter, James C. *Kentucky: Portrait in Paradox, 1900–1950.* Frankfort: Kentucky Historical Society, 1996.

———. *William Goebel: The Politics of Wrath.* Lexington: University Press of Kentucky, 1977.

Knightley, Phillip. *The First Casualty: From Crimea to Vietnam; the War Correspondent as Hero, Propagandist, and Myth Maker.* New York: Harcourt, Brace, Jovanovich, 1975.

Koszarski, Richard. *Hollywood Directors: 1914–1940.* New York: Oxford University Press, 1976.

Langford, Gerald. *The Murder of Stanford White.* New York: Notable Trials Library, 1996.

Lawson, Anita. *Irvin S. Cobb.* Bowling Green, OH: Bowling Green State University Popular Press, 1984.

Lazarus, A. L., ed. *The Best of George Ade.* Bloomington: Indiana University Press 1985.

Lee, Jacob F. "Unionism, Emancipation, and the Origins of Kentucky's Confederate Identify." *Register of the Kentucky Historical Society* 111 (Spring 2013): 199–233.

Lidz, Franz. "Welcome to Farmtopia." *Smithsonian,* May 1915, 76.

Lomax, John A. *Will Hogg, Texan.* Austin: University of Texas Press, 1956.

Long, Ray, ed. *My Story I Like Best.* New York: International Magazine, 1924.

Lucas, Marion B. *A History of Blacks in Kentucky: From Slavery to Segregation, 1760–1891.* Frankfort: Kentucky Historical Society, 1992.

Lundquist, James. *Sinclair Lewis.* New York: Frederick Ungar, 1972.

———. *Theodore Dreiser.* New York: Frederick Ungar, 1978.

Lutholtz, M. William. *Grand Dragon: D. C. Stephenson and the Ku Klux Klan in Indiana.* West Lafayette, IN: Purdue University Press, 1991.

Manchester, William. *Disturber of the Peace: The Life of H. L. Mencken.* Amherst: University of Massachusetts Press, 1986.

Margolies, Daniel S. *Henry Watterson and the New South.* Lexington: University Press of Kentucky, 2006.

Mason, Robert. "The Supreme Court and Press Fashions." *William and Mary Law Review* 22 (1980): 259–79.

Masson, Thomas L. *Our American Humorists.* New York: Moffat, Yard, 1922.

Mathews, Joseph J. *Reporting the Wars.* Westport, CT: Greenwood Press, 1972.

McBride, Joseph. *Searching for John Ford.* New York: St. Martin's Press, 2001.

McLauchlan, Gordon. *A History of New Zealand Humour.* Auckland, New Zealand: Penguin Books, 1989.

Mencken, H. L. *Prejudices: First, Second, and Third Series.* New York: Library of America, 2010.

———. *Prejudices: First Series.* New York: Alfred A. Knopf, 1919.

———. *Prejudices: Second Series.* New York: Alfred A. Knopf, 1920.

Milton, Joyce. *The Yellow Kids: Foreign Correspondents in the Heyday of Yellow Journalism.* New York: HarperCollins, 1989.

Mosedale, John. *The Men Who Invented Broadway: Damon Runyon, Walter Winchell & Their World.* New York: R. Marek, 1981.

Nashaw, David. *The Chief: The Life of William Randolph Hearst.* Boston: Houghton Mifflin Harcourt, 2000.

Neuman, Fred G. *Irvin S. Cobb: His Life and Letters.* Emmaus, PA: Rodale Press, 1938.

———. *The Story of Paducah.* Paducah, Kentucky: Young Printing, 1927.

The New Handbook of Texas. Vol. 3. Austin: University of Texas Press, 1996.

O'Bar, Jack. *The Origins and History of the Bobbs-Merrill Company.* Champaign-Urbana: University of Illinois Press, 1985.

O'Brien, Edward F., ed. *The Best Short Stories of 1921.* Boston: Small, Maynard, 1922.

Pound, Reginald. *Arnold Bennett.* New York: William Heinemann, 1953.

Prentice, George D. *Prenticeana: Or Wit and Humor in Paragraphs.* New York: Derby and Jackson, 1860.

Read, Opie. *I Remember New York.* New York: Richard H. Smith, 1930.

Rinehart, Mary Roberts. *My Story: Mary Roberts Rinehart.* Chicago: E. M. Hale, 1931.

Roberts, Randy. *Jack Dempsey: The Manassa Mauler*. Baton Rouge: Louisiana State University Press, 1979.

———. *Papa Jack: Jack Johnson and the Era of White Hopes*. New York: Free Press, 1983.

Rogers, Will. *The Autobiography of Will Rogers*. Edited by Donald Day. Boston: Peoples Book Club, 1949.

Rourke, Constance. *American Humor: A Study of the National Character*. New York: Harcourt, Brace, 1931.

Ruiz, Jim. *The Black Hood of the Ku Klux Klan*. Lanham, MD: Austin and Winfield, 1998.

Schorer, Mark. *Sinclair Lewis: An American Life*. New York: McGraw-Hill, 1961.

Scruggs, Charles. *The Sage in Harlem: H. L. Mencken and Black Writers of the 1920s*. Baltimore: Johns Hopkins University Press, 1984.

Sellers, Charles, Henry May, and Neil R. McMillen. *A Synopsis of American History*. Chicago: Ivan R. Dee, 1992.

Shipman, David. *The Great Movie Stars: The Golden Years*. New York: Crown, 1970.

Smith, Donald B. *Long Lance: The True Story of an Impostor*. Lincoln: University of Nebraska Press, 1982.

Snyder, Louis L., and Richard B. Morris. *A Treasury of Great Reporting*. New York: Simon and Schuster, 1949.

Sterling, Bryan B. *The Best of Will Rogers*. New York: Crown, 1979.

Stevens, John D. *Sensationalism and the New York Press*. New York: Columbia University Press, 1991.

Stossel, Scott. "My Anxious, Twitchy, Phobic (Somehow Successful) Life." *Atlantic*, January–February 2014, 74–92.

Stowell, Peter. *John Ford*. Boston: Twayne, 1986.

Swanberg, W. A. *Citizen Hearst*. New York: BBS, 1961.

———. *Pulitzer*. New York: Scribner, 1971.

———. *Theodore Dreiser*. New York: Charles Scribner's Sons, 1935.

Tandy, Jeanette. *Crackerbox Philosophers in American Humor and Satire*. Port Washington, NY: Kennikat Press, 1925.

Tebbel, John. *Between Covers: The Rise and Transformation of Book Publishing in America*. New York: Oxford University Press, 1987.

———. *The Compact History of the American Newspaper*. New York: Hawthorn Books, 1963.

Tebbel, John, and Mary Ellen Zuckerman. *George Horace Lorimer and the* Saturday Evening Post. Garden City, NY: Doubleday, 1948.

———. *The Magazine in America: A Compact History*. New York: Oxford University Press, 1969.

———. *The Magazine in America, 1741–1990*. New York: Oxford University Press, 1991.

Thompson, J. Lee. *Politicians, the Press, and Propaganda: Lord Northcliffe & the Great War, 1914–1919*. Kent, OH: Kent State University Press, 1999.

Tobin, Terence, ed. *Letters of George Ade.* West Lafayette, IN: Purdue University Press, 1973.

Toland, John. *No Man's Land: 1918—The Last Year of the Great War.* Garden City, NY: Doubleday, 1980.

Townsend, John Wilson. *Irvin S. Cobb.* Atlanta: Martin and Hoyt, 1923.

Trani, Eugene P. *The Treaty of Portsmouth: An Adventure in American Diplomacy.* Lexington: University of Kentucky Press, 1969.

Tuchman, Barbara W. *The Guns of August.* New York: Ballantine, 1962.

Uruburu, Paula. *America's Eve: Evelyn Nesbit, Stanford White, the Birth of the "It" Girl, and the Crime of the Century.* New York: Riverhead, 2008.

Van Dover, J. K., and John F. Jebb. *Isn't Justice Always Unfair? The Detective in Southern Literature.* Bowling Green, OH: Bowling Green State University Popular Press, 1996.

Waldron, Edward E. *Walter White and the Harlem Renaissance.* Port Washington, NY: Associated Faculty Press, 1978.

Ward, Brian. "Music, Musical Theatre, and the Imagined South in Interwar Britain." *Journal of Southern History* 80 (February 2014): 39–72.

Ward, Richard Lewis. *A History of the Hal Roach Studios.* Carbondale: Southern Illinois University Press, 2005.

Weiner, Ed. *The Damon Runyon Story.* New York: Longmans, Green, 1948.

White, Richard D., Jr. *Will Rogers: A Political Life.* Lubbock: Texas Tech University Press, 2011.

White, Walter F. *The Fire in the Flint.* New York: Alfred A. Knopf, 1924.

———. *A Man Called White: The Autobiography of Walter White.* New York: Viking Press, 1948.

Will Rogers Memorial Commission and Oklahoma State University. *Radio Broadcasts of Will Rogers.* Will Rogers Heritage Trust, n.d.

Wilson, Charles Reagan. *Baptized in Blood: The Religion of the Lost Cause, 1885–1920.* Athens: University of Georgia Press, 2004.

Wilson, Charles Reagan, and William Ferris, eds. *Encyclopedia of Southern Culture.* Chapel Hill: University of North Carolina Press, 1989.

Wilson, Rufus Rockwell. *New York in Literature: The Story Told in the Landmarks of Town and Country.* Elmira, NY: Primavera Press, 1947.

Wood, Amy Louise. *Lynching and Spectacle: Witnessing Racial Violence in America, 1890–1980.* Chapel Hill: University of North Carolina Press, 2009.

Wright, George C. *A History of Blacks in Kentucky.* Vol. 2, *In Pursuit of Equality, 1890–1980.* Frankfort: Kentucky Historical Society, 1992.

Yagoda, Ben. *Will Rogers: A Biography.* New York: Alfred A. Knopf, 1993.

Yardly, Jonathan. *Ring: A Biography of Ring Lardner.* New York: Random House, 1977.

Yates, Norris W. *The American Humorist: Conscience of the Twentieth Century.* Ames: Iowa State University Press, 1964.

Index

Cobb's work on *Mississippi*, 185–86; Cobb's work with Hal Roach, 179–80, 181; *Judge Priest,* 177, 179, 182, 183–85; "Judge Priest" stories made into, 95; last appearances by Cobb, 190; "Southern" movies, 132. *See also* Hollywood

"Moving Throng, The" (column), 15

"Mr. Busybody" (skits), 23

Mt. Vernon Daily Argus, 204

Munsey, Frank A., 96

Munsey's Magazine, 43, 47–48

Murder Day by Day (Cobb), 175–76

Murder of Roger Ackroyd, The (Christie), 175

Murder of Stanford White, The (Langford), 21

"Music" (Cobb), 58

musical comedies, 23

Mussolini, Benito, 154

"My Country, 't Is of Thee" (Cobb), 83

"My Favorite Stories" (column), 137, 146–47

My Story I Like Best (Long), 145

My Wayward Parent (Elisabeth Cobb), 190, 206

Nation (magazine), 86, 123–24

National Battery Company, 149

National Broadcasting Company (NBC), 149, 189

National Parks, The (television program), 1

Native Americans, 6, 63, 166–67

Navajo Indians, 63

Nesbit, Evelyn. *See* Thaw, Evelyn Nesbit

Netherlands, 73

Neuman, Fred G., 5, 181, 198, 201, 202, 203–4

New Deal, 191–92

Newell, Peter, 54, 58

New Orleans Picayune, 109

New Republic, 75

New York City: Cobb's homes in, 35, 36, 136; Cobb's membership in the literary cognoscenti, 24, 37; Cobb's move to in 1904, 15–16; Cobb's "'Twixt the Bluff and the Sound" concerning, 95; Cobb's work with the *Evening Sun,* 16, 17–19; Cobb's work with the *New York World,* 19–22, 23, 25–26, 28, 29–34, 35, 36, 42, 44; Cobb's work with the *Saturday Evening Post* (*see* Saturday Evening Post); Metropolitan Club incident with Sinclair Lewis and Theodore Dreiser, 171–72; Prohibition and the Earl Carroll incident, 154–55; radio broadcasting and, 173; testimonial to Cobb in 1915, 77–79

"New York Day by Day" (column), 181

New York Evening Post, 137, 141–42, 148, 150

New York Evening Sun, 16, 17–19

New York Evening World: Cobb's joins and works as a reporter, 16, 19–22, 23, 25; Cobb's work as a humorist, 28, 29–33, 35, 36

New York Giants, 31–32, 124–25

New York Herald-Tribune, 152–53, 175–76, 200

New York Hilltoppers, 31

New York Journal, 20

New York Lunacy Commission, 21

New York Post, 153

New York Press Club, 88

New York Sun, 12, 19

"New York thro' Funny Glasses" (column), 22, 28, 29, 32

New York Times, 20; acceptance of Cobb's "southern" racism, 82; on Cobb at the dedication of Hotel Irvin Cobb, 165; Cobb on his appearance in *Our Mutual*

Powers, Caleb, 13
Prejudices: First Series (Mencken), 112
Prejudices: Second Series (Mencken), 112
Prentice, George D., 12
Preston, James, 58
Princeton (KY), 9–10
"Principle of the Thing, The" (Cobb),
   156
Prohibition, 123, 124, 144, 154–55,
   162, 176
Prose and Cons (Cobb), 151–53
"Prussian Paranoia, The" (Cobb), 93
Public Nuisance No. 1 (movie), 190
Pulitzer, Joseph, 19, 20, 25, 26, 43,
   139

racism: Cobb's racism and racial
   paternalism, 6–7, 132–35; Cobb's
   racist comments on the Japanese,
   203; Cobb's southern disposition
   and, 82; Cobb's visit to Paris
   in 1914 and, 64; in the early
   twentieth century, 51; English
   views of race in America, 132; Ku
   Klux Klan, 130–32; post–Civil
   War racial violence in the Jackson
   Purchase, 4; racial attitudes in
   Cobb's humor writing, 30–31, 34.
   See also anti-Semitism
radio: Cobb's appearances on, 149,
   173; Cobb's enthusiasm about,
   173; Cobb's *Paducah Plantation*
   program, 189; Will Rogers and, 179
Rand-McNally, 193
Rascoe, Burton, 109, 122–23
Ray Long and Richard R. Smith Inc., 174
Read, Opie, 12, 29
"Rebel Ridge" home, 36, 99–100,
   116–18, 136
Red Book (magazine), 84–85
Red Glutton, The (Cobb), 75
"Red-Handed" (Cobb), 141
Red Likker (Cobb), 162–63, 169

Reelfoot Lake, 59
religion: Cobb and, 7–8, 95
Republican National Convention of
   1920, 123–24
Requiem (Stevenson), 205
Rice, Grantland, 165, 205
Rickard, Tex, 148
Rinehart, Mary Roberts, 74, 94,
   122–23
Rinehart, Stanley, 80–81
Roach, Hal, 177, 179, 180, 181
Robertson, A. T., 95
Robinson, Edward G., 90
Rockefeller, John D., 3
Rockwell, Norman, 46
Rogers, Robert Cameron "Cam,"
   195–96
Rogers, Will: celebrity status in the
   1930s, 182; Cobb and, 166, 179,
   181–82; death of and its impact
   on Cobb, 188–89; the film *Judge
   Priest* and, 177, 179, 182, 183–85;
   film version of "Boys Will Be Boys"
   and, 95; politics and, 191; radio
   program, 179; *Steamboat 'Round the
   Bend* and, 186–88, 189
Roland, Gilbert, 181
Roll Call (Cobb), 201
Roosevelt, Eleanor, 203
Roosevelt, Franklin Delano, 191–92,
   198
Roosevelt, Theodore, 18, 19, 25, 32, 35,
   96, 106
Rothert, Otto, 162
"Roughing It De Luxe" (Cobb), 61–63
Roughing It De Luxe (Cobb), 61–63, 66,
   67, 110
Roustabout Songs (Cobb), 196
Runyon, Damon, 37–38, 100, 119–20,
   140, 148
Russell, Charles, 160, 166
Russell, John, 206
Ruth, Babe, 120

Tombs, 21
Tom Sawyer (Twain), 147
"To Whom It May Concern" (letter by Cobb), 204
Townsend, John Wilson, 59; biography of Cobb and, 128; Cobb dedicates *Sundry Accounts* to, 136; Cobb's correspondence with, 61; Cobb's health in the early 1920s and, 118; on Cobb's recuperation from a gastric hemorrhage, 129–30; as a go-between for Cobb and Mencken, 114; New York City literary scene and, 159; paean to Cobb, Charles Russell, and Will Rogers, 166; report on Cobb's World War I lecture, 77
"Trail of the Lonesome Laugh, The" (Cobb), 47
Trotti, Lamar, 182
Tule Lake Japanese Relocation Center, 203
"Tummies" (Cobb), 54
Turkish Delight (movie), 176
Tuscania (ship), 102, 103
Twain, Mark. *See* Clemens, Samuel
Twilight Club, 76–77
"'Twixt the Bluff and the Sound" (Cobb), 95

"Unaccustomed As I Am—" (Cobb), 76, 85
"Unbroken Chain, The" (Cobb), 156–57
"Uncle Rufus" (Cobb family handyman), 7
Under Sentence (Cobb and Megrue), 90
United Confederate Veterans (UCV), 82–83
Uruburu, Paula, 21

van Gelder, Robert, 200
Veiller, Bayard, 176

Vigilantes, the, 96, 121–22
Vitagraph Studios, 90–91
"Vittles" (Cobb), 58
Volstead Act, 155. *See also* Prohibition
Von Heeringen, Josias, 73

Waldo, Fullerton F., 108
Waldorf-Astoria Hotel, 77, 176
Walker, Lillian, 91
Walker, Stanley, 200
Waller, Tom, 207
"Wall Street's Leap Year" (Cobb), 168
Walthall, Henry B., 184
war correspondents: Cobb as foreign correspondent during World War I, 67–74, 101–7; Cobb's lecturing tours on World War I, 76–77, 107–8; honors and awards received by Cobb, 108–9
Ward, Henry, 197
Ward, Richard Lewis, 180
war dead: Cobb's description of, 69
Washington Street Colored Baptist Church, 108
Watkins, Mel, 184
Watterson, Henry, 12, 17, 50
WEAF radio station, 149
Weil, Adolph, 165
"We of the Old South" (Cobb), 160
"What Irvin S. Cobb Thinks About" (column), 189
"What I Saw at the Front" (speech by Cobb), 76
Whelen, Arlene, 206
"When the Sea-Asp Stings" (Cobb), 102
White, Sanford, 20–22, 23, 24
White, Walter, 132, 135–36
White, William Allen, 51, 200
Whitlock, Brand, 70
"Who's Who at the Zoo" (Cobb), 48
"Why Are Women Like That?" (Cobb), 181